MW00653718

Bad Language

CONTEMPORARY INTRODUCTIONS TO
PHILOSOPHY OF LANGUAGE

Herman Cappelen and Josh Dever

Context and Communication

Puzzles of Reference

Bad Language

Further titles in preparation

Bad Language

Herman Cappelen and Josh Dever

OXFORD
UNIVERSITY PRESS

OXFORD
UNIVERSITY PRESS

Great Clarendon Street, Oxford, OX2 6DP,
United Kingdom

Oxford University Press is a department of the University of Oxford.
It furthers the University's objective of excellence in research, scholarship,
and education by publishing worldwide. Oxford is a registered trade mark of
Oxford University Press in the UK and in certain other countries

First Edition published in 2019

Impression: 1

Published in the United States of America by Oxford University Press
198 Madison Avenue, New York, NY 10016, United States of America

British Library Cataloguing in Publication Data

Data available

Library of Congress Control Number: 2018964270

ISBN 978-0-19-883964-4 (hbk.)
ISBN 978-0-19-883965-1 (pbk.)

Printed and bound in Great Britain by
Clays Ltd, Elcograf S.p.A.

Contents

Contents

Detailed Contents

Preface

Much philosophy of language is an effort to theorize about language as an idealized object and communication as an idealized activity. This is natural because many theoretical advances result from making idealizing assumptions. However, at some point it's important to move away from the idealization and back to the real world. This book is an introduction to some of the linguistic phenomena that come into focus only when standard idealizing assumptions are dropped. We live in a world where speakers constantly lie and are non-cooperative: they say things that make no sense; they insult, bullshit, silence, and coerce each other. This book is an introduction to these darker sides of real-world language use. Alternative titles for this book could be 'Language in the Real World' or 'The Dark Side of Language Use'.

As with the other books in this series, this book is *not* meant to be a comprehensive guide—the dark side of language is too vast for us to cover it all in one book. We don't aspire to comprehensiveness. Instead, we have picked some *topics*, *views*, and *arguments* that we think are *important*, *interesting*, and *instructive*. Our hope is that a reader who has understood and engaged with this selection of material will be in a good position to start engaging with much of the work we don't cover in this book.

The book is written to be accessible to someone with no prior knowledge of the material. It can be used as part of a philosophy of language course or as part of a general introduction to philosophy.

We initially set out hoping to write a single book that could serve as an introduction to philosophy of language. We gave up. We now think that goal is too ambitious for any one book. There is simply too much interesting work that has been done within this field over the last 100 years to cover it all (or even most of it) in a single book. A book that tried to do that would inevitably be so superficial that it would fail to convey to the readers how rich, complex, and important these topics are. To do justice to the field we have set out to write a series of introductions to philosophy of language, each one covering an important topic, each one of which would be a way into the field as a whole. These books aim to provide systematic introductions to important questions, data, theories, and arguments. Those looking for a history of the discipline should look elsewhere.

Acknowledgments

Matthew McKeever was our research assistant for the entire period we worked on this book. He did an extraordinary job (as he also did helping us with the first two books in this series). Similarly, Joshua Habgood-Coote helped a lot with the early stages of this book and gave us many useful suggestions. In the final stages we also got invaluable assistance from Deborah Marber and Matthew Cameron. Our editor at OUP, Peter Momtchiloff, suggested the title for the book and provided much appreciated continuous support.

1

Idealized Communication

In this book we are interested in how language works in the rough and tumble of the real world, full of hucksters, shysters, manipulators, and bullshitters. A central problem in thinking carefully about the role of language in this rough and tumble is that our theoretical tools for analyzing language have been developed using examples of the much more demure setting of the classroom. In the classroom, we are all scholars, and we imagine (or hope) that there is no mere rhetoric, no lies, no deception, and no obfuscation.[1] If we model our theories of language on this setting, then we will tell a highly *idealized* picture about how language works. The highly idealized picture has the advantage of being simple, but its simplicity is a defect when it comes time to step outside the classroom and consider how mere mortals use language. Before we start considering how to use and modify our existing theoretical tools to deal with a decidedly *non-ideal* world, we need to understand what simplifying assumptions went into those tools.

1.1 Seven Typical Idealizations

In what follows we outline some idealizations that have guided many of the efforts to theorize about natural language, communication, and speakers. There is no one set of idealizations that are common to all theorists, but the seven idealizations we sketch below are representative of much contemporary work.

---

[1] Of course, for anyone who has been in a classroom, this is a very idealized picture of what goes on in there, and the idealizations that we discuss below will fail to hold true of many classrooms.

1.1.1 Cooperation

Much work on language takes well-ordered classroom conversations as the model for how language works in general. In the classroom, we are (at least sometimes) engaged in a cooperative and collaborative effort to work out what is true. Paul Grice helped give cooperativeness a central place in theorizing about language by formulating what he called the Cooperative Principle:

> Make your conversational contribution such as is required, at the stage at which it occurs, by the accepted purpose or direction of the talk exchange in which you are engaged.   (Grice (1989): 26)

Grice thinks of the Cooperative Principle as a rule that we expect each other to be following when we speak. As Grice says:

> Our talk exchanges do not normally consist of a succession of disconnected remarks, and would not be rational if they did. They are characteristically, to some degree at least, cooperative efforts; and each participant recognizes in them, to some extent, a common purpose or a set of purposes, or at least a mutually accepted direction.   (Grice (1989): 26)

This gives us our first idealizing assumption:

> **Idealization 1**: Conversation and communication are fundamentally cooperative activities. In a conversation, there is a goal to be achieved, and each participant in the conversation contributes to the conversation in an attempt to further that goal.

It should be clear off the bat that when we describe this as an idealization, we're being generous. Of course, it's far from clear that typical interactions with other people are fundamentally cooperative. This applies as much to linguistic interactions as the rest of life.

Grice's idealized picture has had massive influence on theorizing about language. It is not just the basic picture of conversation as a fundamentally cooperative enterprise; Grice also suggests that if we are being genuinely cooperative in conversation, this has a number of consequences for how we will plan our conversational contributions. In particular, Grice set out four *maxims*, general rules governing how the cooperative speaker will speak:

> **Maxim of Quality**: Try to make your contribution one that is true, by not saying what you believe to be false or saying that for which you lack sufficient evidence.

Maxim of Quantity: Make your contribution as informative as is required for the current purposes, and do not make your contribution more informative than is required.

Maxim of Relation: Be relevant.

Maxim of Manner: Be perspicuous: avoid obscurity of expression, avoid ambiguity, be brief, be orderly. (Grice (1989): 26–7)

Grice's idealized cooperative speaker thus attempts to provide, in a clear way, a relevant and appropriate amount of correct information. And audiences assume that speakers are attempting to provide these things. This gives us a second idealization:

Idealization 2: Speakers attempt to conform to Grice's maxims, and audiences assume that speakers are attempting to conform to the maxims when they interpret their contributions.

1.1.2 Knowledge as the aim

Idealization 1 only tells us that there is *some* goal that we are trying to achieve, and that we are working together toward that goal. But in the classroom, there is a *particular* goal that we are trying to achieve. We are trying to *accumulate knowledge*. Perhaps the topic of the class is the geography of Scotland. One of us knows that Ben Nevis is the tallest mountain in Scotland. Another of us knows that Loch Lomond is the largest lake in Scotland. But before we begin the conversation, our *collective* knowledge about Scottish geography is very limited. Conversation is then intended to correct that deficiency. If we were to pursue the idea that all conversations should be modeled on what well-behaved academics do in the classroom, one might introduce a third idealization:

Idealization 3: The goal of a conversation is to build up a body of knowledge shared by all of the conversational participants.

It should be clear that this is a massive idealization because a lot of people don't care about knowledge: they engage in speech for reasons that have nothing to do with trying to accumulate knowledge. They might want, for example, to embarrass or make fun of or encourage or repress. More generally, speakers can have any number of goals that are unconnected to sharing knowledge.

In later chapters we will return to this point, but for now, let's push on with the idealization. If we assume, for the sake of argument, that the goal of the conversation is to build up a body of knowledge, then we can track how well the conversation is going by tracking how much knowledge we've accumulated so far: the more knowledge, the better. This allows us to assign a kind of 'score' to each conversation. David Lewis (1979) suggests that a conversation is like a baseball game. To play baseball, you have to keep track of what the score is—the score not just in the sense of how many runs have been scored by which team, but in the more expansive sense of telling us the full state of the game: what inning it is, how many outs, strikes, and balls there are, and which runners are on which bases. Actions in a baseball game then regularly change the score, and players need to keep track of how the score is changing. The scoreboard is a public object, shared, tracked, and modified by all the participants in the game. Similarly, says Lewis, language is a kind of game with various kinds of moves which have various effects we can track on the conversational scoreboard. Lewis considers some quite complicated kinds of scoreboards (some of which we'll return to in later chapters), but in our idealized classroom, the only score to keep is the amount of knowledge. We can thus track the state of a conversation by tracking our shared knowledge. This gives us a fourth idealizing assumption:

Idealization 4: The state of a conversation at any point can be modeled by the *common ground* of the conversation: the things which are shared knowledge for all of the conversational participants.

What does it mean for something to be shared knowledge between all of the conversational participants? It's not enough that each participant know that thing. That kind of distributed individual knowledge misses out on the collaborative nature of language. Distributed individual knowledge isn't sufficient for getting us coordinated in important ways. Suppose Alex and Beth are working together to make an omelet. The eggs need to be beaten, and the mushrooms need to be sautéed. If Alex knows these two things need to be done, and Beth also knows that these two things need to be done, but Alex doesn't know that Beth knows, then Alex won't be able to focus on beating the eggs, confident that Beth will sauté the mushrooms. They need to both know what needs to be done, and to both know that they both know what needs to be done. That common ground can be achieved linguistically, by having Alex say, and thereby put on the conversational scoreboard, that in order to make an omelet the eggs need to be beaten and the mushrooms need to be sautéed. This gives us a fifth idealizing assumption:

> **Idealization 5:** The common ground of a conversation is what is known by all the conversational participants, and is known to be known by all of them (and known to be known to be known by all of them, and so on).

If the goal of conversations is to build a body of common knowledge, then we should expect speech to be governed by the norm that we only say what we know. If we assume that speakers follow this norm, this give us a sixth idealization:

> **Idealization 6:** Speakers say only what they know.

Finally, the idealized picture needs to say something about how speakers are able to put things on the conversational scoreboard by saying them. Return again to the classroom where our well-behaved academics are trying to learn about the geography of Scotland. Initially it isn't on the scoreboard that Ben Nevis is the tallest mountain in Scotland. One of us knows that, but it isn't common knowledge to us all. But then the one who knows it says that Ben Nevis is the tallest mountain in Scotland, and it goes onto the scoreboard. She does that by uttering the sentence 'Ben Nevis is the tallest mountain in Scotland.' For this to work we have to make a seventh idealization:

> **Idealization 7:** A common language has words with stable meanings known to all conversational participants, so that speakers can make their communicative intentions manifest by using suitable words.

1.2 Taking Stock and Returning to the Real World

So here is a list of representative idealizations that often govern theorizing about language:

> **Idealization 1:** Conversation and communication are fundamentally cooperative activities. In a conversation, there is a goal to be achieved, and each participant in the conversation contributes to the conversation in an attempt to further that goal.

Idealization 2: Speakers attempt to conform to Grice's maxims, and audiences assume that speakers are attempting to conform to the maxims when they interpret their contributions.

Idealization 3: The goal of a conversation is to build up a body of knowledge shared by all of the conversational participants.

Idealization 4: The state of a conversation at any point can be modeled by the *common ground* of the conversation: the things which are shared knowledge for all of the conversational participants.

Idealization 5: The common ground of a conversation is what is known by all the conversational participants, and is known to be known by all of them (and known to be known to be known by all of them, and so on).

Idealization 6: Speakers say only what they know.

Idealization 7: A common language has words with stable meanings known to all conversational participants, so that speakers can make their communicative intentions manifest by using suitable words.

These kinds of idealizations make for simple models that explain real world phenomena only to the extent the real world corresponds to the idealizations. Consider again Alex and Beth's Scottish geography conversation. Here's a summary of an idealized conversation between them:

Idealized Explanation of a Move in a Classroom-Style Conversation: Alex and Beth enter the classroom friendly and on good terms. They're not there to tear each other down, but to pursue a common goal (Idealization 1). In particular, their common goal is to pool and increase their body of knowledge, with a specific focus in this conversation on the question of what Scotland's geography is like (Idealization 3). At the beginning of the conversation, Alex knows a bit about Scottish geography and Beth knows a bit, but they know separate things and neither of them knows what the other knows, so their common knowledge of Scottish geography is empty. They have no common ground at this point. Alex knows that Ben Nevis is the tallest mountain in Scotland and wants to say something that makes that common knowledge (Idealization 4). She intends cooperatively to follow the Gricean maxims, and to rely on Beth's confidence that she'll be following the maxims (Idealization 2). As a result, Beth will trust what Alex says. Alex knows she can make her intention manifest by picking from the common and stable language words of the right meaning (Idealization 7). Alex thus utters the sentence 'Ben Nevis is the tallest mountain in Scotland.' Since the language is stable and common, Beth knows what intention is associated with it, and since she can assume that Alex has no hidden agenda, she can locate the right communicative intention in Alex. Since Beth knows that Alex will only intend to communicate things she knows (Idealization 6), Beth can use her recognition of Alex's communicative intention as a source of knowledge that Ben Nevis is the tallest mountain in Scotland, and since that's now common knowledge, it becomes part of the common ground and goes onto the conversational scoreboard.

That's a long and complicated story about getting across a small bit of information about a frankly rather small mountain. But linguistic communication is a rather impressive thing (it's like telepathy achieved by moving your lips, or an amazing device for using sound waves to control the neural wirings in another person's brain), and this complicated picture which separates out the many elements of communication has proven very helpful in thinking about language use.

All of this, though, happens in the classroom where things are relatively non-messy. This book is for the most part about what happens when we step outside the classroom and considers a range of questions about what happens when things are not quite so ideal. We focus on questions such as the following:

- What are the various ways in which non-cooperation between Alex and Beth undermines or contributes to their conversation?
- What if one of their goals isn't to build up a body of knowledge, but instead to achieve something that is disconnected from truth and knowledge?
- What happens if one of them speaks, but has no interest in speaking the truth?
- What happens if one of them uses words that mean nothing (and so there's no shared meaning)?
- What happens if they disagree about what the meaning of words are?
- What happens if one of them uses words in order to offend or trigger various emotional reactions?
- How do we understand conversations where one of the participants' contributions are coerced or where one participant is silenced?
- What do we say about cases where it's unclear who the speaker is or what the intended audience is?

In short, the focus of this book is on language use that fails to satisfy the idealizations. It's likely that most use of language fails to satisfy at least one of the idealizations and typically many of the them. That fact raises interesting and complicated questions about why philosophers introduced the idealized picture in the first place. If it fails to describe the majority of speakers and their speech, why did philosophers end up working with theories that make those idealizing assumptions? We return to that question in Chapter 12 where we have more to say about the role of idealizations in theorizing more generally (in the sciences and political theory in particular).

1.3 Some Qualifications

We just gave a broad sketch of some idealization that are often appealed to in theorizing about language and communication. That sketch should be accompanied by a couple of qualifications:

- **First qualification**: We said that these idealizations guide *many* of the efforts to theorize about natural language, communication, and speakers of the last 100 years. We did not say it guided *all* such efforts. More than 100 years of theorizing has generated an enormous amount of literature from varied perspectives. Some of that work (e.g., that inspired by the later Wittgenstein) questions the idealizations.

- **Second Qualification**: We also have not said why these idealizations have governed so much theorizing about language and communication. The answer to this question has at least two parts. One part of the answer is historical: it has to do with the origin of philosophy of language (and linguistics) and the kinds of interests that guided those who founded these disciplines. This is not a history book and so we will refer readers to other sources for that (see suggestions in Further Readings). The second part of the answer, however, is that the theorists that make these (and related) idealizations think they are fruitful. They think that we will develop good theories if we based them on these idealizations. That line of thought is explored further in the last chapter of the book. In that chapter we talk more generally about the value and nature of idealizations in theorizing.

In sum: the purpose of outlining the idealizations is not to write a careful history of philosophy of language, but to create a useful heuristic (an idealization, if you will): it helps us introduce readers to a range of phenomena that are easier to understand and engage with when contrasted with the idealized picture.

1.4 An Overview of the Book

The next ten chapters each deal with various ways in which actual language use diverges from the idealizations set out above.

- The second chapter is about various ways in which speakers communicate content other than what they literally express. We provide a brief introduction to implicatures and presupposition, as well as to what we call 'context control'.
- The third chapter describes various ways in which speakers don't tell the truth. In some cases they make honest mistakes. Sometimes they write fiction. More troubling acts include lying, deception, and misleading. This chapter is primarily an introduction to contemporary theories of these last three phenomena.
- The fourth chapter has two parts. The first is an introduction to contemporary theories of bullshit: it is about people who speak without any regard for truth. The second part is about what we call 'deep bullshit': people who speak without regard to whether what they say makes any sense.
- The fifth chapter is an introduction to the exciting field of Conceptual Engineering: the study of how concepts (or meanings) can be defective and how they can be improved.
- Chapter 6 introduces the reader to contemporary theories of slurs and pejoratives. The various theories are divided into four: Descriptive Content Views, Presuppositional Views, Expressivist Views, and Prohibitionist Views.
- In Chapter 7 we introduce the reader to Lexical Effects: these are the various non-cognitive effects that words have on speakers (think about the how different you feel (or the different associations you get) when you read the words 'fart', 'rose', and 'fascist', respectively).
- Chapter 8 is an introduction to the ways in which generic claims can lead to defective reasoning and the ways in which these expressions can be involved in the promotion of social prejudice and essentializing.

- In Chapter 9 we first describe what happens when a speaker's audience is scattered (for example when she speaks to several people or groups of people simultaneously). We then turn to what happens when the speaker itself is scattered, such as when a group speaks or writes a document (for example a law).
- Chapter 10 starts with a brief introduction to speech act theory and then turns to linguistic oppression (oppression done in speech). We then discuss the phenomenon of silencing. ways to make it difficult or impossible for someone to say what they want to say.
- The eleventh chapter is about the speech act of consent. We discuss what consent is, the advantages and disadvantages of tacit consent, and whether deception can invalidate consent.
- In the twelfth and final chapter of the book we return to the themes from the first chapter in light of the previous discussion. Ten chapters of this book describe the myriad of ways in which speakers don't conform to the idealizations in Chapter 1. Does that mean the idealizations are useless? We compare idealizations about language to idealizations in natural science and political theory.

CENTRAL POINTS IN CHAPTER 1

- What is appropriate speech for the classroom may not be appropriate for the business meeting, date, bar, or political rally. Theorists of language all too frequently concentrate on the former sort of language use, and thus start from an idealized picture of how language works. This book is concerned with how to use the theoretical tools we developed for the study of language in the highly non-ideal real world.
- We noted seven idealizations that philosophers of language and linguists often make. Throughout the book, we will see a range of cases in which these idealizations fail to apply, and at the end we'll step back and see what if anything this means for theorizing about language in general.
- The first idealization has it that communication is a cooperative venture: in a conversation, each participant is working towards a common goal. The second idealization specifies some rules to help people achieve these shared goals: Grice's conversational maxims.
- The next idealizations concern knowledge. They say, respectively, that the goal of conversation mentioned above is to build up a body of shared knowledge, that this can be modeled in terms of a common ground, and that common ground consists of shared knowledge: what is known, known to be known,

known to be known to be known, and so on, by all the participants in the conversation.
- The final two idealizations tell us that speakers say only what they know, and that language has words with stable meanings known to all participants.

Further Reading and Exercises

FURTHER READING FOR CHAPTER 1

Foundational work on conversation is the already mentioned Grice (1989); a readable introduction can be found in chapters 7 and 13 in Lycan (1999). The work of Robert Stalnaker, beginning with (1978), and (1984) and up to the more recent book (2014) is foundational. Lewis (1979) is another work in this tradition, and has been seminal for theorists of non-ideal communication, who have sought to expand his notion of conversational score to make sense of the more malignant things we do with language. Williamson (2000) contains the defense of the knowledge norm of assertion (Idealization 6). For an attempt at creating a theory of language use that departs from many of these idealizations see Sperber and Wilson (1986). For an introduction to the history of philosophy of language see Jason Stanley (2008).

Comprehension Questions

1. Illustrate Idealization 1 with two sample dialogs—one in which it is adhered to, and one in which it is not.
2. Does Idealization 1 strike you as right? Do you think we are cooperative in this way?
3. Give some examples from TV, books, or your recent conversations of cases in which Grice's maxims are violated.
4. Based on the above answer, which, if any, maxim is it worst to violate?
5. What is collective knowledge or common ground? Do we have much collective knowledge?

Exploratory Questions

6. If we understand conversation as a process of building up collective information/common knowledge, how should we understand the role of questions in conversation?
7. Relatedly, consider the following scintillating dialog:
   - Person: Hot today.
   - Person's neighbor: Yes. Hopefully it stays that way!

Are these people trying to build up a body of common knowledge? If not, why not? What are they doing? How prevalent are exchanges like this?

8. In Idealization 5, we claimed that what's important is not just that speakers cooperate in the aim of acquiring knowledge, but of acquiring shared knowledge: it's important not only that they both know p, but also that they both know that they both know p. But we also required that they both know that they both know that they both know that p. Can you think of a reason why this might be so?

9. Idealization 5 says that hearers trust their audience. How frequently do you distrust the person you're speaking to? How does it affect conversation?

10. Justify each of the maxims—why do we need them?

11. Propose some more maxims of conversation.

12. Idealization 6 is close to what philosophers call the knowledge norm of assertion—that one should say only what one knows. Can you think of any reason for preferring this norm to, say, the belief norm of assertion, which says that one should say only what one believes, or the truth norm, which says that one should say only what is true?

2

Three Forms of Non-Ideal Language

We start with some mild deviations from the idealizations in the previous chapter. In the idealized setting, everything going on with communication is overt and on the surface. Here we will consider some small ways in which language and communication can be made devious, with some of the work and some of the machinery hidden from view. A certain amount of deviousness can be a good thing—by hiding things from view, we can make communication faster, more efficient, and easier. But, as we'll see in later chapters, once things get hidden from view, they become potential tools for linguistic manipulation and bad behavior. The specific topics we discuss here involve violations of the idealizing conditions set out in Chapter 1 that have been extensively studied by linguists and philosophers of language. The tools developed to help explain these phenomena will help us explain and describe the more severe forms of non-cooperative communication that we will address in later chapters.

2.1 Devious Intentions: Conversational Implicature

In ideal circumstances, speakers obey (and audiences expect speakers to obey) Grice's maxims of quality, quantity, relation, and manner. In the simplest cases, they obey these maxims straightforwardly, by picking sentences whose conventional meanings give information that is true and relevant. But in more complicated cases, speakers can still be cooperative and follow the maxims, but follow them more indirectly and deviously.

Alex and Beth are preparing for a dinner party. Consider the following dialog:

ALEX: When should I put out the wine?
BETH: The guests are arriving at 7:00.

Beth's response initially looks like it violates the Gricean maxim of relation. Alex has asked a question, and Beth's answer does nothing to address that question. But Beth isn't being genuinely uncooperative. She's caught in a conversational bind. Being a poor enologist, she doesn't know how quickly to expect the wine to warm up or what the ideal temperature is for the wine to be served at. Being cooperative, she wants to obey the maxim of quantity, and supply information that she thinks is true, so she doesn't want to just make up a time. So she says something that looks irrelevant, but she assumes that Alex will assume she is, in fact, doing her best to be relevant. Alex will then understand that Beth, following the maxim of quantity, is providing as much information as she can about the question. Since she hasn't done anything to answer the question directly, Alex can work out that Beth doesn't have any direct answer to it, and in turn can work out that she is relying on Alex's superior enological knowledge to work backward from the time of arrival to the proper time to set out the wine. Alex thus understands Beth as communicating that she doesn't know enough about wines, but Alex does, and can pick the appropriate amount of time that the wine requires to reach ideal serving temperature, and that Alex should set out the wine that amount of time prior to 7:00.

Beth, of course, could just have explicitly said that. But she didn't need to. She was able to exploit the background assumption that she was conforming to the Gricean maxims to communicate more than her words explicitly said. The sentence that she used didn't express a content that by itself would have been relevant, so the assumption that Beth *was* being relevant triggers a search for something more that she might have been saying. This in turn leads to the conclusion that Beth was indirectly communicating that she had no relevant information to provide. In these sorts of cases, Grice says that the speaker is *flouting* the maxims: giving the surface appearance of violating them to force audiences to look for a further communicated content that is, after all, in keeping with the maxims. Beth didn't *say* that she didn't know how long it took the wine to warm up, but she *meant* and *communicated* that. As a bit of technical vocabulary, we say that in such cases the speaker *conversationally implicates* something:

> **Conversational Implicature**: A speaker conversationally implicates that p if they mean that p (they have the Gricean communicative intention of getting their audience to know that p), but they do not explicitly say that p (the sentence they utter doesn't mean that p). Audiences can then work out what the speaker means by assuming that the speaker is (really, despite the flouting) following the Gricean maxims, and determining what communicative intention would make what they explicitly said conform to the maxims.

Conversational implicature is a mild case of communicative deviousness. The speaker is allowing more of the communicative burden than usual to fall on the audience: the audience is not called on only to work out what the sentences used mean, but also to do some psychological calculation, working out why a cooperative speaker would have used those sentences and how their use could have been part of a communicative goal in keeping with the maxims. The example of Alex and Beth involved flouting the maxim of relation, but similar cases can be constructed involving the flouting of other maxims.

2.2 Why Bother with Implicatures?

In the classroom, perhaps no one is devious, and everyone says exactly what they mean. But in actual social interactions, the deviousness of conversational implicature is common. This deviousness can play a number of different functions:

1. One pedestrian reason for using conversational implicatures is that they allow for more brevity in communication. Beth could have said, 'I don't know when to set out the wine because I don't know much about wine, and so in particular don't know either what temperature the wine should be at when drunk or how long it will take the wine to reach that temperature. But I know that you know a lot about wine, and probably do know those things. And from the time of arrival of the guests you can then work out using that knowledge when the wine should be put out. So I'm letting you know that the guests are arriving at 7:00.' But that's a lot to say. If she can get away with just saying 'the guests are arriving at 7:00',

on the assumption that Alex can pretty easily work out the rest, then she's got reason to do so.

Conversational implicature will often involve a trade-off between decreased labor for the speaker (who doesn't have to do to the work of selecting and uttering as many words) and increased labor for the audience (who has to do the extra work of calculating the non-explicit communicative intentions of the speaker). Because there is a trade-off in labor, one effect that conversational implicatures can have is to mark power relations within the conversation. The speaker who communicates by implicature can be revealing (or even signaling) that they are the dominant party in the conversation, and in a position to demand that the audience do the interpretative work. Consider:

> ASSISTANT: When should I schedule your meetings with the ambassador and with the senator tomorrow?
>
> PRESIDENT: There's nothing worse than an officious fool before having coffee.

The president here demands that the assistant do the interpretive work of figuring out that the appointment with the senator (whom the president regards as an officious fool) is to be scheduled later in the day, and thereby also demands that the assistant be tracking enough facts about the president (whom he does and doesn't regard as an officious fool, when he has his coffee) to do that interpretive work. If similarly indirect responses by the assistant to the president wouldn't be tolerated, the facts about who can and can't use the communicative shortcuts of implicature are marking and reinforce the power relations between president and assistant.

2. Conversational implicatures tend to be highly context-specific. Beth's saying 'The guests are arriving at 7:00' implicates that she doesn't know much about wine in the context of Alex's question, but in a different context, it won't have that implication. If Alex says, 'Do we have time for a game of chess?' and Beth replies 'The guests are arriving at 7:00,' Beth will implicate something about the length of chess games, rather than something about her ignorance of wines.

One of the contextual features that influences conversational implicatures is shared knowledge of the conversational participants. To see this, let's invent a little shared background. Alex and Beth have over the years seen all of the Marvel superhero movies in the theater. Not by any explicit design, they've always ended up going out for sushi before seeing each movie. Alex says, 'What are we having for dinner tonight?', and Beth replies 'We're seeing Infinity War tonight!' In saying this, Beth implicates that she and Alex will be having sushi, because that has been the regular association with Marvel movies. (She perhaps also implicates that Alex has noticed the pattern in meals.) But Beth can implicate this by saying 'We're seeing Infinity War tonight!' only because of the rich shared background between her and Alex. Because making and extracting the implicature requires this rich shared background, Beth's decision to communicate by implicature draws attention to the shared background that makes the communication possible. It thus has the secondary effect of bringing Alex and Beth together, of marking them as connected in an important way.

3. On the idealizing assumption that participants in a conversation share a language with stable and mutually known meanings, what is meant by a sentence used by a speaker in that conversation is precise and fully defined. But there are times when we don't want to communicate something precise and fully defined. Alex says, 'Everyone will be at the party tonight.' In doing so, she flouts the maxim of quality—it's obviously not true that literally *everyone* will be at the party. She is thereby conversationally implicating that everyone in some restricted subgroup will be at the party. But Alex herself might not have any particular subgroup in mind. All of their mutual friends? Everyone they invited? Everyone of social importance, for some unspecified standard of social importance? Alex might regard all of these as plausible, but not mandatory, ways of filling out what she was implicating.

Alex's primary goal was, perhaps, to emphasize to Beth the importance of tonight's party. That primary goal isn't itself communicative—it's not that she primarily wanted to get across some precise particular piece of information about the party. By exploiting conversational implicature, then, Alex was able to wave her conversational hands in the general direction of a cluster of contents, any one of which would be sufficient to achieve the primary goal. Alex's linguistic behavior departs in a new way from our idealizing assumptions. She's not only introducing a gap between what she says and what she means, but also stepping away from a model of conversation in which the point of conversation is to have something precise that you mean.

4. Conversational implicature is always devious in the sense that it involves making communicative intentions less than fully manifest (thus

allowing, as in the previous example) the possibility of not always *having* precise communicative intentions). But so far we've been considering examples of implicature that are still basically cooperative: while communicative intentions aren't made fully explicit, the *reasons* for the covertness still involve a cooperative relation between speaker and audience. But once some deviousness has been introduced, it's easy to see how it can be put to less cooperative purposes.

In a successful implicature, there is a communicative intention that's discoverable by the conversational participants, but which isn't made fully manifest by being placed on the conversational record by being given explicit linguistic form. Liz Camp (2018) has drawn attention to a category of utterances she calls *insinuations*, in which a conversational implicature is made with the thought that this lack of manifestness allows a kind of plausible deniability should certain challenges arise. She considers the example of a driver who, when pulled over for speeding, says to the police officer 'I'm in a bit of a hurry. Is there any way we can settle this right now?' The driver is thereby implicating that they are willing to bribe the officer to ignore the speeding violation. But because they don't explicitly *say* this, they maintain plausible deniability. If the police officer responds, 'You do know that it is a serious offense to attempt to bribe the police, don't you?', the driver can respond by denying that they were offering a bribe, and claiming that they were simply asking if there was a mechanism for paying fines on the spot.

Since implicatures require some degree of *mind-reading* in order to calculate what non-manifest communicative intentions speakers have, it's always subject to some chance of error, and a devious and uncooperative speaker can exploit this fact by claiming (falsely) that the audiences have misunderstood their intention. Of course, there's a limit to what plausible deniability can achieve. Perhaps the driver can protect himself from legal sanctions by merely insinuating the bribe (but don't try this at home—we aren't lawyers), but if the insinuating intention is indeed made clear enough that audiences get it, then even if the speaker later disavows that intention, audiences might refuse to accept the disavowal and still hold the speaker socially responsible. To take another of Camp's examples, when a speaker says, 'You know that Obama's middle name is Hussein. I'm just saying', they can deny all they want that they meant to communicate anything negative about Obama, but their audience can nonetheless treat them in the same way they would someone who overtly tries to denigrate Obama by saying 'Obama is a Muslim.'

The insinuator takes advantage of conversational implicature to achieve a kind of higher-level deviousness: there is something they want to communicate, and thus there is a communicative intention they want to be discoverable by their flouting of the Gricean maxims, but they don't want it to be fully epistemically transparent that this is what they're up to, so that they can maintain plausible deniability. But conversational implicature can also be exploited in a more direct way, by someone who *doesn't* endorse what they implicate, but wants to use the implication to mislead their audience. We'll return to this topic in Chapter 3 when we discuss lying and misleading, but consider a famous case of courtroom testimony. In *Bronston v. United States*, Bronston appeared as a witness in a bankruptcy hearing. Bronston had in the past had a Swiss bank account, and wanted to hide this fact from the court. The following exchange occurred:

Q. Do you have any bank accounts in Swiss banks, Mr. Bronston?
A. No, sir.
Q. Have you ever?
A. The company had an account there for about six months, in Zurich.
Q. Have you any nominees who have bank accounts in Swiss banks?
A. No, sir.

Bronston's second answer implicated, by the maxim of quantity, that he had never had a Swiss bank account (because the maxim of quantity would have required him to provide as much relevant information as he had in response to the question). But Bronston was not in fact following the maxim of quantity—he was uncooperatively violating it, rather than cooperatively flouting it. The examiner accepted the (misleading) implicature, and went on.

Of course, Bronston could simply have *lied* and denied having owned a Swiss bank account. But as with insinuations, some level of deniability seems important here. In this case, there was a *legal* question about deniability, since perjury charges were later brought against Bronston when it was discovered that he had had a Swiss bank account. The Supreme Court eventually ruled in Bronston's favor, saying:

There is, indeed, an implication in the answer to the second question that there was never a personal bank account; in casual conversation, this interpretation might reasonably be drawn. But we are not dealing with casual conversation, and the statute does not make it a criminal act for a witness to willfully state any material matter that implies any material matter that he does not believe to be true. (*Bronston v. United States* 409 U.S. 352)

The question of whether the *linguistic* distinction between what is explicitly said and what is merely implicated tracks the *legal* distinction between what creates liability to perjury and what does not isn't entirely clear. The court also considered a hypothetical example of a witness who, having been in a store fifty times, is asked how many times he has been in it and says 'five times'. This might be thought of as a case of a true content with a false implicature—the witness *had* been in the store five times, and then another forty-five times beyond that, and thus merely implicated that he had been in *exactly* five times. But the court suggested that this sort of example *would* be open to perjury charges. The court cast some (reasonable) doubt on whether this was mere implicature, holding that an answer of 'five times' in response to an explicit 'how many' question could be held to explicitly say 'exactly five times'. But the court's ultimate concern seems to have been pragmatic, rather than linguistic. They highlight the fact that the hypothetical example 'contains nothing to alert the questioner that he may be side-tracked' (*Bronston v. United States* 409 U.S. 352). The thought seems to be that the questioner in Bronson's case should have been able to see that Bronson's literal answer wasn't responsive to the question, and pursued the issue further, and that the important legal question is whether the line between perjury and non-perjury is put at a point that places the right level of obligation on the questioners to be thorough in pursuing the information they want.

2.3 Devious Meanings: Presupposition

Conversational implicature is a form of *psychological* deviousness, allowing speakers to be less than explicit, and in certain cases uncooperative and deceptive, about their communicative intentions. But there can also be forms of *deviousness in meaning*. One of our idealizing assumptions in the classroom is that the conversational participants are speaking a shared and stable language, with the meanings of words and sentences common knowledge to everyone. On this picture, when there are no implicatures at issue, the uttering of a sentence contributes some specific bit of information to the common ground.

But some words are more devious in their meaning than others. The word 'cat' is straightforward. Its meaning is (roughly) a kind of animal (the genus Felidae), so its informational contribution is to separate things into two kinds, the cats and the non-cats. But the word 'regret' is less straightforward. Its explicit meaning concerns a certain attitude: to say that Alex regrets stealing Beth's car is to say something about Alex's state of mind. But in saying that Alex regrets stealing Beth's car, we also *get across* that Alex *did* steal Beth's car. We don't explicitly say so, but it wouldn't make sense to say that Alex regretted stealing Beth's car if she hadn't done so.

The word 'regret' is a **presuppositional** word. Presuppositional words have special prior conditions on when it makes sense to use them. 'Regret' is one of a category of *factive verbs*, which presuppose the truth of their complement:

1. Alex regrets stealing Beth's car (presupposes: that Alex stole Beth's car.)
2. Alex forgot that Beth owned a car (presupposes: that Beth owned a car.)
3. Alex was happy that Beth bought a new car (presupposes: that Beth bought a new car.)

None of these sentences with factive verbs explicitly say that their complements are true. It's just that it would be odd and inappropriate to use them if their complements were not true.

One diagnostic symptom of presupposition is that presupposed content persists under negation and other operators. It's odd to say that Alex regrets stealing Beth's car if Alex didn't steal Beth's car. And it's equally odd to say that Alex *doesn't* regret stealing Beth's car if Alex didn't steal Beth's car. This shows that 'Alex regrets stealing Beth's car' doesn't just mean 'Alex stole Beth's car and feels bad about doing so.' If it did mean that, 'Alex doesn't regret stealing Beth's car' would just mean 'It's not true that Alex stole Beth's car and feels bad about doing so,' and in cases in which Alex didn't steal Beth's car, it would be straightforwardly true. The presupposed content is somehow separate from the rest of the content, so when the rest of the content is modified in some way, the presupposed content isn't modified, as we see below. The presupposition remains if the content is questioned, or modified by a tense or modal operator:

4. Alex doesn't regret stealing Beth's car.
5. Does Alex regret stealing Beth's car?

6. Alex used to regret stealing Beth's car.

7. Alex probably regrets stealing Beth's car.

Factive verbs are only one example of presuppositional terms. Once we are on the look-out for the phenomenon, we can find it all over the place in language:

- Change of state verbs: 'Alex stopped/didn't stop smoking' presupposes that Alex smoked.
- Definite descriptions: 'Alex met/didn't meet the king of France' presupposes that France has a king.
- Implicative verbs: 'Alex managed/didn't manage to beat Beth at chess' presupposes that Alex tried to beat Beth at chess.
- Clefts: 'It was/wasn't Alex who stole Beth's car' presupposes that someone stole Beth's car.
- Additive particles: 'Even Alex can/can't solve this problem' presupposes that Alex is at one end of the spectrum with respect to ability to solve the problem.

Presuppositional language combines a *foregrounded, at-issue* content with a *backgrounded, not-at-issue* content. The at-issue content is what the bit of language is overtly about, while the non-at-issue content is what is presupposed. Thus:

Sentence	At-Issue Content	Not-At-Issue Content
Alex doesn't regret stealing Beth's car	Alex feels fine about her actions	Alex stole Beth's car
Alex didn't stop smoking	Alex still smokes	Alex used to smoke
Alex didn't meet the king of France	Alex's day was royalty-free	France has a king
Alex didn't manage to beat Beth at chess.	Beth won the chess game	Alex tried to beat Beth at chess.
It wasn't Alex who stole Beth's car	Alex is innocent	Someone stole Beth's car
Even Alex can't solve this problem	Alex can't solve the problem.	Alex is very good at problem solving.

Devious meanings give rise to devious uses. Presuppositional terms linguistically encode information without putting it out there explicitly.

The use of the presuppositional language is inappropriate when the presupposition isn't met: it's inappropriate to say that Alex doesn't regret stealing Beth's car when Alex didn't steal Beth's car. But it's not inappropriate because it's *false*. Saying that Alex regrets stealing Beth's car when Alex has no regrets is saying something false. It's explicitly putting out a piece of information that's incorrect, and that's not what cooperative people do in conversation. Saying that Alex doesn't regret stealing Beth's car when she didn't steal Beth's car isn't false, it's just odd and inappropriate. It doesn't explicitly put out the incorrect information (that Alex stole Beth's car), it just *acts as if* that information was already out there.

In non-devious cases, the presupposed information *is* already out there. If we've already established that Alex stole Beth's car, then it makes perfect sense to go on and have a discussion about whether she does or does not regret doing so. Our claims about regret will act as if it's already established that Alex stole the car, but that will make sense, because it *is* already established. In these cases, presupposition, like conversational implicature, can be a way of reducing linguistic labor. If our conversation has already established a rich common ground, then we should take advantage of linguistic expressions that rely on that common ground, so that we don't have to keep repeating what we've already established. Using presuppositional language is also a way to keep the conversational participants properly *coordinated* on the common ground. By presupposing that Alex stole Beth's car, we remind people that that fact was part of the common ground, in case anyone was starting to lose track. For this reason it's been suggested that another cooperative maxim is *Maximize presupposition!*—that there is a general preference for presuppositional over non-presuppositional language when the presuppositions are met. Thus, for example, there is something odd about saying:

8. Two of Alex's eyes are open.

rather than:

9. Both of Alex's eyes are open.

'Both' presupposes that Alex has two eyes. When that presupposition is met, and it's part of the common ground that Alex has exactly two eyes, we should prefer to use terms that do rely on that presupposition. Failing to use the presuppositional 'both' as a result tends to create an implicature that Alex has some unexpected number of eyes.

But presuppositions can also be used deviously. Some cases of devious presupposition, like some basic cases of conversational implicature, are relatively innocuous and still fully cooperative. Sometimes it's just more convenient to let certain bits of communication slide in 'under the radar'. Consider the restaurant that displays a sign saying, 'We regret that we cannot accept personal checks.' This sentence presupposes that the restaurant does not accept personal checks. But this isn't a case in which that presupposition was reasonable because the conversational participants all already knew it. Rather, the restaurant is *informing* people that it doesn't accept personal checks, but it's informing them in a devious way, by acting as if everyone already knew that, and assuming that acting that way will allow people to figure out that they don't. In this case the reason for the deviousness is to soften the blow. It's awkward to come out and tell people that you don't trust them enough to accept their personal checks, so you act as if the awkward thing had already been done, and move straight to expressing regret about that unfortunate state of affairs.

Suppose we did not already know that the restaurant didn't accept personal checks. We then read the sign and encounter its presupposition that personal checks are not accepted. In such cases, we will frequently respond by *accommodating* the presupposition. Seeing that the restaurant is speaking *as if* we all already agreed that personal checks are not accepted, we go ahead and accept this, and it becomes part of the common ground. So information can be added to the common ground non-deviously by being asserted and thereby uptaken by the conversational participants, or information can be added to the common ground deviously by being (in some sense illegitimately) presupposed, leading to conversational participants accommodating the presupposition and modifying the common ground to fit it.

In less cooperative cases, speakers can attempt to use presupposition and accommodation to sneak or force information into common ground that other conversational participants might not want there. The crudest version of this occurs in classic cases of presuppositional 'loaded' questions in witness examinations. The attorney who asks the witness 'Had you stopped using cocaine by the summer of 2013?' asks a question that presupposes use of cocaine prior to that summer, so that a 'yes' answer to the question acknowledges that prior use, while a 'no' answer also acknowledges the prior use as well as some use after that summer. Of course, these crude examples are unlikely to be successful. No witness is going to allow themselves to be trapped into an unwanted admission of cocaine use by giving a yes/no answer to the question—they will instead reject the question, replying that they've never used cocaine and thus can't give a yes/no answer.

But the crude examples bring out an important feature of presuppositional content: it can't be challenged *directly*. If a speaker says that Alex stole Beth's car and you disagree, you can challenge what they said by saying 'No' or 'That's wrong' or 'I disagree'. Until that disagreement is resolved, the controverted information won't become part of common ground. But if a speaker says that Alex doesn't regret stealing Beth's car and you disagree that Alex stole Beth's car, you can't challenge by saying 'That's wrong'. That kind of challenge implicitly acknowledges that Alex stole Beth's car, and instead addresses itself to the question of whether Alex regrets it.

Of course, this doesn't mean that presupposing is an unchallengeable way to get information into the common ground. That would give conversational manipulators far too much power. Presuppositions can be challenged, but they can only be challenged in more labor-intensive ways. You have to raise the presupposed content to a higher level of salience, promoting it to at-issue status and then rejecting it. You challenge by saying something like 'Hey, wait a minute. Who said that Alex stole Beth's car? I don't think that's right.' This requires saying more, and being more disruptive of the conversational flow, so there may be some increased tendency for conversational participants to let objectionable presupposed content go by unchallenged, but the challenging is always available.

But because presuppositions are harder to challenge and harder to notice, they may in fact go by unchallenged when the presupposed content is more subtle. Consider a claim like: 'We are facing considerable resistance to our proposed health care reforms, but it's still important that we at least secure caps on prescription drug prices for senior citizens.' The use of 'at least' in this claim encodes a presupposition that the caps on prescription drug prices lie at one end of a spectrum of goals, and thus suggests that those caps are a particularly important goal. But that presupposition isn't so striking and easily characterized as the presupposition of a factive verb, and a conversational participant could easily endorse the claim without particularly noting the presupposition, thus allowing the presupposition to enter into the common ground.

Of course, letting a presupposition into the common ground isn't magically going to make conversational participants accept that presupposition. But the contents of the common ground can shape the future direction of the conversation, and by shaping what is and isn't said can indirectly shape people's attitudes. Compare the two claims:

10. Relief workers are rushing to take aid supplies to disaster-struck regions of Haiti.

11. Relief workers are rushing to bring aid supplies to disaster-struck regions of Haiti.

The change from 'take' to 'bring' marks a change between presupposing a frame of reference centered on Haiti and a frame of reference centered on (e.g.) the United States. By using presupposition to center the frame of reference in one way or another, a speaker can set the conversational scoreboard in a way that encourages describing the relief efforts broadly from the Haitians' point of view or from the Americans' point of view, which can then influence what points about the relief efforts are made.

2.4 Devious Scoreboards: Context Control

In the classroom, the conversational scoreboard has simple contents and simple rules: the scoreboard simply collects the information that has been introduced in the conversation thus far, and is updated after each new assertion by adding the content of that assertion. But outside the classroom a wider range of human considerations drive and shape conversations, and an adequate conversational scoreboard needs to track more than just the information accumulated. The upshot of the examples we give below is that it is possible to change what is true and what is false simply by changing these other features of the scoreboard. We give three examples: questions, commands, and what is possible.

We have been focusing so far entirely on declarative sentences used to make assertions. But there are other kinds of sentences, and other kinds of linguistic acts that can be performed using those sentences. In addition to making assertions, we *ask questions* and *issue commands*. Neither questions nor commands place information on the conversational scoreboard.

But they do *something* to the scoreboard. Roughly the scoreboard tracks, in addition to information accumulated, what our goals in inquiry are and what our to-do list is (there are also elaborate formal theories for both questions and commands, but we won't need the details here).[1] These aspects of the scoreboard can then be adjusted by questions and commands. We can see that the scoreboard is really tracking these things by noting downstream linguistic consequences of questions and commands. Consider the following text:

- Yesterday a policeman and a fleeing suspect got into a fight. He pulled a gun and shot him, and then fled the scene.

The pronouns 'he' and 'him' in the second sentence are ambiguous—this could be the policemen shooting the suspect, or the suspect shooting the policeman. But now suppose that this is said in response to a previous question:

- Alex: Do policemen ever injure suspects during arrests?
- Beth: Yesterday a policeman and a fleeing suspect got into a fight. He pulled a gun and shot him, and then fled the scene.

With the prior question framing what Beth says, the pronouns become unambiguous. That's because when 'he' is the policeman and 'him' is the suspect, what Beth says addresses Alex's question, but when 'he' is the suspect and 'him' is the policeman, what Beth says doesn't address Alex's question. So Alex's question places a new goal of inquiry on the scoreboard, and subsequent moves in the conversation are interpreted in light of that updated scoreboard.

Similarly with commands. Under normal circumstances, the following utterance by Alex is false:

- I'll need to balance a chicken on my head.

But if Beth has just issued the command:

- Place the loudest thing in the room on top of the tallest thing in the room!

---

[1] If you're interested in the details, you could consult Cross and Roelofsen (2018): 2.1 (and references therein) for an introduction to the semantics of questions, and Charlow (2014) for imperatives.

Then Alex's claim, made in the wake of that command, becomes true. Roughly, that's because Beth's command updates to the to-do list of the scoreboard, and claims about what is *needed* are interpreted in light of what the scoreboard represents as our collective agenda for action.

We turn now to a more devious example of scoreboard content and scoreboard control. One of the things that we track in a conversation is *what possibilities we are taking seriously*. Consider an example due to David Lewis in his important paper 'Scorekeeping in a Language Game':

> Suppose I am talking with some elected official about the ways he might deal with an embarrassment. So far, we have been ignoring those possibilities that would be political suicide for him. He says: 'You see, I must either destroy the evidence or else claim that I did it to stop Communism. What else can I do?' I rudely reply: 'There is one other possibility—you can put the public interest first for once!' That would be false if the boundary between relevant and ignored possibilities remained stationary. But it is not false in its context, for hitherto ignored possibilities come into consideration and make it true. And the boundary, once shifted outward, stays shifted. If he protests 'I can't do that', he is mistaken.
>
> (Lewis (1979): 354–5)

Here the sentence 'You can put the public interest first for once' doesn't serve to put a new piece of information on the scoreboard. Rather, it serves to make new possibilities relevant, and thus to enlarge the collection of possibilities on the scoreboard.

On this picture, to say that something must be true isn't to say that it's true in *every single* possibility, but just in the possibilities that are on the scoreboard.[2] So claims about what must be the case can change from true to false as the possibilities on the scoreboard change. If you are in a position to manipulate what the possibilities on the scoreboard are, you can indirectly control what is mutually understood to be possible and impossible.

It's not hard to see that a word like 'must', which is overtly about what is and isn't possible, will have its interpretation influenced by the relevant possibilities on the conversational scoreboard. But other bits of language also look like they are influenced by this aspect of the scoreboard in less obvious ways. Consider counterfactual claims such as 'If Oswald hadn't

---

[2] We see the same behavior with other universal claims. To say, at the party, that everyone is having a good time is not to say that *every single person anywhere* is having a good time, but just that all of a restricted collection of conversationally relevant people are having a good time.

shot Kennedy, he would have won the 1964 presidential election' or 'If a large asteroid hit the earth, it would destroy human life.' Such claims say something about what would have happened in various non-actual possibilities. But it's part of our understanding of these claims that not *every* possibility is relevant. Whether Kennedy would have won the 1964 election is something that can be a matter of serious discussion, examining political trends and speculating on how he would have handled the escalating conflict in Vietnam. But everyone should agree that there are *some possibilities* on which a living Kennedy loses the 1964 election. Consider the possibility that an alien invasion early in 1964 destroys the American government and enslaves all of humanity. If that had happened, Kennedy wouldn't have won the 1964 election.

The possibility of an alien invasion, though, isn't a *relevant* possibility when considering hypotheticals about Kennedy's performance in the 1964 election. Similarly, possibilities in which the laws of gravitation suddenly change and the asteroid bounces off harmlessly aren't relevant when considering hypotheticals about our survival of an asteroid strike. A counterfactual, then, says that every *relevant* possibility (every possibility currently on the conversational scoreboard) that satisfies some qualifying condition (being a possibility in which Oswald doesn't shoot Kennedy) also satisfies some further condition (being a possibility in which Kennedy wins the 1964 election).

As a result, conversational moves that change the scoreboard can thereby change the acceptability of conditionals. Consider:

- Alex: If we leave at 2:00, we'll get to the airport on time.
- Beth: There might be heavy traffic.
- Alex: Good point. We'd better leave early—if we leave at 2:00, we might not get to the airport on time.

On the current picture, what Alex initially says is true, because at that point, the possibility of heavy traffic isn't on the scoreboard. But Beth then puts that possibility on the scoreboard with her 'might' claim. Once on the scoreboard, the conditional is no longer true, and Alex retracts it. This ability to change the acceptability of conditionals then opens up the possibility of interesting devious scoreboard manipulation. What conditionals are true matters to us, because when we make plans, we consider what would happen under various circumstances. Imagine we are trying to decide whether to put a railing along an elevated walkway. At first we think there's no need, because we agree:

- The walkway isn't high, so if someone were to fall off, they wouldn't be injured.

But then the possibilities on the scoreboard get adjusted:

- But there might be older people using the walkway, with more fragile bones.

After adjustment, the acceptability of conditionals changes so that we accept:

- If someone were to fall off, they might break their hip.

Based on this counterfactual consideration, we decide to install a railing. So matters of considerable practical importance can be shaped by how the conversational scoreboard develops.

Shifting the possibilities on the scoreboard has theoretical as well as practical consequences. Here's a rough constraint on knowledge: to know something, we need to have enough evidence to rule out the possibility of that thing being false. Alex is at the zoo, looking out over the zebra pen. She knows that the animal in the pen is a zebra. That's because her evidence is good enough to rule out that it is an elephant or a giraffe or a tiger. She can see its horse-like shape and its distinctive black and white stripes; these features are inconsistent with its being an elephant, giraffe, or tiger. That's not to say that Alex can rule out *every conceivable* non-zebra possibility. There's the possibility that she is in the matrix and there is no animal in front of her at all. But that possibility isn't among the relevant possibilities on the scoreboard, so for current conversational purposes she doesn't have to rule it out to know that the animal is a zebra. But now Beth says:

- Maybe it's a cleverly painted mule.

Beth's utterance changes the scoreboard, and forces the possibility that it's a painted mule to be placed on the scoreboard. Alex's evidence doesn't rule out that possibility, so after Beth's utterance, Alex no longer knows that it's a zebra.

It matters who knows what—it matters to how much we trust each other and accept each other's testimony. If changes in the conversational scoreboard can change who knows what, then conversational control becomes a form of theoretical and practical control. It thus becomes a pressing question who is able to change the scoreboard to what extent.

What possibilities are on the scoreboard also influences the interpretation of causal claims. A lighted match is dropped onto a pile of kindling, and the resulting fire burns down the house. Was the fire caused by the match or by the presence of the kindling? Of course, both are causal contributors (as are thousands of other factors, such as the presence of oxygen in the atmosphere and the absence of a fire suppression system). But our talk about 'the cause' is shaped by what possibilities we are taking to be relevant. We might take the presence of the kindling for granted and view the match as the unusual factor (we always put the kindling there; normally people don't drop matches on it), thus treating the match as the cause of the fire. That's how we will view things if all of the relevant possibilities on the scoreboard have the kindling in place, so that we're only considering the possibility of not having the match applied to the kindling and ignoring the possibility of the match being dropped on a kindling-free floor. Or we might take the presence of the match for granted and view the kindling as the unusual factor (we always drop our lighted matches there; normally people don't store kindling in that spot), thus treating the kindling as the cause of the fire. That's how we will view things if all of the relevant possibilities on the scoreboard have the match in place, so that we're only considering the possibility of not having the kindling where the match lands and ignoring the possibility of the kindling resting on a match-free floor.

What we take to be the causes of things then shapes what we do to change those things. This means that the interpretation of causal claims can be of great political significance. Consider assertions by John McCain and Barack Obama about the cause of the 2008 financial crisis.[3] McCain says:

One of the real catalysts, really the match that lit this fire, was Fannie Mae and Freddie Mac. I'll bet you, you may never even have heard of them before this crisis. But you know, they're the ones that, with the encouragement of Sen. Obama and his cronies and his friends in Washington, that went out and made all these risky loans, gave them to people that could never afford to pay back.

---

[3] The following quotations are from the second Obama/McCain presidential debate on October 7, 2008. The transcript can be read here: <http://edition.cnn.com/2008/POLITICS/10/07/presidential.debate.transcript/>.

Obama, on the other hand, says:

Let's, first of all, understand that the biggest problem in this whole process was the deregulation of the financial system. Sen. McCain, as recently as March, bragged about the fact that he is a deregulator.

We can thus see McCain and Obama as wrestling for control of the conversational scoreboard. Both Fannie Mae/Freddie Mac and financial deregulation were financial contributors to the crisis. But McCain and Obama are trying in different ways to set the relevant possibilities on the scoreboard to shape what we take to be 'the cause' of the crisis and thereby affect what political action we take in response to it.

2.5 From the Devious to the Bad

In this chapter we've been stepping away slightly from the idealizations of the first chapter. These small deviations from those idealizations remain within the territory that philosophers of language have studied extensively and developed sophisticated tools for. We've gotten a first look at some of those tools here: implicatures, presuppositions, and sophisticated conversational scoreboards. These more sophisticated tools in turn allow speakers to do more sophisticated things with the language. But so far none of this falls into what we mean by the category of *bad language*. The speakers in this chapter are a bit more devious and sneaky than those of the previous chapter, but they are still basically guided by the idealized picture—they are cooperative speakers working together to meet some beneficial conversational end. Tools that can be used to those beneficial ends can also be abused, though. In the coming chapters, we'll look at a number of cases in which idealization crumbles away entirely and we have various forms of non-cooperative, malicious, and otherwise ill-intentioned speakers.

CENTRAL POINTS IN CHAPTER 2

- In this chapter we begin our tour through non-idealized language use. We first consider implicatures, where one takes advantage of the idealized framework to communicate more quickly, effectively, or, sometimes, deviously. One can, for example, overtly flout one of the maxims introduced in the previous chapter and on that basis trust that one's hearer can work out why one did so, and what one's conversational aim was.

- We can flout maxims for good or for ill. Sometimes, we might do it just to speed up conversation. Thus if you ask me if I want to play tennis, and I reply that it's raining, by seemingly flouting the maxim of relevance I simultaneously convey both that it's raining and that I accordingly don't want to play, and do so more succinctly than if I had said 'I don't want to play because it's raining.'

- But sometimes we can do it deceptively, as when we're asked how many donuts we had, and, although we had fourteen, answer, truthfully, that we had one (it's truthful because we did have one; we just had thirteen others we chose not to mention). We thereby flout the maxim of quantity, in the hopes of hiding our gluttonous ways.

- Another linguistic maneuver we can use for good or ill is presupposition. Some words have special conditions on when it makes sense to use them. So if I say that I stopped eating donuts, it presupposes that I previously ate donuts, in the sense that, if I didn't previously eat donuts, what I said makes no sense. But it's not clear that what I said was false if I never ate donuts. Rather, it seems like it's not evaluable for truth and falsity.

- Sometimes presuppositions are conversationally useful. As with implicatures, they trade on shared knowledge and that allows brevity. I can say to you that after I stopped eating donuts I lost some weight, and that's quicker than saying 'As you know, I used to eat donuts and no longer do, and as a result I've lost weight.'

- But sometimes they can be used maliciously. Thus I might attempt to denigrate my healthy eating friend Peter, who has always avoided deep-fried sugary things, by saying 'He's so smug about his eating habits but, unlike me, he hasn't stopped eating donuts and other such fatty foods.' Such an utterance can lead to bad effects: if my audience aren't aware of Peter's eating habits, they'll come to presuppose that he formerly and presently eats donuts. But I'm somewhat absolved of the responsibility for their coming to have these false beliefs: after all, it's not like I directly said something false about Peter.

- Yet another way to guide conversations to whatever purposes, good or ill, we may have is by manipulating the conversational scorecard. We assumed, in Chapter 1, that the scorecard just recorded collective knowledge, but on more sophisticated accounts it does more. For example, it might record the *to-do list* of the conversational participants: the actions they are required to perform. One can add to the to-do list by uttering imperatives, like 'Tidy your room!' And this also updates the record of collective knowledge, because it becomes collectively known that Alex needs to tidy her room. So, again here, we can bring claims to the conversation without explicitly uttering a declarative sentence that expresses them.

Further Reading and Exercises

FURTHER READING FOR CHAPTER 2

There's a lot of material on conversational implicatures. Much of Grice (1989) is seminal. Introductory accounts can be found in textbooks like Lycan (1999), while overview articles are Davis (2014) and Blome-Tillmann (2013). There's also a vast literature on presupposition. Beaver and Geurts (2014) is a good place to start, as is Simons (2006); more advanced but exhaustive is Beaver (2001). Discussion of context sensitivity in general can be found in Cappelen and Dever (2016) and for the context sensitivity of knowledge in particular Lewis (1996).

Comprehension Questions

1. Think of dialogs like Alex and Beth's that violate the other maxims and give rise to implicatures.
2. Give some examples of implicatures, perhaps from your experience or tv shows or catchphrases.
3. We said that implicatures can both serve to mark distance in a relationship—when they convey power—or to mark closeness, by making salient a shared context. Give examples of each.
4. Both presupposition and implicature involve, in some sense, a claim being put forward without being outright said. What are the differences and similarities between the two phenomena?

Exploratory Questions

5. We noted the important phenomenon of presupposition *accommodation*: this is where a hearer, on encountering a sentence which presupposes something they didn't previously believe, comes silently to accept it. Do you think this goes on often in day-to-day conversation? Can you think of the last time you either accommodated or caused someone else to accommodate a proposition?
6. Can you think of other linguistic phenomena that should be recorded on a conversational scoreboard?
7. A lot of humor depends on the use of implicature and presupposition. What are some examples of jokes and/or comedic dialogs that exploit implicature and presupposition?

3

Messing with the Truth

Telling the truth played a big role in our idealized picture of communication. It comes up in both Idealizations 3 and 5:

Idealization 3: The goal of a conversation is to build up a body of knowledge shared by all of the conversational participants.

Idealization 5: Speakers in a conversation speak, and are expected to speak, truthfully. Hearers in a conversation trust, and can be expected to trust, what speakers say.

It clearly comes up in Idealization 5; that it comes up in Idealization 3 follows from the fact that a body of knowledge is, among other things, a body of truths, since if something is known, then it is true.

The significance of truth is also at the core of Grice's theory. His Maxim of Quality says:

Maxim of Quality: Try to make your contribution one that is true, by not saying what you believe to be false or saying that for which you lack sufficient evidence.

Many forms of non-ideal, defective, communication involve *not* telling the truth. This chapter is about the various ways that can happen.

3.1 Speaking Falsely

3.1.1 Speaking falsely 1: making mistakes

The first thing to note is that assertions of falsehoods are ubiquitous in speech for a very simple reason: we're often wrong about what the world is like. We are cognitively restricted creatures. The world is difficult and confusing. Very often we get it wrong. We keep making mistakes. But we still form beliefs. Creatures like us will often investigate whether p is the case, find some evidence that leads us to believe that p is the case, then end up believing that p is true, even when p is false. Believing that p is true makes us more inclined to assert that p and thus to tell others that p. In doing so we think we are acting in accordance with Idealizations 3, 5, and the Maxim of Quality. But we are not. This—our fallibility—is the central source of false assertions. It causes us to fall short of the idealizations, but it doesn't involve speakers *wilfully* violating these norms: the speakers are trying to say things that are true, but they get it wrong. They have good intentions, but that is not good enough: sometimes the world just won't cooperate, no matter how much work we put into it. So our fallibility and the assertion of falsehoods it leads to, is not in itself a violation of the idealizations mentioned above: we still try to speak the truth and to build up a body of shared knowledge. We're just really bad at it (because we're not that smart).

3.1.2 Speaking falsely 2: not trying hard enough

The above observation, however, isn't a license for just saying whatever you believe, no matter what. There's a great deal of philosophical literature on just how much of an *effort* we should expect people to put into checking whether their beliefs are true before telling others about them. Recall Grice who says you should not ' . . . say what you believe to be false' or ' . . . that for which you lack sufficient evidence.' This does seem to be an important element of communicative practice. But what is the right amount of effort? Does that question have a stable answer?

Suppose you just find yourself believing that A is a criminal, but you have no good reasons for thinking it. It's a hunch you can't shake. There's something shady about the guy, you feel, but you can't put your finger on it. In this situation it wouldn't be reasonable to go to the police and tell them that A is a criminal. You also shouldn't tell your friends. That you happen to believe it—based on a hunch—is not good enough reason to tell others that A is a criminal. If you *did* go around telling others and it turned out to be wrong, you couldn't defend yourself by saying: 'But I believed it to be true and so I *tried* to speak the truth.' Note that even if your hunch turned out to be right, you could have been legitimately criticized for telling others that A is a criminal: you didn't have a good enough reason for saying it. Trying to say what you believe to be true isn't good enough—you also have to make an effort to establish what the truth is. In this case, a hunch is not good enough.

However, it's hard to pin down exactly what the requirement on evidence gathering is. Most likely it varies with the context your speech takes place in. Here is some evidence of that variability: There are settings in which saying something based on a hunch is perfectly okay, even encouraged. Philosophical conversations can serve as an illustration: sometimes in casual philosophical conversation (e.g., not exam settings) you can have a hunch that p is the case, and that's good enough for asserting that p. These are settings in which the aim of the conversation is to try out ideas and in those conversations, having a hunch that something is true is good enough reason for saying it (and then we commit to trying to find support for it later in the conversation).

One factor that might play a role here is the practical impact of the speech. Casual philosophical conversation has minimal practical impact and so standards for evidence gathering are low. If the context in which you speak is one where your speech will have very severe consequences—say you're a doctor making a diagnosis that will lead to immediate surgery—then you should make a serious effort to gather evidence. If the context is one where what you say has very little impact—like casual philosophical conversation—then less is required.

The claim we just made—that the evidential requirement on saying that p varies with context—is controversial. Some philosophers (most recently and notably Williamson 2000: chapter 11) think there are constitutive rules for what he calls 'assertion', rules such that if you don't follow them, you are not making an assertion (he compares these to the rules of chess: it's not chess unless played according to the rules of chess). According to Williamson, the rules of assertion are very strong: you should assert that p only if you know that p. Your evidence must be strong enough to count as knowledge. If that is the case, then any assertion of a falsehood will be a violation of our norms of assertion (because in order for you to know that p, it has to be the case that p—'A knows that p' implies that p is true).

3.1.3 Speaking falsely 3: fiction

There's another familiar way to mess with truth (i.e., to violate Idealizations 3, 5, and the Maxim of Quality): fiction. Should literature, movies, plays, poetry, and so on, be described as defective forms of communication because they seem to consist of falsehoods (such as the falsehood that there's a place called Westeros where dragons roam)? Most of us are inclined to deny this: there's nothing wrong with literature. On the contrary, some think literature is one of the pinnacles of speech. If that is right, then our idealized picture is wrong since it seems to entail that fiction is a very bad form of speech: it consists for the most part of speakers saying things that are entirely made up. Truth does not constrain it at all. So the puzzle is this: if fiction is indeed not defective communication, *why* is it not given that it diverges so radically from the idealizations set out in Chapter 1?

We don't have a full answer to this question—maybe in a way it's fine to say that literature is defective in various ways, but we'll mention three features of fiction that help respond to the puzzle (much more on the semantics of fictional discourse can be found in our companion volume Cappelen and Dever (2018): chapter 3).

First, fiction is *parasitic* on the idealized picture in Chapter 1. A rough partial characterization of fiction goes like this: 'Fiction involves a form of pretense: in it, we pretend to do what we normally do when we speak.' It's pretense and part of what it pretends is that there's normal speech. But then in order for there to be fictional communication, there has to be non-fictional communication first. The former builds on the latter (since it, in part, pretends to be the latter). This doesn't directly answer the puzzle, but gives a hint: fiction isn't ideal communication, but it is a form of communication you can engage in when non-fictional communication is already established.

Another part of the answer is that fiction is typically *marked* as fiction. That something is fiction is typically strongly signaled: we have conventions that mark novels, short stories, etc. as such. Fictional stories about Donald Trump are not printed in the *New York Times* in the same way that articles about his politics are. If the *New York Times* published a fictional story about Trump being a murderer in the same format as their political articles, and they didn't mark it as fiction, they would be sued for defamation. It would be no defense to say: 'You misunderstood, that was just fiction, we sometimes publish short stories like *The New Yorker* does. This was one of our short stories.'

A nice illustration of this is the outrage caused by the 1938 radio program *The War of the Worlds*, Orson Wells's dramatization of H. G. Wells's novel. It was broadcast on the CBS network and presented as a series of news bulletins that follow an alien invasion of Earth. The news bulletins describe how the aliens gradually start taking over the world and (according to the fictional news stories) how this is causing global panic and destruction. This radio program was initially marked as fiction: at the beginning of the show audiences were told that it was a fictional story. The problem was that many people tuned into the show after that introduction and all they encountered were what appeared to be genuine news updates about an alien invasion of Earth. This triggered massive (non-fictional!) panic: people didn't realize that it was fiction and the broadcaster was widely criticized for this. What this illustrates is that we have conventions in place that require fictional speech to be marked as such. To mark fiction as fiction is to alert the audience to the fact the aim of expressing literal truths has been suspended. This undermines the idea that fiction is a form of deception or lying.

A final part of the answer to our puzzle is that there *is* a kind of truth that does matter in fiction: let's call it truth in fiction. According to David Lewis (1978), we should regard all fictional statements as starting with a tacit 'In such and such a fiction: . . . ' and then in place of ' . . . ' comes the fiction. The point that fiction must be marked or signaled provides some evidence of that: it has to be made salient that there's a tacit 'in the fiction' qualifier in front of the story. If some version of that view is right, then we can say that fictional claims (the claims that include the 'in such and such fiction' up front) are true: they are true if the claims made are true in the fiction. The statements that follow the tacit 'in such and such fiction' are false: it's not true that Sherlock Holmes lived on Baker street, but it is true that *in the Sherlock Holmes* stories, Sherlock Holmes lived on Baker street. Of course, this requires us to have a notion of 'truth' in fiction and requires us to think that all fictions start with a tacit 'In such and such a fiction . . . ', both of which are controversial assumptions. It would take us too far afield, however, to attempt to defend these assumptions here.

Putting all this together we get at least a partial answer to our puzzle: fictional communication is marked as pretending to be non-fictional speech and so while it violates the idealized norms from Chapter 1 it does so in an open way. Moreover, it respects some version of a truth in fiction principle, and although it is pretensive speech, within the pretense it respects the idealized norms.

3.2 Lying and Misleading

We turn now to ways of messing with truth that are more serious and problematic: lying and misleading. There's an extensive literature on how to define lying and how to distinguish it from being merely misleading. We start our discussion of this topic by some remarks about the current discussions of these issues.

3.2.1 Lying and misleading: why we should not aim for reductive necessary and sufficient conditions

Those discussions often take the following form: Someone proposes a set of necessary and sufficient conditions of the form:

- A lies just in case C.

Importantly, 'C' doesn't itself contain 'lie'—so the aim is often to find *reductive* necessary and sufficient conditions. The conditions we get— i.e., the C above—is articulated without using 'lie'. For example, the Stanford Encyclopedia entry for 'Lying and Misleading' is structured around the following definition:

To lie =df to make a believed-false statement to another person with the intention that the other person believe that statement to be true.

Each such proposal triggers a massive amount of counterexamples, showing that such proposed conditions fail to capture the notion of lying. Call this the Reductive Counterexample Game. We start this section with a little sermon on philosophical methodology: in almost all areas of philosophy is it unwise to play the Reductive Counterexample Game. This is so for two reasons:

- First, we have no good reason to think that our language contains words that when combined will exactly pick out what 'lie' picks out. We don't have that for 'red' or 'love' (if you don't believe us, try to think of reductive definitions for them!) and in general there's no good reason to expect language to have such resources. A word can come into existence in something like the following way: we observe people doing something and we say: 'let's call that kind of thing lying.' There's no reason to expect that our language already contains a bunch of words that can be used to pick out just that kind of act.
- Second, once we have introduced a word for a certain kind of act— say, once we have introduced 'lying' in the way described above— there's no good reason to think we know what kind of thing it is. Its

nature could be entirely different from what we think it is—we have no more direct insight into the nature of lying than we have into the nature of chocolate or democracy. The Reductive Counterexample Game assumes that we do: it assumes that when we are presented with examples, we have a kind of intuitive insight into whether it is a lie or not. But that's bad methodology. It takes theory and investigation to figure out what lies are, not intuitive reactions to examples.

With that little sermon out of the way, here's how we will proceed. The literature on lying and misleading is valuable in that it has provided us with a very broad and rich range of illustrations of acts in the vicinity of lying and misleading. Let's not worry too much about what exactly falls under 'lying' and what under 'misleading, but not lying'. Instead we'll draw attention to some important distinctions between cases that might cut across these.

3.2.2 Can you lie by saying something true?

As a matter of autobiography, we approached this literature with the expectation that lies must be false—we thought that in order to lie, you had to say something false. Interestingly, those writing on this topic tend to dispute this. There's a consensus that you can lie while saying something true. Here are some cases that motivate this view:

(1) A is harboring B from the Nazis. The Nazis come to A's house. B, hearing this, flees out the window, although A does not know that he has fled. The Nazis ask whether A is harboring anybody; he replies no. He tells the truth, but it seems like he is lying. (Faulkner (2007))

(2) In a foregone age in which people believed in spontaneous generation, Robert is asking his friend Thomas advice before taking an exam. Robert asks, 'Where do rats come from?' Thomas believes that rats are generated spontaneously by wet dirt, and he knows that this is the answer that will be taken as correct on the exam. But he wants Robert to fail the exam and so he tells him, 'They are born by other rats.' Robert trusts Thomas's response and gives it as his answer on the exam, which he thereby fails. (Stokke (2018))

The consensus view among those writing on lying is that in both cases the speaker is lying despite saying something true.

It's worth considering an alternative to that description: in these cases the agent *tries*, but fails, to lie. After all, it must surely be possible to try to lie, but fail: one can try but fail to do pretty much anything. To see this, consider the following. For a person to lie, several kinds of things must be the case. Some of these are internal (i.e., they depend on the agent's mental states and decisions) and some are external (i.e., they depend on non-internal factors about the world). We'll talk about some of the internal conditions below, but one way to think about lying is to take falsity to be an external success condition (i.e., a condition that's independent of a person's decisions and mental states). So in these cases the speaker is doing all he can, so to speak, to lie, but because he's confused about what the world is like, he fails.

In the spirit of what we said in our little sermon, the significant point here isn't whether we classify this as 'lying' or 'trying to lie, but failing'. What is important is that there are these two varieties and that lying might have both internal and external success conditions—in some cases you can fail to lie because you're wrong about what the world is like.

3.2.3 Does lying involve deception?

A natural thought about lying is that it involves deception: on this view an internal success condition on lying is that the liar intends to deceive the audience. It turns out that it's more complicated than that—there's at least something lying-like (something in the neighborhood of lying) that doesn't involve an intention to deceive. These are often called 'bald-faced lies'. Thomas Carson ((2006): 290) gives the following example:

The Cheating Student
A student accused of cheating on an exam is called to the Dean's office. The student knows that the Dean knows that she did in fact cheat. But as it is also well known that the Dean will not punish someone unless they explicitly admit their guilt, the student says, even though she knows that the Dean will know she is not speaking the truth, purely to avoid punishment:

1. I didn't cheat.

Let's not worry too much about whether this is 'really' lying. Instead, note that something clearly lying-like has taken place here, but the intention to deceive is missing. It's importantly different from the typical cases of lying, and illustrates the richness and variety of lying-like phenomena.

3.2.4 The moral neutrality of lying: white lies?

So maybe deception isn't a crucial feature of the cluster of phenomena we are concerned with. Let's consider another prima facie plausible such feature. It's natural to think that it's in the nature of lying that it be done maliciously or with some kind of bad intention. It turns out that's not true either. There are lies that involve kindness. The most obvious examples are so-called 'white lies', when you lie to make someone feel better. When your friend asks how her very expensive new coat looks and you say 'Looks great' even though you think it looks horrific, you're being kind.

It's tempting to think that in such cases you are doing something that's a bit wrong—it's a bit immoral—but that this badness is outweighed by the good you are doing in making your friend feel better. However, it's not clear that this is the right way to think about the situation. An alternative view is this: making your friend feel good is just the right thing to do, end of story. There's no more moral badness involved than there is when the doctor gives you an injection. Is the doctor being a little bit immoral because she inflicts a bit of pain? If there's a god keeping score, would she subtract points from the doctor each time she inflicts some pain (but then add many more points on the plus side because what she's doing is overall good)? If you think not, then analogously you could think that white lies show that lying, as such, has no moral valence. It's morally neutral—sometimes good, and sometimes bad. It all depends on why you do it and what the effects are. We return to these two ways of thinking about lying below when we compare lying and misleading.

3.2.5 The gray areas between lying, misleading, and deception

Quite a bit of work has gone into trying to precisely demarcate the distinction between lying and deception. Deception is a broader category than lying. You can deceive someone to think you are at home by programming the lights to turn on and off. In this case you get someone to have a belief (the belief that you are at home turning the lights on and off) that you know to be false, but you do it without lying. If A puts on a nurse's uniform in order to get people to think he's a nurse, he is not lying, but is deceptive.

Being misleading is again different from both: this is often used to single out cases where the speaker doesn't say something false, but intentionally communicates something false. There are interesting issues that come up when thinking about the gray area between lying and being misleading and in the rest of this chapter we discuss three examples that could be described either as speakers lying or as speakers being misleading. The goal is to show how hard it is to draw these distinctions.

3.2.5.1 IMPLICATURES AND LYING

In Chapter 2 we mentioned a note in the Supreme Court's Bronston ruling where they considered a hypothetical example of a witness who, having been in a store fifty times, is asked how many times he has been in it and says 'five times'. The witness *had* been in the store five times, and then another forty-five times beyond that. In some way the witness communicated that he had been in the store *exactly* five times. The court suggested that this sort of example *would* be open to perjury charges. If it is a case of perjury, then it's natural to also describe it as a case of lying. If it is a case of lying, then one can lie without asserting: the witness communicates the falsehood that he or she has been in the store no more than five times, but doesn't assert it outright.[1]

This of course opens the door to a range of borderline cases where it's less clear what we should put weight on: what was asserted or what was otherwise communicated. Consider the following sentences used in advertisements for New Winston cigarettes:

- Yours have additives. 94 percent tobacco 6 percent additives. New Winstons don't. 100 percent Tobacco. True taste. No BULL.
- Thank you for not smoking additives. No BULL. 100 percent tobacco. True taste.
- Still smoking additives? Winston straight up. NO ADDITIVES. TRUE TASTE.

The advert is trying to communicate that Winston cigarettes are healthier than others because they don't contain additives. The facts, however, are these: they don't contain additives (that's true), but that does not make them healthier (so it's false that they are healthier

---

[1] Is this really lying or misleading? We say: it doesn't matter. What matters is that we understand what happened, the salient features of the case, and that it can be assessed. The Supreme Court was able to assess it as (possible) perjury independently of deciding whether it's misleading or lying. What's crucial is that the speaker didn't assert the false claim: he asserted something true and in so doing, communicated something false (and knew that he did that).

cigarettes). So what the advert says is true, but what it communicates is false. The Federal Trade Commission threatened to take Winston to court, and Winston relented, adding a disclaimer to the effect that lack of additives doesn't mean their cigarettes are healthier (see Carlson and Sedivy (2011): 151ff. for discussion of this case). Did the company lie or was it merely being misleading? There might be no clear answer: the ordinary language expressions are sufficiently indeterminate and flexible (see Chapter 6 for how terms are often modulated and shaped in context) that both descriptions seem apt, and it's hard to think of a conclusive argument for the ad being one and not the other. But if the company was lying (because it was intended to communicate something the speakers knew was false), then, again, we see that it's not necessary that lying involve assertion: the lie in this case, if there is one, is merely implicated.

3.2.5.2 PRESUPPOSITIONS AND LYING

A closely related phenomenon can be generated by exploiting what we in Chapter 2 called presuppositions. Suppose someone says: 'Jones has not stopped beating his dog.' And suppose Jones never beat his dog: he is a very kind owner. There's definitely something a bit off with what the speaker said, since it presupposes that Jones previously beat his dog. Has the speaker lied or merely been misleading? Again, there doesn't seem to be a clear answer, but if this might be a case of lying, it would be another case of lying without assertion (since presupposing something doesn't involve asserting it.)

3.2.6 What's worse, being a liar or being dishonest?

Andreas Stokke says:

...a large number of philosophers throughout history have assumed that the distinction between lying and merely misleading is fundamental to what Williams (2002) calls 'the morality of truthfulness.' Aspects of this view are built into legal systems in which lying (perjury) is punishable while merely misleading utterances are not punishable if they are not also lies. Similarly, many religious systems incorporate a strict prohibition on lying, while other forms of deception are sometimes seen as permissible. Although moral traditions as well as individual writers on lying have disagreed about whether lying is ever morally acceptable, the consensus has been that lying is always morally worse than merely misleading.   (Stokke (2013): 352)

We have raised a bit of doubt about this above. We suggested that white lies are morally fine: they involve no wrongness. Even if you think a white lie involves a tiny bit of immorality, it surely has to be very minor: white lies are uttered all the time for all kinds of minor reasons— sometimes to make someone feel good for a fleeting moment, some- times to avoid a difficult conversation topic, and so on. If lying is intrinsically bad, the badness has to be super tiny, and not enough to sustain the heavy claims that Stokke summarizes (but doesn't assert in his own voice) above.

In the contemporary literature on lying and misleading, philosophers have drawn attention to a series of cases where it doesn't seems right to say that lying is worse than misleading. Here is an example from Jennifer Saul (2012): 73):

> George plans to kill Frieda. Frieda is allergic to peanuts and George makes some food for her that contains tons of peanut oil. Frieda is a bit concerned and she asks George whether the food is safe for her. Now compare two answers:
> 1. The food is safe—it won't make you sick.
> 2. The food contains no peanuts.

According to Saul, George isn't more morally blameworthy if he utters 1 than if he utters 2. Both can lead to Frieda dying. There's no deep moral difference between George using 1 or 2 when answering. Accordingly, the tradition that Stokke describes in the passage above is mistaken: we should not assume that lying is fundamentally worse than other ways of deceiving. This is pretty obvious given that white lies are lies (and if they are bad at all, it must be an extremely tiny bit of badness).

3.3 Is Respect for Truth Fundamental to All Communication?

So far in this chapter we've looked at a variety of sources of false speech. People make mistakes, they make up stories, and they lie or mislead. When all these are taken into account, it might look like truthful speech isn't even the normal or typical form of communica- tion. Saying something true is on par with saying something funny. Some utterances are funny, some are not. Some are true, some are not.

Being true is no more special than being funny. This view is obviously very different from the idealized picture of communication we presented in Chapter 1. We can distinguish between two opposed views of the role of truth in communication:

> *Truth Special*: Some of the most prominent traditions in philosophy of language assume that communication is possible only if there's a convention or norm to the effect that speakers tell the truth (or at least try to tell the truth). This is reflected in the idealizations we outlined in Chapter 1. According to such views, truth telling is especially important—it's in some sense a necessary condition on communication. Communication would break down if people didn't, in general, respect the norm of telling the truth.

> *Truth Not-Special*: But there's another way to think about the role of truth in communication: telling the truth is often nice and helpful, but not constitutive of communication. We could speak and communicate without a norm or convention of truth telling. We call such views *Truth Not-Special Views*. We end this chapter with a few arguments for and against each of these positions.

Many philosophers endorse some version of Truth Special. One version of this view holds that we couldn't say anything unless we accepted the norm of aiming to tell the truth. If we didn't accept that norm, we would not be engaging in the act of speaking or saying or asserting. Those acts are constituted by acceptance of that norm. As an analogy, consider the game of chess. You're not playing chess if you move chess pieces around on a chess board without following the rules of chess. To play chess is to adopt the rules (the norms) of the game of chess. Truth telling, on such views, is as closely connected to the act of saying as the rules of chess are to the playing of chess.

3.3.1 Lewis on conventions of truthfulness and trust

The philosopher David Lewis is an influential proponent of Truth Special. According to Lewis, that we have a shared language is a matter of shared conventions. The basic idea seems obvious enough. First, it's natural to think that the words we use mean what they mean as a matter of conventions. If we had different conventions, the sentence

- Spraspr muligrliæ saøøøruf

could mean that the cat is on the mat. If we had different conventions, the sentence:

- The cat is on the mat

could mean that the rat is on the mat (if we had a convention to use 'cat' to talk about rats). It's because we have the conventions we do have that 'the cat is on the mat' means that the cat is on the mat.

Working out a correct theory of linguistic conventions is difficult and we can't go into that rich topic in detail here. However, putting aside a range of complications, Lewis's view is that the relevant conventions are conventions of what he calls 'truthfulness and trust'. English speakers rely on the convention that they don't utter any sentences of English that are not true in English (and so they avoid uttering any English sentences that they believe to be false). To be trusting in English is to form beliefs in a certain way: to attribute truthfulness in English to others, and so to tend to respond to another's utterance of any sentence of English by coming to believe that the uttered sentence is true in English.

On Lewis's view, this commitment to a convention of truthfulness and trust is what makes us English speakers. If we didn't have those conventions, we couldn't speak English (or any other language). More specifically, if we consistently uttered sentences that we didn't believe to be true (and consistently distrusted the speech we heard), we couldn't speak a language. This view would also help us understand lying: lying works because people have a convention to believe what others say. If there was no such convention, then lying wouldn't work.

3.3.2 Wilson and Sperber on why truth is not special

The Truth Not-Special proponents reject this Lewisian view. According to Truth Not-Special, we could have people speaking and saying things to each other, even cooperating, without a commitment to truth telling. For example, Wilson and Sperber (2002) and Cappelen (2011) defend the view that acts of saying something are normatively neutral. There could be speakers who spoke English and just tried to be funny or just cared about something that didn't track truth. The commitment to truth telling isn't, on these views, constitutive of speaking a language.

Wilson and Sperber's argument for this view focuses on what they call 'loose or approximate uses'. Consider normal utterances of 1–4

(1) The lecture starts at five o'clock.

(2) Holland is flat.

(3) Sue: I must run to the bank before it closes.

(4) Jane: I have a terrible cold. I need a Kleenex.

As Wilson and Sperber note:

> these utterances are not strictly and literally true: lectures rarely start at exactly the appointed time, Holland is not a plane surface, Sue must hurry to the bank but not necessarily run there, and other brands of disposable tissue would do just as well for Jane. Such loose uses of language are very common. Some are tied to a particular situation, produced once and then forgotten. Others may be regular and frequent enough to give rise to an extra sense, which may stabilize in an individual or a population.   (2002): 592)

Loose and approximate speech is ubiquitous. Is it defective? Does it fall short of the ideal or the convention that we are committed to? Would we as hearers prefer the strictly true statements in (1*)–(4*)?

(1*) The lecture starts at or shortly after five.

(2*) Holland has no mountains and very few hills.

(3*) Sue: I must go to the bank as fast as if I were running.

(4*) Jane: I need a Kleenex or other disposable tissue.

For Wilson and Sperber the answer is clearly: no. They say: 'In most circumstances, the hearer would not be misled by strictly untrue approximations such as [(1)–(4)], and their strictly true counterparts in [(1*)–(4*)] would not provide him with any more valuable information. Indeed, since these strictly true counterparts are typically longer, the shorter approximations may be preferable' (2002): 593). They conclude that 'loose uses of language present few problems for speakers and hearers, who are rarely even aware of their occurrence; but they do raise a serious issue for any philosophy of language based on a maxim or convention of truthfulness' (2002): 593).

These considerations in no way settle the debate between Truth Special and Truth Not-Special. Lewis, for example, tried to provide an account of what made meaning possible: how we manage to give words and sentences with meaning. To refute this view one needs more than a few examples. Ideally, an alternative account of the nature of meaning is needed. That debate is the topic of the final book in this series (Cappelen and Dever forthcoming).

CENTRAL POINTS IN CHAPTER 3

- In this chapter we were concerned with truth. Truth certainly seems important to communication, but frequently speakers show a disregard for truth. We explored some ways in which they do so, before asking whether truth is really that important.
- We first considered some mundane cases in which we seem to disregard truth by speaking falsely. We might do so simply because we're wrong, which we often are, in big and small ways. This might be because we don't put enough effort into finding out the truth, which might be the case if not much turns on whether we're right or not (it's no big deal if I say, incorrectly and without checking, that the next bus is at 12:30 and it's not, provided the buses are relevantly frequent). Or we might be telling a fictional story.
- We then went on to consider more serious instances of disregarding truth: lying and misleading. We pointed out that the exact definition of lying is unclear, but that the goal is not to find a precise definition.
- We then considered some important questions about lies, such as whether one can lie by telling the truth, and whether lying necessarily involves deception. We pointed out that there's arguably no clear distinction between lying and other lying-like phenomena.
- We ended by considering if truth is indeed as important to communication as it may seem. We noted that some people (such as David Lewis) think that truth is fundamental to speaking a language in that if the members of a community didn't typically try to speak the truth, that community wouldn't count as speaking a language. We contrasted that view with others who think that speaking the truth is an optional feature, not a *sine qua non* of communication.

Further Reading and Exercises

FURTHER READING FOR CHAPTER 3

Helpful overview articles on lying and related topics are Stokke (2013) and Mahon (2015), while some recent monographs are Saul (2012) and Stokke (2018). Michaelson and Stokke (2018) is a useful collection of papers. Lewis's seminal work on convention is his (1969).

Comprehension Questions

1. Do you agree with the sermon on philosophical methodology about looking for reductive definitions?

2. Think of some more cases of (apparently) lying by telling the truth. What do you think of the view that in this case they're merely trying to lie?
3. Give some more examples of lying using presuppositions or implicatures.
4. Give some more examples of loose or approximative speech à la Wilson and Sperber.

Exploratory Questions

5. Kant, famously, really didn't like lying. Imagine a murderer shows up at your door and asks if there's anybody in the house, so he can kill them. If you say no, Kant thinks, you do wrong because you lie, even though you save the person's life. Do you agree with this?
6. You buy a ticket for the lottery. The chances of winning are extremely slim. Is it okay to say, without having seen or heard about the draw:
   • I didn't win the lottery.

If not, why not? Does this support the knowledge norm of assertion? If so, can you think of similar cases that cause problems for it?

7. Do you think that Truth is Special or do you think it's Not-Special?
8. We claimed that fiction isn't deceptive. But there are tricky cases. David Peace's novel *The Damned United* was clearly marked as a work of fiction, but it discussed real life events (concerning football manager Brian Clough). Someone whom it discussed threatened to sue the publisher for libel, and the publisher edited the text in response. Do you think we should say that Peace was lying in his fiction? If not, what, if anything, was he doing wrong?

4

Bullshitting and Deep Bullshitting

This chapter has two parts: the first provides an introduction to *bullshit* and the second to what we'll call *deep bullshit*. We explore both of these and elaborate on the difference between them.

4.1 Bullshit

Bullshitting is yet another way to mess with truth. People who bullshit are different from people who are liars. Must of what we have to say in the first part of this chapter draws from Harry Frankfurt's classic work *On Bullshit* (2005). It'll be useful to start with some illustrations. Politics is a great source of examples: During the presidency of Barack Obama there were many people in the USA who said that Obama was not born in America. Maybe some of them believed it, but many of them didn't: they said it in order to have an effect on their audience. That effect was what mattered to them, not the truth of what they were saying. During the 2016 election campaign, there was a widespread story connecting a chain of restaurants and leading democratic politicians to sex-trafficking. Again, maybe a few of those spreading this story believed it, but most of them did it for other reasons. In both these cases the following is a plausible story about what was going on with at least some of these speakers:

> *Plausible story about what goes on:* They didn't believe what they said and they didn't disbelieve it either. It simply didn't matter to them whether it was true or false. They also chose not to look for evidence for and against the claims.

About a similar case, Frankfurt says that the problem is not that the person has made a careless mistake: 'Her laxity, or her lack of care, is not a matter of having permitted an error to slip into her speech on account of some inadvertent or momentarily negligent lapse in the attention she was devoting to getting things right.' The fundamental flaw, says Frankfurt, is that the bullshitter

... offers a description of a certain state of affairs without genuinely submitting to the constraints which the endeavor to provide an accurate representation of reality imposes. Her fault is not that she fails to get things right, but that she is not even trying.   (Frankfurt (2005): 32)

This, the essence of bullshit according to Frankfurt, is a good way to describe one of the most troubling features of a great deal of political speech.

So understood, bullshitting is importantly different from lying, as Frankfurt points out:

That is why she (the Bullshitter) cannot be regarded as lying; for she does not presume that she knows the truth, and therefore she cannot be deliberately promulgating a proposition that she presumes to be false: Her statement is grounded neither in a belief that it is true nor, as a lie must be, in a belief that it is not true. It is just this lack of connection to a concern with truth—this indifference to how things really are—that I regard as of the essence of bullshit.   (Frankfurt (2005): 20)

One way to see the difference between a liar and a bullshitter is to note that a liar must care about whether what he says is true or false, while the bullshitter need not: he just says things without regard to their truth value. The bullshitter speaks, but isn't guided by or motivated by a desire to track the way the world is:

It is impossible for someone to lie unless he thinks he knows the truth. Producing bullshit requires no such conviction. A person who lies is thereby responding to the truth, and he is to that extent respectful of it. When an honest man speaks, he says only what he believes to be true; and for the liar, it is correspondingly indispensable that he considers his statements to be false. For the bullshitter, however, all these bets are off: he is neither on the side of the true nor on the side of the false. His eye is not on the facts at all, as the eyes of the honest man and of the liar are, except insofar as they may be pertinent to his interest in getting away with what he says. He does not care whether the things he says describe reality correctly. He just picks them out, or makes them up, to suit his purpose.   (Frankfurt (2005): 55)

So understood, bullshitting violates a number of the idealizing conditions we outlined in Chapter 1:

1. Bullshitting is uncooperative, meaning that It violates idealization 1, according to which communication is fundamentally cooperative;

2. Bullshitting violates the Gricean Maxims (Idealization 2), because the bullshitter does not aim to make her contributions true (violating the maxim of quality), or maximally informative (violating the maxim of quantity);
3. The Bullshitter does not aim to share knowledge, so violates Idealization 3 which says that the goal of conversation is to share knowledge;
4. Because the bullshitter speaks without regard to the truth of what she says, even when what she says is true, she doesn't know it, meaning that she says things that she doesn't know (violating Idealization 6), and that whatever she adds to the common ground is not known (Idealizations 4 and 5).

4.1.1 'Bullshit is a greater enemy of truth than lies are'

According to Frankfurt, the bullshitter is *worse* than the liar. This is because the liar cares about truth—she is sensitive to truth and facts. The bullshitter just doesn't care. It's of no significance to her:

Someone who lies and someone who tells the truth are playing on opposite sides, so to speak, in the same game. Each responds to the facts as he understands them, although the response of the one is guided by the authority of the truth, while the response of the other defies that authority and refuses to meet its demands. The bullshitter ignores these demands altogether. He does not reject the authority of truth, as the liar does, and oppose himself to it. He pays no attention to it at all.
(Frankfurt (2005): 60–1)

The lack of concern with truth exhibited by the bullshitter can have corrupting long-term effects, according to Frankfurt. When someone gets used to speaking without any concern for truth, she will over time lose the habit of paying attention to the facts. This, again, can be dangerous. Someone who is losing the ability to be sensitive to the facts can, in the long run, lose touch with reality. So bullshitting can be a very dangerous and damaging activity to engage in on a regular basis (though of course occasional, recreational, bullshitting will have few or no bad effects).

4.1.2 Why so much bullshit?

Politicians aren't alone in being bullshitters. There is a huge amount of bullshit and very many bullshitters. As Frankfurt points out:

One of the most salient features of our culture is that there is so much bullshit. Everyone knows this.   (Frankfurt (2005): 1)

He's right, but that raises the question: why is there so much bullshit? A clue to this is in the passage from Frankfurt above: the bullshitter is bullshitting (making things up) to serve his or her purposes. Such purposes could be of all kinds. In the case of politicians bullshitting it could be done in order to diverge attention away from negative coverage. They might, for example, have hoped that by uttering bullshit about Obama, they could swing some votes. That of course is a very specific set of purposes and each instance of bullshitting will be motivated differently.

Frankfurt points to a structural feature that tends to generate bullshit: People must often talk about some topic that they don't know anything about: 'Bullshit is unavoidable whenever circumstances require someone to talk without knowing what he is talking about. Thus the production of bullshit is stimulated whenever a person's obligations or opportunities to speak about some topic are more excessive than his knowledge of the facts that are relevant to that topic. This discrepancy is common in public life, where people are frequently impelled—whether by their own propensities or by the demands of others—to speak' (Frankfurt 2005: 63). This happens quite frequently. Frankfurt says that politics is an important source of bullshitting: citizens are supposed to have views about political issues. Such issues are very, very complex and extremely hard to understand. Most citizens don't have time or energy or interest in exploring these extremely difficult issues, but they still feel compelled to talk. So they talk about political issues, but without much regard to truth or evidence. Communication on the internet has many of these characteristics as well: there's endless opportunity to express views about topics one is ignorant of and there's a certain social pressure to contribute. The result is a massive amount of bullshit being produced on a regular basis. It's not unlikely that most of what's written on social media is bullshit.

4.1.3 Some concerns about Frankfurt's definition of bullshit

According to Frankfurt, the bullshitter has no concern for truth. He or she just makes things up to suit his or her purpose. Here's a challenge to that view:

> *Objection to Frankfurt's account of bullshit*: it fails to distinguish bullshitting from storytelling. Someone who tells a story has, in some sense, no regard for truth and she's just making it up. Good storytelling is often characterized by a complete indifference to truth or to fact or to any aspect of reality.

What this shows is that we need some additional distinction to characterize the genuine bullshitter. There are many ways one could try to
distinguish the storyteller and the bullshitter:

1. The bullshitter typically intends to mislead—she is not open about
   her bullshitting. The bullshitter is typically pretending to be a
   normal conversation partner.[1] It can become clear that she is not
   a normal conversation partner, but the initial effect is in almost all
   cases based on the audience expecting a non-bullshitting conversation partner (a conversation partner who sticks to the standard
   conversational norms (see Chapter 1)). In the case of fiction, that's
   typically not the case. The fiction writer is, typically, clear that
   she is telling a story and so that typical conversational expectations
   are lifted.[2]
2. Another important difference between bullshitting and storytelling
   is that the storyteller has a kind of concern with truth: as we saw,
   she cares about what we called 'truth in fiction'. That's a difficult
   notion to make precise (for which see Lewis 1978, for example), but
   it's a pre-theoretically clear enough idea to use as a contrast: there's
   no corresponding constraint on the bullshitter. Some of the world's
   most prominent bullshitters are not even constrained by consist-
   ency. They will happily tweet that p one day, then tweet that not-p
   the next day, and then when asked about how they can hold both p
   and not-p, they will just shamelessly respond with some irrelevant
   statement, q.

4.2 From Lying, Misleading, and Bullshit to Fake News

The notion of 'fake news' plays a big role in contemporary public debates
(and debates about public debates). Some argue that fake news helped get
Donald Trump elected to the US presidency in 2016. Others argue that
fake news contributes to a dangerous political polarization and to a
degenerated political discourse. This chapter is about messing with the

---

[1] And in the few cases where she is not, it's more a case of pretend play.
[2] We've put 'typically' a lot in this passage because there are exceptions here, but a case
can be made that the exceptions are parasitic on the typical cases.

truth and fake news does that. Exactly how does fake news mess with truth? How is it related to lying, misleading, and bullshitting? Those notions are theoretically useful, but as we will argue below, it is much less clear that 'fake news' is a useful notion—it might instead be a notion we should try to get rid of.

First note it is in no way a new phenomenon that journalists (like other people) sometimes lie, mislead, and bullshit. The messengers who delivered news between provinces in Ancient Rome would often deliver misleading, incomplete, and deceptive information. While the technology was different (horses and papyrus) it's hard to argue that it's not closely related to what today is called fake news. In the first half of the twentieth century many were concerned about how new technologies such as electric wires and the telegraph would affect the reliability of news. In 1925 *Harper's* magazine published an article called 'Fake News and the Public' expressing concern about how news received through electrical wires would be hard to verify: 'An editor receiving a news item over the wire has no opportunity to test its authenticity as he would in the case of a local report.'[3]

So fake news is not news. So far, we haven't tried to answer the question of what fake news is. How should 'fake news' be defined? Some examples of how the expression is used in regular (non-theoretical) speech are given in a 2018 *Vanity Fair* article called 'The 6 Fakest Fake-News Stories of 2017'. It references false claims that 25 million fraudulent votes had been cast for Hillary Clinton in the most recent presidential election, reports that Justin Bieber said 'the music industry is run by pedophiles' to a Bible study group, and also highlights Donald Trump's frequent use of the expression 'fake news'.[4] These are paradigm cases, which could be multiplied at will (and can be, if you care to google the term).

The concept of fake news has increasingly been of interest to the more theoretically-minded. Philosophers and others have tried to figure out what 'fake news' means as it is used in these contexts and innumerable other recent uses. Here are some proposed definitions. We lean heavily

[3] <https://shorensteincenter.org/combating-fake-news-agenda-for-research/.>.
[4] <https://www.vanityfair.com/news/2018/01/the-6-fakest-fake-news-stories-of-2017>.

here on Joshua Habgood-Coote's very helpful paper 'Stop Talking about Fake News!' (Habgood-Coote (2019)):

- 'Fake news' expresses the property of being false and (presented as) news.[5]
- 'Fake news' expresses the property of being (completely) false, intended to deceive, and created for financial gain.[6]
- 'Fake news' expresses the property of being false news that is produced knowingly.[7]
- 'Fake news' expresses the property of being false news that is circulated with the intention to mislead and to be spread.[8]
- 'Fake news' expresses the property of being claims from fake news sources (i.e., first we define 'fake news sites', then anything they produce falls under 'fake news').[9]

These all treat fake news as involving some combination of lying and misleading by journalists. What's distinctive about fake news is the role of the journalist, the way their information is produced and circulated.

Can we say that one of these proposed definitions is correct and the others wrong? If being correct means that it captures the meaning of 'fake news' as it is used by most politicians and journalists, it will be very hard to determine which definitions is correct. We would have to look at thousands of uses and see which proposal best explains those uses. Some philosophers (Habgood-Coote and Tallise) argue that the expression is used in so many ways by so many different people with such different agendas that no one definition can capture all those uses. Habgood-Coote argues that 'Fake News' is linguistically defective: it does not have a stable descriptive content and it is not clear what is expressed by sentences that contain the term. He suggests that we should, for that reason, abandon the term. In other words, it would be better if we stopped using it, rather than try to find a stable meaning for it.

Skepticism about the usefulness of the term 'fake news' can be supported by an observation that traces back to the reporter Craig Silverman. Silverman says:

---

[5] (Montgomery-McGovern 1898), (Allcott and Gentzkow 2017), (Collins 2017).
[6] (Silverman and Alexander 2016), (Silverman 2017).
[7] (Klein and Wueller 2017), (Lilleker 2017), (McIntyre 2018).
[8] (Rini 2017), (Gelfert 2018).
[9] (Levy 2017), (Aikin and Talisse 2018), (Lazer et al 2018).

The end of 'fake news' as I knew it came on Jan. 11, 2017, when Donald Trump—master of branding—redefined the term to mean, effectively, news reports he didn't like. (Silverman (2017))

What Silverman is getting at here is that the term 'fake news' often is used in an expressive way. Thus consider the tweet from Trump we quoted above ('... 91% of the Network News about me is negative (Fake)'). It's used to express the speaker's dislike of a piece of news. On this view, the expression does not have a descriptive role at all. This same idea is also developed by Robert Tallise who says that there is no such a thing as fake news: 'the term is best regarded as a political slur'. Tallise makes two points (i) 'fake news' often functions as a slur (see Chapter 6 for further discussion of what slurs are) and (ii) 'fake news' is a slur we don't need. You could of course agree with (i) but not (ii): some slurs are not so bad—a case could be made that 'asshole' and 'sucks' are useful, at least in some contexts. So it doesn't follow from being a slur that we should get rid of it.[10]

However, on balance there is a strong case to be made that 'fake news' is superfluous. The argument is based on the combination of a–c:

a. The expression is used in varied and in part inconsistent ways.
b. The expression is used both descriptively and expressively—and it's not clear when it is used in what way.
c. Finally, and this is important, there's nothing we can say with expression 'fake news' that we can't equally well say using other expressions: take a look at the definitions proposed above and note that they describe phenomena that are easily identified without using 'fake news'.

If all of a–c are true, then it's a reasonably strong case for the view of Tallise and Habgood-Coote: we are better off without the expression 'fake news'.

4.3 Deep Bullshit (i.e., Nonsense and Gibberish)

The expression 'bullshit' in natural language isn't very precise and what Frankfurt has offered us is a precisification of one way to use that expression. As G. A. Cohen (2002) points out there's a use of 'bullshit'

---

[10] <https://www.3ammagazine.com/3am/theres-no-such-thing-as-fake-news-and-thats-bad-news/>.

that Frankfurt doesn't engage with. Frankfurt's bullshitter is one who doesn't care about truth. Cohen's bullshitter, on the other hand, doesn't even care about making sense. That second form of bullshit is even more fundamental. Let's call it 'deep bullshit'. The deep bullshitter will utter words and combinations of words that we can describe as nonsense or gibberish. They might appear meaningful, but on closer inspection they are not.

Deep bullshitting is a violation of what might be the most important of the idealizing assumptions in Chapter 1. that the words and sentences we utter have a meaning (Idealization 7). It is only when this condition is satisfied that we can grasp what others are saying. It's only then that they can say something true or false.

In the rest of this chapter we describe some of the various ways this most fundamental of the idealizing assumptions might fail. Some of the questions we'll address are:

- How can speech be meaningless?
- Why would someone produce deep bullshit, i.e., speech that's meaningless?
- How much deep bullshit is there?

4.3.1 How can there be meaningless speech?

Meaningless speech has two basic sources:

- Source 1: Meaningless words
- Source 2: Meaningless combinations of meaningful words.

Our focus will be on the first, which Lewis Carroll's 'Jabberwocky' is a classic illustration of. Here is the second stanza:

> 'Beware the Jabberwock, my son!
> The jaws that bite, the claws that catch!
> Beware the Jubjub bird, and shun
> The frumious Bandersnatch!'

This stanza contains a number of words that Lewis Carroll just made up. 'Jabberwock', 'Jubjub', 'frumious', and 'Bandersnatch' mean nothing. Note that, inspired by Lewis Carroll, someone could utter sentences containing these meaningless words. In so doing she could give the appearance of producing a meaningful sentence, but really her words mean nothing. She might, for example, tell her her friends: 'You must shun the frumious bandersnatch and beware of the Jabberwock.' The friends might think she is saying something (they don't know that these words are meaningless and they trust the speaker), but in fact she is not saying anything. If this were to happen, then there would be the illusion of meaningfulness and the illusion of information being conveyed. This deep bullshitter is not messing with truth. The person who says, 'You must shun the frumious bandersnatch and beware of the Jabberwock' doesn't say something false. She doesn't say anything at all so there's nothing there that can be either true or false.

So far we have not said anything about the deep bullshitter's intentions— we haven't said that deep bullsitters don't care about speaking meaningfully. Recall the bullshitter: she was characterized by an indifference to truth. That's a description of what she cares about. We have three kinds of deep bullshitters—three different ways of speaking meaninglessly:

(i) You could speak meaninglessly on purpose (as in the case we just imagined where someone uttered 'You must shun the frumious bandersnatch and beware of the Jabberwock' knowing that it means nothing and intending to deceive the audience).

(ii) You could speak meaninglessly by accident: if, for example, one of the audience members trusts the speaker who says 'You must shun the frumious bandersnatch and beware of the Jabberwock,' and then repeats this sentence to others because the audience member thinks you are (a) saying something, and (b) that what you are saying is true.

(iii) Finally, it could also be done with indifference—in the same way the bullshitter is indifferent to truth the deep bullshitter can be indifferent to whether her speech is meaningful.

Bullshitting, according to Frankfurt, is widespread. Is deep bullshitting equally widespread? Is there a lot of nonsense? Some philosophers think so. The extent to which people speak meaninglessly will depend on what you think it is for a word to have meaning. In what follows we go through a few traditions in philosophy of language according to which there might be quite a bit of nonsense.

4.3.2 Carnap and logical positivists on nonsense

We'll start with the philosopher Rudolf Carnap and his famous paper 'The Elimination of Metaphysics Through the Logical Analysis of

Language' (1959). In its most abstract form, Carnap's argument in this paper has two steps:

Step 1. An account of the conditions that must be satisfied for an expression (and so a sentence in which that expression occurs) to be meaningful.

Step 2. An empirical claim about which expressions satisfy the conditions for being meaningful according to the account in Step 1.

These two steps can be instantiated in any number of ways, depending on what one thinks meaning is and which expressions one thinks satisfy the conditions required for meaningfulness according to that theory. Carnap's implementations were these:

Step 1-C. Carnap adhered to the verificationist theory of meaning, according to which 'the meaning of a sentence lies in its method of verification. A statement asserts only so much as is verifiable with respect to it' ((1959): 76).

Step 2-C. Carnap then went on to make a number of claims about terminology that didn't satisfy the conditions in Step 1. His primary focus was terms used by other philosophers.

According to Carnap, much of Western philosophy fails to satisfy the conditions for meaningfulness. He says, for example:

Just like the examined examples 'principle' and 'God,' most of the other specifically metaphysical terms are devoid of meaning, e.g. 'the Idea,' 'the Absolute,' 'the Unconditioned,' 'the Infinite,' 'the being of being,' 'nonbeing,' 'thing in itself,' 'absolute spirit,' 'objective spirit,' 'essence,' 'being-in-itself,' 'being-in-and-for-itself,' 'emanation,' 'manifestation,' 'articulation,' 'the Ego,' 'the non-Ego,' etc.   (Carnap (1959): 67)

Carnap concludes that 'the alleged statements of metaphysics which contain such words have no sense, assert nothing, are mere pseudo-statements' (1959: 67). He goes further, arguing that all normative speech is nonsense as well:

[T]he same judgment must be passed on all philosophy of norms, or philosophy of value, on any ethics or esthetics as a normative discipline. For the objective validity of a value or norm is (even on the view of the philosophers of value) not empirically verifiable nor deducible from empirical statements; hence it cannot be asserted (in a meaningful statement) at all . . . It is altogether impossible to make a statement that expresses a value judgment.   ((1959): 77)

If Carnap were right, it would be tragic: some of the greatest minds of human history have spent their entire lives having the illusion of thought, having conversations that meant nothing and writing books that meant nothing. It's not just the intellectuals: anyone who thinks or talks about morality or esthetics will be in the same situation: they have the illusion of thinking and of speaking in meaningful sentences. When we try to talk and think about morality or esthetics, we fail because there's no content there.

4.3.3 Nonsense in contemporary theory of meaning

Not many contemporary philosophers endorse Carnap's verification theory of meaning. They either think that the theory itself isn't verifiable (and so is internally inconsistent) or that there are plenty of unverifiable sentences that are meaningful (for example sentences about the far past). As a result of the rejection of this view, many philosophers of language have become less interested in the possibility that much of our speech is nonsense. But that is a mistake. No matter which theory of meaning you endorse, it could be the case that much of our language is defective: that it has no meaning. A theory of meaning has the form:

> **Condition on Meaningfulness:** For an expression, E, to be meaningful it must satisfy conditions C.

There are many accounts of what C amounts to and there is very little agreement amongst philosophers and linguists on these conditions. However, it is worth noting that none of these theories *rule out* that many of the expressions we take to be meaningful are really meaningless. It's an entirely open question how much nonsense there is. Here is one illustration of that: many philosophers think that C include facts about the past: how expressions were introduced (through dubbings or descriptions) and facts about how the expression has been passed along in communicative chains (see Kripke (1980) for this view; Cappelen and Dever (2018) is a textbook presentation of it). This view is one of the dominant views in contemporary philosophy. The view implies that if expressions had defective introductions, then they are meaningless. And if something has gone wrong in the communicative chain, then, again, the expression is meaningless. The details of this aren't important, but what is important is that this *can* happen and we have no empirical evidence to help figure out how often it happens. And so it goes more generally: any theory of meaning will require that some condition is satisfied in order for an expression to be meaningful and none of the leading theories of meaning are accompanied by systematic evidence that the condition is always or typically satisfied. So it's an open question how much nonsense there is.

So far this is very abstract—it's focused on the theoretical possibility of nonsense. Do we have concrete reason to think that any significant domain of speech is defective in this way? We'll consider some candidates from theoretical speech and some from ordinary language.

4.3.4 Theoretical gibberish and charlatans

We will start off our series of illustrations close to home. Some philosophical texts are considered very, very hard to understand. They are written with extensive philosophical jargon and with very convoluted sentence structure. Since the writers of such texts often are people in positions of some authority, such as famous academics, there's a tendency to assume that such texts always have a meaning. But don't make that assumption. In a famous experiment, the physicist Alan Sokal submitted a paper full of gibberish (meaningless sentences) to the journal *Social Text*. The editors of the journal accepted the paper for publication. In doing this, Sokal proved that a paper consisting for the most part of gibberish can be read by editors and then published. This of course is a one-off event, but Sokal, with a co-author Jean Bricmont, went on to write an entire book documenting nonsense in texts by famous philosophers. Their aim was not to undermine philosophy as such, but to document and warn against charlatanism:

We are not attacking philosophy, the humanities or the social sciences *in general;* on the contrary, we feel that these fields are of the utmost importance and we want to warn those who work in them (especially students) against some manifest cases of charlatanism. In particular, we want to 'deconstruct' the reputation that certain texts have of being difficult because the ideas in them are so profound. In many cases we shall demonstrate that if the texts seem incomprehensible, it is for the excellent reason that they mean precisely nothing.
(Bricmont and Sokal (1999): 5)

Their book is filled with illustrations of primarily French intellectuals from the twentieth century writing sentences that mean nothing. Here's an example from the French philosopher Jacques Lacan. Lacan writes (this is taken from Bricmont and Sokal):

I will posit here the term 'compactness.' Nothing is more compact than a fault [*faille*], assuming that the intersection of everything that is enclosed therein is accepted as existing over an infinite number of sets, the result being that the intersection implies this infinite number. That is the very definition of compactness.

The intersection I am talking about is the same one I put forward earlier as being that which covers or poses an obstacle to the supposed sexual relationship. Only 'supposed,' since I state that analytic discourse is premised solely on the statement that there is no such thing, that it is impossible to found [*poser*] a sexual relationship. Therein lies analytic discourse's step forward and it is thereby that it determines the real status of all the other discourses. Named here is the point that covers the impossibility of the sexual relationship as such. Jouissance, qua sexual, is phallic—in other words, it is not related to the Other as such. Let us follow here the complement of the hypothesis of compactness. (Bricmont and Sokal (2003): 21)

Sokal and Bricmont comment: 'although Lacan uses quite a few key words from the mathematical theory of compactness . . . he mixes them up arbitrarily and without the slightest regard for their meaning. His "definition" of compactness is not just false: it is gibberish' (Bricmont and Sokal (2003): 21).

The general point here is this: whatever one might think of the particular cases that Sokal and Bricmont discuss, it's certainly possible that some of those cases and many others are meaningless. This is significant: it means that very bright people—people whose job it is to think and do research—can be fooled into thinking that strings of words that mean nothing are meaningful. It also means that there are conversations that consist in some people uttering words that mean nothing and others responding with more words that mean nothing. If this goes on a lot, it's a very depressing state of affairs and an important task is to find diagnostics for nonsense to try and root it out.

Meaninglessness of this kind can be generated intentionally or by accident. Let's introduce the term 'charlatan' for someone who does it intentionally. A charlatan is someone who intentionally engages in deep bullshitting: a speaker that intentionally speaks meaninglessly in order to deceive the audience into thinking the speech is meaningful. Sokal and Bricmont don't take a stand on whether for example Lacan is a charlatan in our sense. They say, 'Do these abuses arise from conscious fraud, self-deception, or perhaps a combination of the two? We are unable to offer any categorical answer to this question, due to the lack of (publicly available) evidence' (Bricmont and Sokal (2003): 5).

Two final points about Sokal and Bricmont and the possibility of widespread meaninglessness in theoretical texts:

1. Sokal and Bricmont had no theory of what they call 'nonsense', 'meaninglessness', and 'gibberish'. Their accusations of charlatanism were not backed up by a theory of meaning that provided a theoretical framework for drawing the distinction between the meaningful and that which has no meaning. We get no sharp diagnostic, for example, for distinguishing between blatant falsity and gibberish. This is to be expected because they are not philosophers of language and so had no refined philosophical tools available to them. However, the lack of an appeal to such distinctions makes their work somewhat unsatisfying from the point of view of philosophy of language. The view would have been philosophically deeper and more valuable had it been incorporated into a theory of the nature of nonsense.

2. The target of Sokal and Bricmont's investigation was a handful of French intellectuals. Their sample was very restricted and their diagnostic tools were basically their intuitions about meaningfulness. There's no reason whatsoever to think that the kind of meaninglessness they claim to find in their select texts can't also be found in places other than France and in traditions and fields very different from those investigated by Sokal and Bricmont. It could be a characteristic of any domain inquiry at any point in time and at any place. It's unlikely (though not impossible) that only French people are susceptible to such deception. People from Sweden, USA, Peru, Belgium, China, and really anywhere can be bamboozled in the way the readers of those texts were. The real lesson from their work is that all of us should constantly be on the alert for gibberish.

4.3.5 Meaninglessness in ordinary language: 'race' as an illustration

In the previous section we gave examples of gibberish in the work of some French philosophers. But we don't need to go to France or obscure philosophy to find meaninglessness. Maybe entirely ordinary terms—terms we use on a day-to-day basis—can turn out to be meaningless. If many of the words we all learn as part of basic English are meaningless, that would not make all those of us using those terms into intentional deep bullshitters, but we would be uttering gibberish on a regular basis. We could still care about making sense, we just fail at it, for no fault of our own. The rest of this section explores that option.

As an illustration of this possibility, we consider the term 'race' and the various claims philosophers working on the metaphysics of race have made about the deficiencies of this term. On some views, the term is so defective that it's close to meaningless and should be discarded. If this is true about 'race', the conclusion generalizes. The tradition we focus on is typically described as 'eliminativism' or 'skepticism' about race. To get a sense of that view, consider the question: what does 'race' denote? What does it pick out? That's very hard to answer. There are three dominant views in the literature:

A1. It denotes some kind of biologically characterized group—a population with shared genetic or other biological traits

A2. It denotes nothing: the aim was for it to denote populations that share genetically significant features, but there are no such things.

A3. It denotes a social kind—a social construct.

Here is an argument for A2 from one of the most prominent 'race' theorists, Kwame Anthony Appiah. Appiah begins by noting 'the biological referent would simply be groups defined by skin color, hair, and gross morphology, corresponding to the dominant pattern for these characteristics in the major subcontinental regions: Europe, Africa, East and South Asia, Australasia, the Americas, and, perhaps, the Pacific Islands' (Appiah (2002): 101). He goes on to say:

This grouping would encompass many human beings quite adequately and some not at all: but it is hard to see of what biological interest it would be, since we can study the skin and gross morphology separately, and there is, at any rate, a good deal of variation within all these areas, in skin, hair color, and the morphology of the skull. Certainly, this referent would not provide us with a concept that was central to biological thinking about human beings. And, once more, in the United States, large numbers of people would not fit into any of these categories, because they are the products of mixtures (sometimes long ago) between people who do roughly fit this pattern, even though the social distinctions we call 'racial' in the United States do, by contrast, cover almost everybody. And so, if we used this biological notion, it would have very little established correlation with any characteristics currently thought to be important for moral or social life. The bottom line is this . . . you can get various possible candidates from the referential notion of meaning, but none of them will be much good for explaining social or psychological life, and none of them corresponds to the social groups we call 'races' in America.   (Appiah (2002): 101)

Now suppose you think that if 'race' denotes anything, it denotes a biological kind. You then have an argument for the view that 'race' denotes nothing: if it denotes anything, it denotes a biological kind, but there isn't a biological kind for it to refer to. So it denotes nothing. We thought there was some unified biological phenomenon here, but we have discovered that there isn't.

This leaves a lot of questions open. In particular we have done nothing to rule out answer A3 above. But put that aside for now. For the purpose of this chapter—illustrating meaningless terms in natural language—what is important is that A2 is one of the most influential views of 'race'. With that in mind, let's think about what we should say about sentences that contain the word 'race': 'x and y are of the same race', or 'Race plays an important social role in US history.' If 'race' denotes nothing, what should we say about these sentences? There are two main options:

1. We can say that all such sentences are false because they presuppose that 'race' denotes something (and that's a false presupposition).

or

2. We can say that these sentences are meaningless: we tried to introduce such terms in order for them to denote a certain kind of biological kind, but we failed, and so we failed to give the term a meaning.

Maybe 2 is true, maybe not. It's at least a live option. And it illustrates a more general point made above: the conditions for being meaningful can be quite demanding. We, as speakers, don't know that those conditions are satisfied. Sometimes we just have to trust others (as in the case of Lacan above, where it turned out that trusting him was a bad idea). Sometimes it depends on what the world is like: we have meaningfulness only when the world is a certain way (for example when there's the presence of certain biological traits among certain groups of people). Sometimes there's a kind of logical incoherence to terms that are important to us. If any of these claims are right, then we have no guarantee that terms like 'democracy', 'love', or 'cool' are non-defective. For each of these cases what's needed is an account of two things:

1. An account of what it takes to be so defective as to be meaningless, i.e., a procedure for distinguishing between meaningfulness and meaninglessness. In order to get that, you need an entire theory of meaning.

2. You then need detailed investigation of whether particular expressions ('race', 'truth', 'good', 'beautiful', 'free', etc.) satisfy the conditions of meaningfulness.

Currently we simply have too little understanding of both issues to be able to rule out that there's a lot of nonsense speech. Getting clearer on this is an important task for current research into mind and language.

4.3.6 Can there be illusions of thought?

Before we leave deep bullshit behind, we'll consider one reason for holding that widespread, unrecognized gibberish is impossible. The argument says that if unrecognized gibberish were possible, then there would be *illusions of thought*, but there can't be illusions of thought, so there can't be unrecognized gibberish. Here is the argument in a bit more detail:

1. Suppose sentence containing 'race' are meaningless and that this is unrecognized, i.e., speakers and hearers think that they speak meaningfully.
2. If that is the case, then speakers and hearers will also have the illusion that they are entertaining thoughts when they utter sentences containing 'race'.
3. If the sentence is meaningless, then there is nothing there to think, so there has to be the illusion of thought. So when they utter and interpret 'Jill is the same race as Alex' they will think that they are entertaining the thought that Jill is the same race as Alex, but that's not really a thought (because 'Jill is the same race as Alex' is meaningless).
4. However, illusions of thought are impossible: you can't think you're thinking a thought and not be doing so. Whether or not you are thinking something must surely be something you can't be wrong about. If you think you are thinking something, then you *are* thinking something!

Some version of this argument might motivate resistance to the hypothesis that there's widespread nonsense in ordinary and theoretical speech. However, step 4 in the argument is less obvious than it might seem at first blush. Recall Lacan, the French philosopher who might have been a charlatan. Much of what Lacan said was meaningless. For example, consider again his utterance of:

Nothing is more compact than a fault, assuming that the intersection of everything that is enclosed therein is accepted as existing over an infinite number of sets, the result being that the intersection implies this infinite number.

This means nothing. Nonetheless, Lacan's followers thought it did. Those who read this work and repeated it to others (by, for example, teaching it to others, writing papers about it, etc.) thought they were entertaining thoughts when they read it and repeated it. This is prima facie evidence that there can be illusions of thought. Another illustration: suppose we are told by an authority figure that we should shun the frumious bandersnatch. We believe what she tells us and we tell others that they should shun the frumious bandersnatch (much like Lacan told his disciples things and they passed them on). In so doing, we try to think a thought: the thought that we should shun the frumious bandersnatch. We can't succeed because that's not a real thought. What we have, instead, is the illusion of thought. When we have that illusion, there will of course be real thoughts associated with the illusion, such as the thought *that there's some kind of animal that I should shun*. That and related thoughts will go through our heads when we have the illusion of thinking that we should shun the frumious bandersnatch. One possibility is this: whenever there's an illusion of thought, it is accompanied with some associated genuine thoughts.

CENTRAL POINTS IN CHAPTER 4

- This chapter, which follows on from the last one, was concerned with two other phenomena that evince a disregard for truth: bullshit and what we call deep bullshit.
- One produces bullshit if one utters things without caring for their truth or falsity.
- Deep bullshitting is our term for saying things that don't even make sense (and so can't be true or false).
- We gave reasons for taking deep bullshit seriously. You might think that true nonsense is few and far between, confined to such things as Lewis Carroll's obviously meaningless poem Jabberwocky. We pointed out that some serious twentieth-century philosophers, such as Carnap, Wittgenstein, and related figures, proposed that many paradigmatic questions of philosophy were in fact nonsense.

- We noted that even if one doesn't like their reasons for thinking this, still it's necessary to be open to the possibility that nonsense is more widespread than we think. It could be that our theory of meaning places requirements for an expression to be meaningful that are often not met, even though we don't realize this.
- We went on to consider some cases of nonsense. We quoted some gibberish passages from Lacan, someone whom many people have taken and continue to take seriously. Scholars of Lacan, like it or not, will often find themselves reading and sometimes speaking nonsense.
- Meaninglessness isn't confined to French theorists. Another example we considered was the word 'race'. Some theorists think that it fails to stand for anything: were it to stand for anything, it would stand for a biological kind, but there is no such kind for it to stand for. When we talk about race, then, we're talking about nothing.
- We ended by considering an objection to the view that much speech might be nonsense: if that were true, then much thought would also be impugned. If one gives voice to a thought in speaking, then, if one utters nonsense, it's plausible to think that there's no thought one is expressing, and so one is merely under the illusion of thinking in such cases.

Further Reading and Exercises

FURTHER READING FOR CHAPTER 4

Frankfurt (2005) made bullshit famous for philosophers. A readable account of the logical positivists' views about meaninglessness is A. J. Ayer's *Language, Truth, and Logic* (1936). To assess whether meaninglessness is widespread, you need to assess various contemporary theories of meaning—Lycan (1999) is a readable (if slightly dated) introduction. For philosophy of race, see Haslanger (2000) and Mallon (2004). For illusions of thought, see Cappelen (2013).

Comprehension Questions

1. How does bullshit differ from lying?
2. Is there a sharp distinction between being a bullshitter and being careless (as we often are)? How much bullshit do you think you produce?
3. Pick up (browse to) a newspaper('s website) and start reading. Stop reading when you first find bullshit. What was it and how long did it take you to find?
4. We quoted Frankfurt as saying, 'it is impossible for someone to lie unless he thinks he knows the truth.' Do you think this is right? Explain your answer.

5. We noted a couple of reasons for bullshit—it can be advantageous, and people are expected to have opinions about complex things they don't know enough about. Can you think of other reasons?

6. Can you think of any other words like 'race' that might be meaningless?

Exploratory Questions

7. What do you think of Carnap's view? Do you agree that talk of esthetics and morals is meaningless? Is it important if they are?

8. Are we too harsh on Lacan? How would you respond if someone were to pick out a passage of particularly impenetrable analytic philosophy and claim it was meaningless?

9. Pick a philosophical term that you think is meaningless—one about which the debate is a pointless waste of time. Give reasons why you think this.

5

Conceptual Engineering

The previous chapter argued that in some cases there might be no meanings to share because speech is nonsensical. In this chapter we discuss cases where there are too many meanings, but no *shared* meaning. We focus on cases where conversation partners disagree over what meaning a word should have. These are conversational settings that diverge from the idealized picture in Chapter 1 not in that there's an absence of meaning, but in that there are too many alternative meanings and no consensus on which one to settle for. Some philosophers see these fights over meanings as central to large swathes of public and theoretical discourse. We start with some illustrations and then explore the underlying theories in more detail.

5.1 Introduction to Conceptual Engineering: We Care about What Words Mean

We just said that in many cases there are too many meanings that words could have, and it matters which one we choose. Here are some illustrations to make this vivid.

- **Debates over 'rape':** In many places and at many times, the term 'rape' is used in such a way that it is impossible for a husband to rape his wife.[1] In some cases this is motivated by the idea that a wife is the property of the husband. In other cases it is motivated by the idea

---

[1] It may or may not shock you to learn that as late as 1962, the Model Penal Code—a sort of blueprint of the law, used by legislatures in the US when writing laws—didn't recognize marital rape as a criminal offense. The Wikipedia page is a useful place to begin researching this: <https://en.wikipedia.org/wiki/Marital_rape>.

that to enter into a marriage is to give open-ended consent. Most of us reject that definition of 'rape': we think it is the wrong way to construe 'rape'. This isn't the only disagreement about the meaning of 'rape'. At the time of writing this book, there are ongoing intense debates about just what kind of activities should be classified as 'rape'. In short: there are very many related meanings that 'rape' could have and many people care passionately about which one it should have.

- **Debates over 'marriage':** At the end of the twentieth and beginning of the twenty-first centuries in many Western countries there were fierce debates over how to construe the meaning of the word 'marriage'. Should it or should it not include same-sex couples? This is, at least in part, a disagreement over what the word 'marriage' should mean. Many of those who advocate for same-sex marriage would not accept that a new word, say 'Schmarriage', be introduced to cover same-sex couples. They want the word 'marriage' to have a meaning that includes them—the meaning that excludes same-sex couples is wrong, they say.[2] More generally, there are a broad range of related meanings 'marriage' could have and which one it has matters a great deal.

- **Debates over 'person':** What's a person? Some people think a fetus should be included and others disagree. Among those who think a fetus shouldn't be picked out by 'person', there's disagreement over what *should* be picked out. This issue, or at least a version of this issue, has been at the core of the debate over abortion in the US. One way to think of this debate is as in part a debate over what the word 'person' should mean.

- **Debates over 'torture':** Is waterboarding a form of torture? This is a matter of intense dispute. Some think 'torture' should be used in such a way that waterboarding is included and some think not. Again, one way to think of this is as a debate over what 'torture' ought to mean.[3]

---

[2] Of course *some* would be happy with another label—say 'domestic partnership'.

[3] For this case, see Plunkett and Sundell (2013). These are all cases where there are important social debates that in part concern how words should be used. Peter Ludlow's book *Living Words* (Ludlow (2014)) provides a rich source of additional examples of this phenomenon. Another source of additional examples is Cappelen (2018).

These cases make clear that meaning choices matter. Many people care passionately about them. The study of how we assess and improve concepts is central to the field called *Conceptual Engineering.*

The reader might have noticed that the examples above—'rape', 'marriage', 'person', and 'torture'—are all taken from social, political, and legal contexts. They are cases where there have been fierce and emotionally charged public debates. That, however, is not the only domain in which the choice of word meanings is important. Consider the following philosophical questions:

- What is freedom?
- What is lying?
- What is word meaning?
- What is knowledge?
- What is evidence?
- What are intuitions?

Here are two ways to think about the debates over those questions:

- **The First Way**: According to this view, each of the words 'freedom', 'lying', 'word meaning', 'knowledge', 'evidence', 'intuition', and so on, has a fixed meaning and the philosopher's aim is to figure out what that meaning is and then describe it. The correct theory is the one that gets the actual meaning right. On this view, there is just one correct answer to each of these questions. 'Knowledge', for example, has a fixed meaning in English and a good theory of knowledge describes that meaning.
- **The Second Way**: According to this view, there are many things each of these words *could* mean and the debate about these issues is best construed as (at least in part) a debate over which of these meanings is best. The goal, on this view, isn't simply to describe the meaning that each of these words happens to have been assigned in English. The aim is just as much to answer a normative question: what meaning *should* they have? On this view, the different answers to the question, 'What is knowledge?' are best construed as different proposals for what that word should mean, or what the best concept of knowledge would be.

The conceptual engineer advocates for the Second Way and in the next section we turn to an argument for the importance of the Second Way.

5.2 The Master Argument for Conceptual Engineering (and a Little Bit of History)

Here is an argument for why conceptual engineering (the assessment and improvements of meanings) is important for everyone who thinks and talks, and in particular for all parts of philosophy:[4]

The Master Argument:

1. If W is a word that has a meaning M, then there are many similar meanings, $M_1, M_2, \ldots, M_n,$ W could have.
2. We have no good reason to think that the meaning that W ended up with is the best meaning W could have: there will typically be indefinitely many alternative meanings that would be better meanings for W.
3. When we speak, think, and theorize it's important to make sure our words have as good meanings as possible.
4. So no matter what topic you are concerned with, you should assess and ameliorate the meanings of central terms. That is to say, you should engage in conceptual engineering.

This line of thought can be found throughout the history of philosophy. Consider, for example, the following passage from the German philosopher Friedrich Nietzsche:

Philosophers . . . have trusted in concepts as completely as they have mistrusted the senses: they have not stopped to consider that concepts and words are our inheritance from ages in which thinking was very modest and unclear . . . . What dawns on philosophers last of all: they must no longer accept concepts as a gift, nor merely purify and polish them, but first make and create them, present them, and make them convincing. Hitherto one has generally trusted one's concepts as if they were a wonderful dowry from some sort of wonderland: but they are, after all, the inheritance from our most remote, most foolish as well as most intelligent ancestors. This piety toward what we find in us is perhaps part of the moral element in knowledge. What is needed above all is an absolute skepticism toward all inherited concepts.   (Nietzsche (1968): 220–1, section 409)

Nietzsche here advocates a radical form of skepticism about all our inherited concepts: we should take none of them for granted and subject all of them to critique. He sees conceptual engineering as core philosophy. The meanings we have are, according to Nietzsche, the result of an obscure and dubious history. According to Nietzsche, the right attitude is complete mistrust of what that history has produced.

---

[4] This is from Cappelen (2018) and Cappelen (forthcoming).

Many of the leading philosophers in the twentieth century endorsed versions of the Master Argument for conceptual engineering, but for reasons other than those given by Nietzsche:

- In one of his central works, Gottlob Frege constructed an improved language—the *Begriffsschrift*—the aim of which was to 'break the domination of words over the human mind' (Frege (1879), Preface to the *Begriffsschrift*). Ordinary language, according to Frege, is so defective along so many dimensions that it has obscured our thoughts and in order to think clearly we have to replace it with an improvement. This was obviously an impressively ambitious exercise in conceptual engineering.
- The aim of Ludwig Wittgenstein's early work—*Tractatus Logico-Philosophicus*—was to draw a line between what could be said and what could only be shown. You shouldn't, according to Wittgenstein, try to say what can only be shown. The aim of telling philosophers (and others) about the legitimate and illegitimate uses of language is a fundamentally normative aim.
- We've mentioned the philosopher Rudolf Carnap before—he is the one who claimed much of philosophical and ordinary speech is meaningless (see Chapter 4). He was also an advocate of what he calls 'explication'. This is an effort to improve our conceptual apparatus. The idea is to take a term that suffers from various deficiencies—Carnap focuses on what he calls 'vagueness' and 'indeterminacy'—and then improve them along various dimensions. Here is how Anil Gupta describes the process of explication:

> An explication aims to respect some central uses of a term but is stipulative on others. The explication may be offered as an absolute improvement of an existing, imperfect concept. Or, it may be offered as a 'good thing to mean' by the term in a specific context for a particular purpose.   (Gupta (2015): §1.5)

5.3 Some Challenges for Conceptual Engineers

The Master Argument raises a range of extremely interesting and challenging questions. In the rest of this chapter we briefly explore three of them:

- In what sense can meanings be defective?
- Doesn't a change in meaning make people talk past one another?
- Is meaning change within our control?

5.3.1 Challenge 1: in what sense can meanings be defective?

The project of conceptual engineering relies on the assumption that one meaning can be better than another and that a meaning can be improved. What are the relevant kinds of virtues and vices? There are not that many attempts to systematically answer this in the literature, but Cappelen (2018) provides a partial taxonomy. He distinguishes between two broad categories.

Category 1: Intrinsic badness: the meaning itself is defective.
Category 2: The meaning has negative effects.

Paradigms of Category 1 include the following:

Slurs. The meaning of 'bitch' or 'kike' might be intrinsically bad. These are examples of morally objectionable meanings. Just what that means we explore in Chapter 6. However, it's worth noting that in this case we have two options: 'elimination' (we eliminate the use of the expression) or what is often called 'reappropriation' (which involves a form of amelioration).

Excessively vague or indeterminate terms. At least for certain purposes, it is natural to think that vagueness and indeterminacy are important defects and that amelioration involves some form of precisification.

- Incoherence or inconsistency: many philosophers claim that certain meanings are incoherent or inconsistent. The philosopher Peter van Inwagen, for example, thinks our concept of freedom is incoherent. He says:

  There are seemingly unanswerable arguments that . . . demonstrate that free will is incompatible with determinism—and there are seemingly unanswerable arguments that . . . demonstrate that free will is incompatible with indeterminism. But if free will is incompatible both with determinism and indeterminism, the concept 'free will' is incoherent, and the thing free will does not exist.
  (van Inwagen (2008): 327–8)

- The philosopher Kevin Scharp has argued that most central philosophical concepts are incoherent and that what philosophers should do is create replacement concepts, i.e., improved meanings. When that is done, philosophy is over. He writes: 'My view is that philosophy is, for the most part, the study of inconsistent concepts . . . Once enough progress has been made to arrive at a set of relatively consistent concepts for some subject matter, it gets outsourced as a science.' (Scharp (2013): 3)

What these diverse cases have in common is the idea that the meaning of a word has some kind of intrinsic defect. This is the respect in which they contrast with Category 2 defects.

Category 2 defects focus not on the intrinsic properties of the meanings, but on the effects of those meanings. This category is extremely diverse. The category potentially includes *any* negative or positive effect of thinking and talking with a certain meaning. Some illustrations:

- As we will see in Chapter 8 some philosophers and psychologists argue that describing social kinds using expressions called 'generics' can result in faulty reasoning and biased attitudes. If this is right, that's a defect of generics and a reason for either improving them or replacing them.
- Suppose the meaning of 'marriage' excludes same-sex couples. This can have the effect of perpetuating certain kinds of discrimination of such couples. That's an example of a social and political defect.
- Suppose the meaning of 'rape' is such that it cannot apply to people who are married. You might think that's a bad meaning for 'rape' because it affects people's behavior and attitudes in deeply harmful ways.
- Suppose our use of gender terms contributes to a certain social structure that's unfair or unjust. If so, that's an effect of the meanings of our existing gender terms. If you think the current meanings of those terms have important negative effects, you should be motivated to ameliorate those meanings.

We will elaborate some more on this last example and provide an illustration of a proposed amelioration. One of the world's leading experts on conceptual engineering is the philosopher Sally Haslanger (see for example, her (1999) and (2000), which are collected, among other relevant papers, in her (2012)). One of Haslanger's most influential proposals is that we change the meaning of the words 'man' and 'woman' in ways that she thinks will contribute to positive political and social change. One of her concrete suggestions is this: we should build into the very definition of 'woman' that a woman is socially subordinated on the basis of perceived gender. This leads her to the surprising conclusion that, using 'woman' as she proposes, feminists should aim for the elimination of women:

> Roughly, women are those subordinated in a society due to their perceived or imagined female reproductive capacities. It follows that in those societies where being (or being presumed to be) female does not result in subordination along any dimension, there are no women. Moreover, justice requires that where there is such subordination, we should change social relations so there will be no more women (or men). (This will not require mass femicide! Males and females may remain even where there are no men or women.)   (Haslanger (2012): 8–9)

Haslanger thinks this proposed change in meaning will have positive effects on how each of us think of ourselves. Here is what she writes more generally about her proposals for how to engineer our gender and race concepts:

> ... by appropriating the everyday terminology of race and gender, the analyses I've offered invite us to acknowledge the force of oppressive systems in framing our personal and political identities. Each of us has some investment in our race and gender: I am a white woman. On my accounts, this claim locates me within social systems that in some respects privilege and in some respects subordinate me. Because gender and racial inequality are not simply a matter of public policy but implicate each of us at the heart of our self-understandings, the terminological shift calls us to reconsider who we think we are.   ((2000): 47)

As should be clear from this passage, it is the positive effects of the new meanings (and correspondingly negative effects of the old) that motivate her project.

One way to see more generally the importance of Category 2 defects is to notice the various ways that the meanings we have shape our thoughts and actions. Burgess and Plunkett (2013a) describe these effects as follows:

> ... our conceptual repertoire determines not only what beliefs we can have but also what hypotheses we can entertain, what desires we can form, what plans we can make on the basis of such mental states, and accordingly constrains what we can hope to accomplish in the world. Representation enables action, from the most sophisticated scientific research, to the most mundane household task. It influences our options within social/political institutions and even helps determine which institutions are so much as thinkable. Our social roles, in turn, help determine what kinds of people we can be, what sorts of lives we can lead. Conceptual choices and changes may be intrinsically interesting, but the clearest reason to care about them is just that their non-conceptual consequences are pervasive and profound.   (Burgess and Plunkett (2013a): 1096–7)

They are right. The meanings/concepts we have affect our lives in many, many ways. That is one reason why it is very important to make sure that the meanings we have are as good as they can be. And that's why conceptual engineering is important.

5.3.2 Challenge 2: doesn't meaning change result in verbal disputes?

Why keep the same linguistic expression when you are changing the meaning? Why, for example, should Haslanger continue to use the word 'woman' with a new meaning, rather than employing a new expression, say 'woman*', to mark the distinction with her new, ameliorated meaning? After all, those using 'woman' with Haslanger's proposed meaning plausibly express different thoughts from those who were using it with the pre-amelioration meaning. This is bound to create massive confusion when the ameliorators try to talk to the non-ameliorators to say what people said pre-amelioration. Wouldn't everything be much easier if we marked the distinction in meaning by a distinction in lexical item?

A closely related challenge is this: when we change the meaning of a term, say, 'woman', haven't we just changed the topic? If that is so, Haslanger is no longer talking about the same thing as those using 'woman' with its old meaning. That seems very unfortunate: it could have potentially negative effects on communication. Jennifer Saul ((2006): 141) makes this problem vivid with the following example. We are to imagine Amanda has taken a feminist philosophy course and learned about and accepted Haslanger's theory. She accordingly starts using 'woman' and 'man' in the way Haslanger suggests. She utters to her friend Beau:

(1) All women are subordinated by men.

Now, Beau doesn't know anything about Haslanger's meaning and so he doesn't use 'woman' the way Amanda does. Here are some hard questions for Haslanger (and for ameliorators more generally):

- What has Amanda said to Beau? Has she said what Beau would say using this sentence or has she said what Haslanger would say?
- Suppose the answer is that Amanda has said what Haslanger would say using (1). Now imagine that Beau tells someone else what Amanda has said. Beau says: 'Amanda said that all women are subordinated by men.' What has Beau said here?

These are very tricky questions and there is no consensus among conceptual engineers about how they are best answered. Here we will briefly outline two answers.

Appeal to Topics. Cappelen (2018) answers these challenges by introducing what he calls *topics*. Topics, according to Cappelen, can be stable while word meanings change over time. This is what happens when the meaning change is topic-preserving. So suppose the meaning of a term like 'woman' has changed over time (maybe because of a Haslanger-style proposal). The challenge is to explain how those who use 'woman' before and after the change can talk to each other. The answer is that there's a topic—women—that's more coarse grained than the meaning of the word 'woman', so speakers can use that word with somewhat divergent meanings, but talk about the same topic—they can talk about women despite using 'women' with different meanings. The challenge for this kind of view is to develop a satisfactory theory of topics and to explain when meaning change is topic-preserving and when it is not. Those questions are answered in Cappelen (2018).

Embrace of Conversational Chaos/Disruptions. Sterken (forthcoming) proposes a view according to which these kinds of conversational breakdowns—or 'disruptions' as she calls them—should be embraced. It can be part of the conceptual engineer's goal to create a bit of conversational chaos because that can get conversational partners to stop and reflect on meanings. One of the things the conceptual engineer wants to promote is more awareness of ways in which language can be problematic. Communicative disruptions, on Sterken's view, can help promote such awareness. So in response to the kinds of question Saul asks ('What did Beau say?' 'How can Beau tell others what Amanda said?'), the conceptual engineer should embrace confusion: there are no easy answers. These kinds of communicative disruptions can be part of the intended effect of conceptual engineering.

5.3.3 Challenge 3: is meaning change within our control? The Dynamic Lexicon vs the Austerity Framework

So far we have seen that meanings matter: it makes sense for us to care about the meanings our words have. That raises two important questions:

- Who gets to decide what meanings we have?
- And are meanings the kinds of things that we have control over? Can we change them at will?

We saw, for example, a proposal from Haslanger about what 'woman' ought to mean. Presumably, those who agree with Haslanger would want to change current meanings and replace them with these improved meanings. They would want to engage in linguistic activism. This is, indeed, how Haslanger construes part of her work. It is intended to have practical impact—she doesn't want her work to consist of entirely theoretical reflections. For activism to make sense, however, meanings must be the kind of things we can change. The meaning of 'woman' would have to be somehow within our control. The questions we address in the rest of this chapter are: 'Do we have that kind of control?' and 'What would meanings have to be for us to have control?'

We look at two theories of meaning change: Peter Ludlow's Dynamic Lexicon (Ludlow 2014) and Cappelen's Austerity Framework (Cappelen 2018). The two frameworks are radically different: according to Ludlow, meanings are the kinds of things we can change and control more or less at will. According to Cappelen, our ability to control linguistic meaning is minimal and linguistic activism is futile.

5.3.3.1 LUDLOW ON THE DYNAMIC LEXICON

Ludlow advocates a view of language and communication that will strike many as congenial to the project of conceptual engineering. Ludlow starts with observations of what he calls 'the extreme context sensitivity of language'. He rejects the idea that languages are stable abstract objects that we learn and then use. According to Ludlow, human languages are things that we build on a conversation-by-conversation basis—he calls them 'micro-languages'. He rejects the idea that words have stable and fixed meanings that we can come to learn. According to Ludlow, word meanings are dynamic. Shifts of meaning do not just occur between conversations, they also occur within conversations—and that is often the purpose of conversations. At the core of Ludlow's view is a thesis he calls Meaning Control:

> The doctrine of Meaning Control says that we (and our conversational partners) in principle have control over what our words mean. . . . If our conversational partners are willing to go with us, we can modulate word meanings as we see fit.
> (Ludlow (2014): 83)

If this view is right, then in each conversation we create new meanings and, if we can get our conversation partners to go along, we're in control of the meaning of the words we use.

According to Ludlow, the power relations between conversation partners affect who gets to decide on the meaning of the micro-language (the language of that conversation). In this framework it becomes important who has the most knowledge, who is recognized as having the most authority, and so on. The internal power dynamic of conversations becomes central to an understanding of how meanings are shaped.

Ludlow's view is controversial along many dimensions. We'll briefly mention two worries:

- First, it's unclear what kind of control we really get in Ludlow's framework. You might be in control of the meanings of words in your little momentary micro-language, but the next moment, when a new micro-language evolves, it's all up for grabs again. Similarly, not only do you lack control over your future micro-language, you also lack control over the micro-languages of the people you're not speaking to. You have no influence, for example, on the conversation taking place next door. Any meaning modulation is at best both momentary and restricted to you and your conversation partners.
- Second, note that Meaning Control makes meaning dependent on a group, those Ludlow calls 'conversational partners'. The extent to which any *one* is in control will depend on who is included in the group of conversational partners. Suppose, when one writes a paper (or a book like this one), one is thinking of people *in the past*, people *in the future*, and also *people existing now that I will never meet or know about*, as my conversational partners. According to the doctrine of Meaning Control, we have control over meaning modulations only insofar as we can get this diverse group to coordinate. This coordination is unlikely to happen when you write a paper, since coordinating with people in the past, the future, and with people you'll never meet is practically impossible. So even within Ludlow's framework, there's at least the potential for total *lack* of control over meaning modulation. Further, this kind of broad audience is the norm, not the exception. We don't intend for our conversations to be isolated linguistic events, disconnected from what has been said in the past and what will be said in the future

or said in disconnected conversations. Our speech is always continuous with speech in the past. Our speech is often a reply to or follow up on something someone said, or it presupposes parts of what has been said in the past. And often, our speech is intended for people to think about and talk in the future, it's intended to be passed along to other people, and it's intended for consumption in unpredictable ways. In slogan form: *there's no such thing as conversational solipsism*. With that in mind, the right way to understand 'conversational partners' is broad, and so the doctrine of Meaning Control, properly interpreted, doesn't mean that *we* are in control, because the audience one needs to negotiate with is entirely open-ended.

5.3.3.2 CAPPELEN ON THE AUSTERITY FRAMEWORK

A view of conceptual engineering that contrasts sharply with Ludlow's is developed in Cappelen's *Fixing Language: An Essay on Conceptual Engineering*. Cappelen is an advocate of the view that normative reflection about language and meaning is important. He thinks much of language is defective and can be improved along various dimensions. However, he is a pessimist about what we can think of as *conceptual engineering activism*: according to his Austerity Framework, the meaning of words is fixed by facts we speakers have very little or no control over. They are, for example, determined by facts about the past and by inscrutable patterns of use over a long period of time (involving very many people). Cappelen rejects Ludlow's notion of micro-languages and his focus is on our ability to change or introduce meaning into natural languages, such as English, Chinese, and Norwegian. A central part of his framework involves two observations he calls 'Inscrutable' and 'Lack of Control':

Inscrutable. The facts that determine what meanings our words have and how these meanings can change are typically not accessible to us. We typically have no way to get information about the facts that affect the meanings of specific words, say 'race', 'woman', 'marriage', 'freedom', 'love', and 'friendship'. The relevant facts are hidden in the past and depend on the accumulation of uses by indefinitely many people over time—uses of words that we have no way to get information about. So the meaning-determining facts are typically inscrutable to us.

Lack of Control. As a corollary of Inscrutable, no one of us (or group of us) has any control over how meanings evolve. It's a bit like large-scale social change: it depends in part on how humans behave along various dimensions, but there's an inscrutable interaction between indefinitely many agents, natural events, accidents, etc. over long periods of time: a collection of facts that no one of us or group has any significant degree of control over.

Cappelen distinguishes between *the foundations for meaning* and *the superstructure of meaning*. The *foundations* are the facts that make it the case that our words mean what they mean. The *superstructure* consists (at least in part) of our beliefs, hopes, preferences, intentions, theories, and other attitudes about meanings (what they are and what they ought to be). Here are two important related questions:

1. How, if at all, does the superstructure affect the foundation?
2. How much of a discrepancy can there be between the superstructure and the meaning facts?

These are under-explored questions that have massive implications for conceptual engineering. According to Cappelen, what people say, think, propose, wish, and debate about meanings has very little influence on what words mean. The superstructure has little effect on the foundation and there can be a significant discrepancy between superstructure and the foundation. This is not to say that meanings are unaffected by the superstructure. Our various mental states and beliefs have some effect on meaning, but in unpredictable and inscrutable ways. This disconnect has significant implications for the practice of conceptual engineering. If Cappelen is right, the way to change meanings isn't to change people's beliefs (or wishes or preferences) about meanings. It is to act directly on the foundation. We don't know much about how to do that.

Cappelen's position is familiar from other normative domains: theorists often develop views of how things ought to be and what a just society is, without accompanying such views with an instruction manual for how to make the world that way. Moral philosophers have theories about what it is to act morally, but they don't accompany those theories with an instruction manual for how a specific immoral person, say Bob, should go about becoming more moral. Moral philosophers are not self-help gurus or therapists. Many political philosophers develop theories of what kind of social structures would be just, but in doing so they're not at the same time telling you how to make Canada or the Republic of Congo more just. And so it goes. There's a long and distinguished tradition of engaging in reflections about how things ought to be without these reflections being constrained by the availability of relevant facts or our control over these facts.

Cappelen agrees that limitations on our ability to improve our concepts is troubling. We are animals who pride ourselves on our rationality. The ability to think and represent is at the core of that rationality. That ability enables us to recognize both that our own concepts are defective and that there isn't much we can do about it. We can observe these defects, describe them, reflect on them, and think of ameliorative strategies. But careful thinking also reveals that such reflection is ineffective. Amelioration might happen, but if it does, it has little to do with our intentional efforts. Our intellect can diagnose itself, figure out a cure, but is helpless when it comes to doing anything. Emphasizing this highlights an important limitation on human rationality and intellect.

CENTRAL POINTS IN CHAPTER 5

- In the previous chapter we considered problems that arise from an expression's having no meaning. In this chapter we consider a somewhat related problem: cases in which a word has a meaning, but that meaning isn't good enough. This is the domain of the approach to philosophy known as *conceptual engineering*, to which this chapter is an introduction.
- We begin by pointing out that what words mean matters. If a word doesn't have the right meaning—as 'rape' and 'marriage' didn't until recently—we should change it.
- We noted that this perspective offers us a new way to understand paradigm philosophical debates. A question like 'what is knowledge?' can be approached in two ways. On one way, the aim of inquiry is to find out what 'knowledge' actually means: what conditions are needed for something to count as an instance of knowledge. On the other, the aim is to determine what 'knowledge' *should* mean.
- We went on to consider some challenges for this project of engineering new meanings or concepts. We considered what it is for one meaning to be better than another, the worry that changing the meaning of a word would result in widespread confusion because not everyone would know about the change of meaning, and, most fundamentally, the concern that meaning isn't something that we can change.
- We considered two opposing views as to whether meaning change is indeed possible: Ludlow's Dynamic Lexicon vs Cappelen's Austerity Framework.

Further Reading and Exercises

FURTHER READING FOR CHAPTER 5

Burgess and Plunkett (2013a, 2013b) and Cappelen and Plunkett (forthcoming) are good overview articles. Cappelen (2018) is the first monograph devoted to conceptual engineering and it introduces the topic comprehensively, taxonomizes the field, and furthers the debate in numerous ways. Much of Sally Haslanger's work, as collected in her (2012), is devoted to conceptual engineering. Scharp (2013) argues that we should conceptually engineer the concept of truth. Burgess, Cappelen, and Plunkett (forthcoming) is a useful series of articles on the topic.

Comprehension Questions

1. What is conceptual engineering? How is it a different approach to philosophy?
2. Think of other socially or politically important contested terms like 'rape' and 'torture'. Do you think debates about the meanings of such terms are frequent?
3. What do you think of the master argument for conceptual engineering? Explain your answer.
4. Do you think we should be worried about the thought that changing meaning leads people to talk past one another? Explain your answer.
5. Can you think of any conversations you've had recently where you've modulated meanings temporarily in the way Ludlow suggests?

Exploratory Questions

6. Do you agree with Nietzsche that we should be skeptical about our inherited concepts?
7. Try to come up with Haslanger-style definitions of politically or socially important terms. Alternatively, try to find problems with Haslanger's definition of 'woman'. Does it include or exclude people it shouldn't, in your view?
8. Cappelen (2018) defends the *topic* response to the problem of continuity by considering the way we report speech. For example, say Alex watches a video from twenty years ago of her grandmother giving a speech where she says 'marriage is important'. And say Alex, today, also says 'marriage is important'. Then it's fine to say the following:
   - Alex and her grandmother both said marriage is important; so they said the same thing.

But the meaning of 'marriage' has changed in the last twenty years: now, in a lot of places, it can apply to same-sex couples. If this is so, then two people can say the same thing by uttering the same sentence, even if the meaning, in some sense, of that sentence has changed. Cappelen thinks that the explanation for this is that both Alex and her grandmother were talking about the same *topic*, even if the precise meaning of 'marriage' has changed. On this basis, he thinks that we can avoid verbal disputes while engaging in conceptual engineering, provided the topic (as reflected in the ability to report people before and after the change as saying the same thing) stays the same. What do you think of this line of argument?

9. Do you side with Ludlow or Cappelen on the matter of control?

6

Slurs and Pejoratives

6.1 Introduction

There are a lot of things that you'll never hear said in the classroom, but that people in the real world say, sometimes with alarming frequency. There are straight insults, from the pedestrian 'bastard' and 'fucking asshole' to the Shakespearean flourishes of 'swollen parcel of dropsies' and 'whoreson obscene greasy tallow-catch'. There are expletives used as intensifiers, as in 'fucking awesome' and 'damn annoying'. There is the distressing range of pejoratives we have developed based on race ('dago', 'gook', 'pickaninny', 'limey', 'ofay') or on gender and sexual status ('bitch', 'faggot', 'breeder') or on religion ('papist', 'fundie', 'hymie') or on social status ('nerd', 'redneck', 'square') or on disability ('retard', 'spastic', 'crip').[1] (Presumably there are some other categories in which we linguistically encode our hatred for each other that we've overlooked here.) On the flip side of these dysphemic terms are euphemisms meant to make things sound nicer than they really are, from the political 'collateral damage' and 'extraordinary rendition' to the scatalogical 'Montezuma's revenge' to the topical 'hiking the Appalachian trail'. There are dogwhistles and code words meant to evoke responses from

---

[1] These are offensive terms, and shouldn't be bandied about casually. We won't, of course, be *using* them to describe or label anyone. But even the *mention* of such terms can reasonably give offense. As a result, sometimes discussions of slurs focus on particularly mild slurs (archaic slurs like 'boche', slurs with somewhat less cultural vitriol behind them like 'chav', or slurs targeting more empowered groups such as 'geek'), or make use of euphemistic reference to slurs ('the N word', 'a slurring term for promiscuous women'), or use schematic or fictional examples ('consider a slur S'). Nevertheless, we will be mentioning these terms in abundance. We worry that theorizing when the offensive terms are hidden away runs the risk of inadvertently minimizing the power of slurs and endorsing a theory that can't properly account for that power. The opening paragraphs of Geoffrey Pullum's paper 'Slurs and Obscenities' (2018) makes more extensively the case for the approach we are taking here.

specific subgroups, like 'welfare queen', 'Dred Scott', 'inner city', 'international bankers', 'states' rights', and 'super-predator'.

In this chapter, we consider the question of what these words mean, considering potential lessons about what an adequate theory of meaning for a language would have to look like to be able to account for this range of examples. The philosophical literature has focused especially on the meanings of slurs and pejoratives, so the views we consider will typically start with these cases, but we'll also consider whether proposals made to deal with slurs can be extended to insults, euphemisms, and dogwhistles. One point to keep in mind throughout is that there may be no simple one-size-fits-all solution. Maybe slurs have one kind of meaning and insults another, or maybe some slurs have one kind of meaning and other slurs another. So we may need to combine resources from all of the approaches we consider.

6.2 Descriptive Content Views

Perhaps no special theory of meaning is needed for slurs. Just as 'assassin' (for example) serves to describe someone in a certain way, perhaps the slur 'hillbilly' also serves to describe someone in a certain way. But in what way? We start with the observation that slurs are *targeted*. There is good reason to think that 'hymie' doesn't mean the same thing as 'Jew'. The first, after all, is a slur, and the second is not. But there is some kind of connection between the two terms, because Jews are the specific group being slurred by the term. The bigot who calls a Jew a hymie is doing something morally and linguistically wrong. But the bigot who calls a Buddhist a hymie is, in addition to all of that, profoundly confused. Let's then say that 'Jew' is the *neutral counterpart* of the slur 'hymie'. A *descriptive* theory of slurs then holds that the meaning of a slur is some (offensive) elaboration of its neutral counterpart.

The immediate challenge to the descriptivist is then to give a theory of what this elaboration is. As a starting point, consider the following excerpt from an 1890 *Popular Science* article called 'What Shall We Do with the "Dago"?':

What shall we do with the 'dago'? This 'dago,' it seems, not only herds, but fights. The knife with which he cuts his bread he also uses to lop off another 'dago's' finger or ear, or to slash another's cheek. He quarrels over his meals; and his game, whatever it is, which he plays with pennies after his meal is over, is carried on knife at hand. More even than this, he sleeps in herds; and if a 'dago' in his sleep rolls up against another 'dago,' the two whip out their knives and settle it there and then; and, except a grunt at being disturbed, perhaps, no notice is taken by the twenty or fifty other 'dagoes' in the apartment. He is quite as familiar with the sight of human blood as with the sight of the food he eats. His women follow him like dogs, expect no better treatment than dogs, and would not have the slightest idea how to conduct themselves without a succession of blows and kicks.

(Morgan (1980))[2]

Not all speakers and audiences will link the word 'dago' with this exact, or so specific a, set of images, but the word will typically evoke something along these lines, and perhaps we can extract the elaborating content of the slur from these sorts of images. The neutral counterpart of 'dago' is the disjunctive 'Italian, Spanish, or Portuguese' (for convenience, 'southern European'). The imagery in the above passage centers primarily on a propensity for violence, so perhaps 'dago' means something like 'southern European who is prone to violence'. Let's note two strengths of this descriptivist approach:

1. Because different slurs can have different descriptive contents, the view can capture the slurring specificity of different terms. 'Chink' and 'papist', for example, don't *just* say something bad about the Chinese and Catholics respectively. They say different things about the two different groups, depending on the specific bigoted stereotypes associated with each. So 'chink' means something like 'Chinese and shifty, money-grubbing, and untrustworthy', while 'papist' means something like 'Catholic and overly loyal to the Pope'.

Descriptivism is also well-positioned to explain why some slurs and insults are more offensive than others. To call someone a jerk, for example, is less severe an insult than to call them a motherfucker. Descriptivism can capture this difference by modifying the *strength* of the insult meaning:

- 'Jerk' = 'person prone to mildly inconsiderate behavior'
- 'Motherfucker' = 'person who regularly acts with complete indifference to the feelings of others'.

---

[2] The full text can be read here: <https://en.wikisource.org/wiki/Popular_Science_Monthly/Volume_38/December_1890/What_Shall_We_Do_with_the_Dago%3F>.

Slurs also vary in strength—calling someone a spic is more serious than calling someone a limey. Some of this is presumably explained by power disparities in the targeted group, but some of it also can be accounted for by varying how offensive the descriptive component of the meaning is.

2. The descriptivist theory explains why the bigot is straightforwardly wrong in their use of language. When the bigot says, 'A family of dagos moved in next door', according to the descriptivist he says something like 'A family of southern Europeans prone to violence moved in next door.' Since the bigot's new neighbors are not prone to violence, the bigot speaks falsely.

However, there are also a number of problems with the descriptivist approach:

1. One concern comes out through reflection on the previous point. Most southern Europeans, like most people everywhere, are not particularly prone to violence. But there are going to be *some* southern Europeans who are violent (just as there are some northern Europeans who are violent—any sizeable group is going to contain some instances of any human failing). If Lucius Vorenus is a violent southern European, then descriptivism says that it is true to say that Lucius Vorenus is a dago. The racist is right, then, in thinking that some people are dagos (and also in thinking that all dagos are violent, since all violent southern Europeans are violent). The racist's error, on this view, is in concluding too quickly that people are dagos, not in thinking that there are dagos in the first place, or that 'dago' is a reasonable way to classify the world. This may well be less error and more correctness than we want to allow the bigot.

This concern might point to the need for a more sophisticated view of what the descriptive content of a slur is. Perhaps 'dago' means 'one of the southern Europeans, all of whom are prone to violence'. Then it's not true to say that violent Lucius Vorenus is a dago, because he is not one of a group all of whom are violent. Chris Hom (2012) has proposed a sophisticated variant of this idea, suggesting that what is needed is a *normative* feature, roughly of the form 'deserving of bad treatment and negative evaluation simply by virtue of being in the relevant group'. Since, for example, no one is deserving of bad treatment and negative evaluation simply by virtue of being southern European, no one satisfies the description 'is southern European and is therefore deserving of bad treatment and negative evaluation'. If that's what 'dago' means, then there are no dagos. Call the resulting view *normative descriptivism*.

2. Descriptivism starts with the neutral counterpart of a slur and then augments it with some form of offensive description. But it's not clear that all slurs have neutral counterparts. Lauren Ashwell (2016) has argued that some gendered slurs, such as 'slut', have no neutral counterpart, because there is no way to pick out the specific group of women targeted by that slur without making a moral judgment about that group. Some racial slurs, such as 'oreo' and 'twinkie', don't target all of a racial group, but only some subset of that group—in both cases, something like a subset that's seen as inappropriately interested in assimilating to some other group. We might then think that there's no neutral way to pick out the subgroup—that the very isolation of the subgroup already requires buying into an objectionable racist ideology. Antirealists about race (people who don't think that any of our racial terms pick out real categories in the world) might think this about *all* racial slurs.

Looking beyond slurs, the same worries could be raised about insults. What is the neutral counterpart of insults like 'asshole' or 'mother-fucker'? (There are, of course, flatly literal descriptive contents to these terms, and it's possible to envision a theory of insults on which that's the right meaning for the terms, so that the insulter is either a flagrant liar or quite metaphorical. That's perhaps the right thing to say about 'swollen parcel of dropsies'.) Insults in general seemed designed not to denigrate someone *because of a category they belong to*, but just to denigrate them.

But thinking about insults might also help us see how the descriptivist could respond to this worry. *Many* slurs have neutral counterparts, so that's a natural place to start in giving the descriptive meaning of a slur. But it's not clear that we have to have a neutral core to every slur—some slurs could do nothing but attribute offensive features.

3. On the other hand, some terms in this vicinity seem to lack anything but a descriptive meaning. Dogwhistles, for example, look particularly mysterious on the descriptivist view. The whole point of a dogwhistle is to use a term that communicates one thing to one group and another thing to another group. 'Dred Scott' needs to call to mind a wrongly decided nineteenth-century Supreme Court case on race for one group, but call to mind a model for the eventual overturn of *Roe v. Wade* for another group. It's not clear, though, that 'Dred Scott' carries any descriptive meaning other than referring to the *Dred Scott* case, and thus not clear that the descriptivist can provide a meaning for it that explains

its dogwhistling effects. Similarly, it's unclear what the descriptivist view will say about expletives like 'fucking'. What's the descriptive meaning for 'fucking' in 'fucking awesome' and 'fucking asshole' and 'I can't fucking stand him'? Something like 'very' is tempting for 'fucking awesome', but not grammatically suited to 'fucking asshole'. Perhaps the descriptive view should just say that the expletive 'fucking' is meaningless and contributes nothing to the meaning of sentences in which it appears, or simply hold that while slurs are explained by the descriptivist view, expletives are not.

4. The most serious problem for descriptivist views arises from cases of embedded occurrences of slurs. The simplest example is negation. According to the descriptivist, when someone says 'That person is not a gook,' they are saying (something like) 'that person is not both Korean or Vietnamese and deserving of bad treatment and negative evaluation by virtue of being Korean or Vietnamese.' This will then be true—trivially true, because *no one* is deserving of bad treatment by virtue of being Korean or Vietnamese. But this seems like the wrong result. Slurs like 'gook' are so defective that it's bad to say that someone *isn't* a gook as well as bad to say that someone *is* a gook. Rather, the non-bigot just recognizes 'gook' as a defective term, and doesn't do any sort of classification using it.

Other sorts of embedded uses of slurs create the same problem. It's a consequence of the descriptivist view that it's true to say 'If someone is a wetback, they ought to be condemned,' because 'wetback' just means 'illegal immigrant deserving of bad treatment and negative evaluation by virtue of being an illegal immigrant', and anyone who is deserving of bad treatment is, trivially, deserving of bad treatment. The descriptivist will think that there are no wetbacks, but will think that if there were, they ought to be poorly treated. Again, it seems like such conditionals ought not come out true. The descriptivist says that the question, 'Is that person a slut?' just is the question 'Is that person someone deserving of condemnation for their sexual activity?', and thus that it's a question that a non-bigot could ask. But it seems like the non-bigot should recognize that even *asking* whether someone is a slut is somehow already to be implicated in a bigoted perspective.

In general, a slurring term continues to have its slurring effect, and thus continues to be unacceptable to use, even when embedded in various logically complex constructions such as negation, conditionals, and questions. A good theory of slurring will predict that embedded slurs still slur, but no form of descriptivism seems to do so.

The general problem is that on the descriptivist views, there's nothing deeply *wrong* with slurs. They are perhaps terms that don't actually apply to anything, because they apply only to things having normative features that the right moral views show nothing could have. But there are lots of terms that don't apply to anything ('unicorn', 'phlogiston', 'round square'), but which are still respectable parts of the language.

In the next few sections, we will consider other views on the meanings of slurs designed to help solve the problem of embeddings. First, though, we note one other interesting and intricate feature of slurs, that creates a difficult challenge for all views on the meanings of slurs. Many slurs give rise to *appropriative uses* Slurring terms will often be co-opted by members of the targeted group, who start using the slur in a non-slurring way among themselves. This is often an attempt to defuse the slur by giving it a positive valence and to insist on the value of the targeted group by treating all terms for it as positive. 'Queer' is perhaps the most prominent example of appropriation—at this point, the term has been so thoroughly appropriated that the earlier slurring sense has almost disappeared. Other terms retain both a slurring and a non-slurring sense ('dyke' and 'homo', for example). The details of appropriation are subtle and varied. Often appropriated slurs are available only to members of the targeted group—they can use the appropriated slur inoffensively, but those outside the group cannot use the term without slurring. Sometimes appropriation aims to eliminate both the general offensive nature of the slur and the specific negative descriptive content of the slur. But in other cases appropriation seeks to retain the offensiveness (to claim as a badge of pride for the slurred group that they give offense to those who oppress them) or to retain or ironically endorse the negative descriptive content (to reclaim those descriptive features as in fact of positive rather than negative value, or to strengthen group status within the targeted group by emphasizing the way they have been characterized by others).

Appropriation is a difficult phenomenon for any view that gives slurs a distinctive (and especially a distinctively defective) meaning. If descriptivism is right and 'dyke' means something like 'lesbian and deserving of bad treatment because of being lesbian', how can appropriation of the word be possible? Whether you are lesbian or not, it's hard to see how you could call someone else lesbian and deserving of bad treatment because of being lesbian without giving offense, or at least causing confusion. Perhaps appropriation happens by creating another homonymous word—a new word 'dyke' is created meaning simply 'lesbian' (or 'lesbian and deserving good treatment because of being lesbian'), and the appropriators use the new word rather than the old word. But this explanation has difficulty in making sense of dialogs such as:

- Alex: You're a dyke!
- Beth: Damn straight, and proud of it, too!

Beth clearly wants the appropriated use of 'dyke', but presumably Alex has used the slurring term, not the appropriated one. How can Beth sensibly *agree* with Alex, then?

6.3 Presuppositional Views

A central problem with descriptivist views is that they didn't capture the thought that there was something wrong with even trying to categorize the world using slurs. On descriptivist views, slurs, like other terms, simply pick out certain (possibly empty) groups of individuals. According to such views, it might be wrong to think that there *really are* people picked out by the slurs, but it doesn't look like merely using the categorization does anything wrong. We'll now consider some views that take as their central motivation capturing this thought that slurs have gone wrong from the very beginning—that in some sense it's wrong even to have them in the language, even if they are never applied to anything.

On a presuppositional view, a slur *says* one thing and *presupposes* another. 'Dago', then, might *say* 'southern European', but *presuppose* that all/most southern Europeans are violent. (Or that southern Europeans are deserving of negative treatment by virtue of being southern European, or something else along these lines. Just as the descriptivist has many options about what the elaborative descriptive content of a slur is, presuppositional views have many options about what the presupposed content is.) Given that view, a non-bigot won't use the word 'dago', because they won't be willing to accept the false presupposition. We thus capture the idea that there's something deeply wrong with slurs. Slurs don't *just* divide the world up into categories—they are part of a project of dividing up the world that starts with bigoted and offensive assumptions built in.

What does a presuppositional view say about a claim like 'Lucius Vorenus is a dago'? Such a claim will say something true (that Lucius Vorenus is southern European), but presuppose something false (that all/most southern Europeans are violent). So we should consider what we make of claims that say something true but presuppose something false. As noted in Chapter 2, claims with false presuppositions strike us as odd and inappropriate in various ways. Thus consider:

- *Alex doesn't regret stealing Beth's car.* This claim presupposes that Alex stole Beth's care. If Alex didn't, we'll probably find this claim odd or inappropriate, and want to object 'Hey, wait a minute—Alex didn't steal Beth's car.' However, we could make sense of someone who wanted to insist on it. ('Of course Alex doesn't regret stealing Beth's car. She didn't steal it, so how could she regret stealing it?')
- *Alex bought a new Mercedes, too.* This claim presupposes that someone else also bought a new Mercedes. If no one else did, we'll probably understand perfectly well what's being said, but require the speaker to rephrase things to eliminate the false presupposition.
- *Even Alex can't solve this problem.* This claim presupposes that Alex is especially good at solving problems. If she isn't, we'll probably accept the claim, but lodge a mild dissent from the presupposition. ('Well, I wouldn't say Alex was especially good at problem solving, but I see what you mean.')

These aren't terrible models for how we might react to the use of a slur, but they're not perfect, either. When the bigot says, 'There are more and more papists in this neighborhood,' we want to lodge some kind of dissent, but it's not clear that 'There certainly are a lot of Catholics living here, but I wouldn't say that Catholics are dangerously loyal to the pope' is the right form for the dissent to take.

Presuppositional views are well designed to deal with embedded slurs, because presuppositional meaning is a kind of meaning that 'projects out' from embeddings. The factive presupposition of 'regrets that' persists when 'regrets that' is placed under a negation, or in the antecedent of a conditional, or in a question. Similarly, the slurring effect of 'dago' persists when 'dago' is placed under a negation, or in the antecedent of a conditional, or in a question. That's exactly what we'd expect if the slurring effect was the consequence of a presupposed meaning. But the details here get complicated. Consider two problem cases:

- Presuppositions typically don't project out of 'believes that' and 'says that' contexts. The sentence *Charles said that Alex doesn't regret stealing Beth's car* doesn't presuppose that Alex stole Beth's car, although it might presuppose that Charles *thinks* that Alex stole Beth's car. But it's not obvious that the same is true of slurs. Does a sentence like *Nigel said that the new store is owned by a Paki* involve slurring by the speaker, or just slurring on Nigel's part? Judgments can be mixed and unclear in these cases, but views that say that the speaker slurs don't fit well with a presuppositional account.
- Presuppositions can be 'screened off' by, for example, mentioning them in antecedents of conditionals. The sentence *If Alex stole Beth's car, then Alex definitely regrets stealing Beth's car* does not presuppose that Alex stole Beth's car—that presupposition has been screened off by the antecedent. But it doesn't look like slurring effects can be screened off in the same way. The sentence *If southern Europeans are violent, then I don't want any dagos living around here* is just as offensively slurring as the simple uses of 'dago'. Again, this doesn't fit well with a presuppositional account.

The basic picture here is that the slurring effects of slurs are more persistent than the presuppositional effects of presupposition triggers. If that's right, then presuppositional language isn't quite the right model for slurs.

6.4 Expressivist Views

Descriptivist and presuppositional views have in common that slurs communicate some substantive (false) information about the world beyond the neutral counterpart. Presuppositional views differ from descriptive views just in putting that information in a different (presupposed) position, in an attempt to deal with the problem of embedding. But it could be that this common informational assumption is mistaken. We have considered above various descriptivist suggestions for what the descriptive content of slurs is. But in considering these options, it's hard to avoid thinking that none of them really seems quite right. 'Redneck' means *something like* 'rural and ignorant and uncultured', but it surely doesn't mean *exactly* that. That proposal is both too specific (is the slurring practice committed to rednecks always being poorly educated?) and not specific enough (it fails to capture the full richness of the bigoted stereotype that lies behind the 'redneck' label). But many attempts to improve on that descriptivist proposal tend to recreate the same problems. As with metaphors, there seems to be something *ineffable* about the content of slurs. Any attempt to state clearly what the metaphor or the slur says leaves one feeling that the heart of the thing has been left out. One aspect of the ineffability of slurs is that the descriptive paraphrases seem to leave out the full *nastiness* of the slur. No matter what the descriptive content proposed, that content said without the slur lacks the same emotional impact.

Perhaps, then, we need to look to language whose role is to *express* rather than *describe*. Consider the word 'ouch'. It is appropriate to say 'ouch' when you are in pain, but the word 'ouch' doesn't *mean* that you are in pain. If it did, it could make sense to respond to an utterance of 'ouch' by saying 'that's false', and it would be possible to say things like 'Yesterday, ouch', or 'If ouch, I'll take an aspirin'. 'Ouch' doesn't *describe* your pain—it *expresses* it.

'Ouch' is a purely expressive term, but other bits of language combine expressive and descriptive functions. Chris Potts has developed a multi-dimensional account of language that distinguishes descriptive and expressive dimensions. Potts discusses examples such as:

1. That bastard Kresge is famous.

This sentence has the descriptive content that Kresge is famous. The descriptive content is informational, saying something about how the world is. 'That bastard', on this view, contributes nothing to the descriptive content. But the sentence also has the expressive content of expressing a negative attitude toward Kresge. The expressive content isn't informational—it's not saying how the world is, but expressing how the speaker feels about part of the world.

Expressive content, unlike descriptive content but like presuppositional content, escapes from negation. If Alex says, 'That bastard Kresge is famous,' expressing her negative attitude toward Kresge, and Beth likes Kresge and wants to reject Alex's negative attitude, she can't do that by saying 'That bastard Kresge isn't famous.' That sentence won't express a positive attitude toward Kresge. It continues to express the negative attitude, and rejects only the descriptive part of Alex's claim that Kresge is famous.

But expressive content has an even stronger tendency than presuppositional content to escape embeddings. Consider Potts's discussion of the sentence *Whenever I pour wine, the damn bottle drips*:

> The bottles can vary with the choice of pouring events. One might expect the meaning of *damn* to vary as well, so that the example would assert that in all situations *s* such that the speaker pours wine in *s*, the bottle in *s* drips in *s* and the speaker is in a heightened emotional state in *s*. But that paraphrase is consistent with the speaker feeling no special expressive attitude in the context of utterance, but rather only in wine-pouring situations. That is not what we intuit, though. Rather, we infer from the speaker's use of *damn* that he is in a heightened emotional state *right this minute*.   (Potts (2007): 171)

Similarly, expressive content can't be screened off by conditionals in the way that presuppositional content can. 'If I have a negative attitude toward Kresge, then that bastard Kresge is famous' doesn't block expression of the negative attitude; it just makes for a very odd assertion. This feature of expressive meaning fits well with the full extent of the tendency of slurs to escape embedding, and also helps explain the expressive immediacy of slurs—when a slur is used in, for example, the past tense, the speaker is nevertheless expressing a current, not a previous, attitude.

However, a purely expressive theory isn't faithful to all the ways that slurs are used. Camp (2013) has observed that there can be 'innocent' uses of slurs—slurs can be used by people embedded in a bigoted culture, who have picked up the language and perhaps some of the attitudes of that culture, but who often use that language calmly and neutrally, not *intending* any slurs. Camp gives examples such as:

2. I'm glad we have so many spics at our school: they always bring the best food to our fundraising functions.

3. I wonder whether Japs like to cuddle their babies as much as Chinks seem to.

There's no doubt that these speakers are (perhaps despite their intentions) slurring the targeted groups. But they don't seem in using the slurs to be expressing an immediate negative attitude toward the slurred group. If an expressivist theory gives slurs an expressive dimension of displaying some hostile, derogatory, or otherwise negative attitude, then these speakers are somehow misusing the slurs. The speakers are morally wrong to use the slurs, but given that they have used them, they don't seem to be linguistically wrong in the way that they are using them.

6.5 Prohibitionist Views

Descriptive, presuppositional, and expressivist accounts of slurs all try to capture what is distinctive about slurs by saying something about the *meaning* of slurring terms. Prohibitionist accounts, on the other hand, hold that what's distinctive about slurs isn't an aspect of their meaning. Rather, what's distinctive is the simple fact that slurs are words that there is a rule against using.

The idea of prohibitionism is most easily seen not with slurs, but with expletives like 'fuck'. Why does 'fuck' have the particular complicated role that it does? 'Fuck' can be a positive intensifier ('fucking awesome'), a negative intensifier ('fucking asshole'), a neutral intensifier ('can't fucking stand him'), a simple expression of strong emotion ('fuck!' as an expression of anger, joy, fear, disgust, or surprise), and a verb of aggression ('fuck him!'). We could look for a meaning (or a cluster of meanings) that explains these uses. Or we could just say that 'fuck' is a *prohibited word*—something that one is not supposed to say in polite company—and that its use, through violating that prohibition, creates an effect of shock and intensity. The speaker who says 'fucking awesome' rather than simply 'awesome' must be so swept away by the awesomeness that they can't be bothered with the pedestrian matter of following conventional rules.

Prohibitionism then extends this picture to slurs. Why is 'dago' a slur but not 'southern European'? According to prohibitionism, it's because there is a rule against the use of 'dago'. Speakers who use 'dago' despite this rule mark themselves in certain ways—they can't be bothered to use a permissible rather than an impermissible term for southern Europeans. That's enough to explain why the use of the prohibited 'dago' conveys some attitude toward southern Europeans, but why is the conveyed attitude a negative attitude? Why can't 'dago', like 'fuck', have both a positive and a negative valence?

The answer lies in the *source* of the prohibition. If the use of 'dago' is prohibited, who is it that has prohibited it? Where did this rule come from? The prohibitionist picture is that it is the *targets* of the slurs that do the prohibiting. Southern Europeans make clear that they don't want to be called 'dagos', and since they reasonably have authority over what they are called, that's enough to make the use of 'dago' prohibited. Someone who then uses the word anyway marks themselves as unconcerned to follow the rule. But a disregard for the rule in turn signals a disregard for the rule creators. Since the rule is a rule introduced by southern Europeans (the slur targets), to use 'dago' is to display that you don't regard southern Europeans as worthy of enough respect to bother following their rules.

Prohibitionism gives a natural explanation for the embedding behavior of slurs. If the use of a slur is prohibited, then it's prohibited, whether the slur occurs in a simple sentence or is embedded in a complex construction. In fact, prohibitionists push the embedding argument a step further. On any of the views previously discussed, a mere quotational mention of a slur has no slurring effect. That's because merely mentioned words don't invoke any of their meaning properties. So on the earlier views, there should be nothing problematic about saying things like:

4. 'Spic' begins with an 's'.
5. 'Chink' is a slurring term for Chinese people.
6. The store had a sign saying 'No Homos!'

But in fact, many people find it very uncomfortable to say such things, and take offense at hearing them said. (Thus the use of the slur euphemism 'the N word', which is itself starting to achieve prohibited status.) Prohibitionism can explain this: if the rule is just a rule against saying the word, then the rule prohibits quotational mention just as much as it does direct use. (If anything, prohibitionism will face a reverse problem of explaining why non-quoted uses of slurs are *worse* than quoted mentions.)

Since prohibitionism isn't a theory about the meaning of slurs, but rather a theory about the rules of permissible use for slurs, it is silent on the question of what the truth conditions of slurring claims are. It might be natural, however, to combine prohibitionism with the view that 'dago', for example, is true of (but forbidden to apply to) southern Europeans. Prohibitionism might *need* this commitment in order to explain why it's southern Europeans who are authoritative in prohibiting the use of 'dago'. The prohibitionist then holds that the bigot speaks truly saying that all Chinese are chinks, but simply hold that the bigot shouldn't say what they are saying.

A central worry about prohibitionism is that it seems to reverse the order of explanation. We want to say that slurs are prohibited because they are slurring, but the prohibitionist tells us instead that slurs are slurring because they are prohibited. Pursuing this worry can lead us to a more satisfying view that shares important similarities with prohibitionism. If the prohibitionist is right, and slurs are slurring because they are prohibited, it raises the question of why the words were prohibited in the first place. Consider the word 'pickaninny'. It's now a slur targeting (roughly) black children, but there is some evidence that the word began life as a neutral word for children, deriving from the Portuguese *pequinino* and spreading through various African communities connected to Portuguese trade. (Even if the history is wrong in this case, words certainly sometimes transition from non-slur to slur.) How, then, did 'pickaninny' come to be prohibited? The full history is surely enormously complex, but it looks like the story goes something like this. White communities began, especially through their contact with slaves, to pick up the word and to use it specifically for black children (since they were encountering it in that context). Those uses then got entangled with bits of racist ideology. Children's books would be written, for example, featuring racist caricatures of black children being called 'pickaninnies'. At some point the association of the word with the way that racist speakers were using it became strong enough that the original black community disavowed its use, causing it to be prohibited by the relevant authoritative group.

But once we see a story like this, it's unclear how much the added step of *prohibiting* is bringing to the picture. Suppose we've reached a point at which there is a long history of racist uses of 'pickaninny', uses in conjunction with degrading and dehumanizing depictions of black children. That history has become prominent enough that it's hard, especially if you are in the right community, to hear the word without having a cluster of offensive uses coming immediately to mind. This looks like it already does the work of explaining why the word slurs. It slurs because it invokes a troubled and racist history. It's offensive because it offends by invoking that history.

As we saw in the discussion of expressivist views, there can be 'innocent' uses of slurs, uses by people who have no intention of communicating or expressing anything negative. But the speaker's intentions don't have any influence over the history of the word, so even 'innocent' uses can reasonably offend. And if a speaker is aware of the history, then whether their communicative intentions are innocent or not, they do something offensive in deliberately using a term they know offends.

We might thus slightly generalize prohibitionism. The generalized view agrees that the explanation of slurring isn't to be found in the meanings of slurs, but holds that there's nothing more general to be said than that slurs are words with histories that create certain kinds of negative effects. A few observations about this generalized view:

1. It's easy to worry that the view does too little to explain the offensiveness of slurs by making their slurring a 'mere psychological effect', rather than a real part of the meaning. But to think this is to underestimate the powerful effects of history and culture. Certain slurring terms can't be heard without immediately calling to mind in the audience a host of vivid images (from personal experience, from film and television, from oral history) of the Southern redneck sneering the term while holding a shotgun, of white-robed figures yelling the term while tying a noose to a tree, of the Northern factory owner contemptuously spitting out the term while sending in strike-breaking scabs, and on and on. Being confronted by that wave of images and ideas can be far more powerful than anything that's given in the 'mere semantics' of the words.

2. The generalized view is also useful in explaining dogwhistles and euphemisms. Why can support for social policies be driven down by saying that they benefit 'inner city youth'? Because the use of 'inner city' immediately invokes scenes from *The Wire*—the dealer on the run-down corner calling 'Pandemic!', the homeless man wandering by with a half-empty bottle of cheap wine, and so on. Countless stories of the intractable ills of contemporary urban life spring to mind. With these images of hopelessness forefronted, who would want to waste resources on problems that our cultural stories tell us can't be fixed? Why is 'extraordinary rendition' useful as a euphemism for 'sending to another country for torture'? Because it avoids the word 'torture', loaded with bad associations, and because the technical and managerial sound of 'extraordinary rendition' brings to mind images of competence and success.

Notice that dogwhistles and euphemisms aren't prohibited, so original prohibitionism, unlike the generalized version, has nothing to say about them. Prohibitionism has the opposite problem with terms like 'ain't'. 'Ain't' is prohibited in a very straightforward sense—schoolchildren are regularly told not to use it. But it doesn't thereby become a slur. The generalized view, on the other hand, will observe that 'ain't' has a long history linking it to specific social groups (roughly, the working classes and the American South), and that that history gives rise to various effects, so that use of the word is associated with informality and lower education.

6.6 Final Thoughts

The naive classroom view of meaning is informational—the job of each sentence is to tell us something about how the world is, and so the job of words is to describe bits of the world so that sentences using those words can say things about those bits. This chapter has been an exploration of some of the most radical deviations from the calm language of the classroom—we've been interested in the words we use to vent our bitterest bile, to throw in each other's face the ugliest parts of our sordid history, to curse and spit at the world, and (iron-ically) often to try to paper over all of that ugliness with euphemistic language. A central question then is how much we need to change the informational paradigm of the classroom in order to account for this language, red in tooth and claw. We've seen in this chapter answers to this central question going in two different directions. Some theories (descriptivist, presuppositional, end expressivist accounts) build the bile into the theory of meaning in various ways, giving us new more complicated and sophisticated meanings that deviate from the class-room's calmly descriptive meanings in increasingly elaborate ways. Other theories (prohibitionism) give up on specifically *linguistic* the-orizing at this point. The bile isn't encoded into our language, but rather resides in us, and emerges through the way that we interact with the language. The question of which of these two broad approaches is correct is then a complicated mixture of questions of detail, examining how well the different approaches deal with the specifics of how slurring behaves, and big picture questions, thinking about what the final scope of a theory of language ought to be, and how that theory should give way to and interact with theories of human psychology and sociology.

CENTRAL POINTS IN CHAPTER 6

- In this chapter of *Bad Language* we consider bad language: slurs, swear words, dysphemisms, insults, codewords, and more. Our aim is to introduce some of the problems philosophers and linguists face trying to theorize about such expressions, and present some theories about how these expressions work.
- We first consider descriptive content views of slurs and related terms. According to this sort of view, slurs have a clear descriptive meaning. Thus 'dago' might mean something like 'southern European who is prone to violence'. We considered some good features of this view, such as the fact that sentences like 'A family of dagos moved in next door' come out (almost certainly) false, since it's (almost certainly) false that a family of southern Europeans prone to violence moved in next door (just because most southern Europeans aren't prone to violence).
- There are problems with the descriptive content view, though. If you call a southern European who *is* prone to violence a 'dago', you have spoken correctly, which seems wrong. Moreover, there are serious problems with the view when it comes to embedded slurs. Putting a slurring sentence under a negation, as in 'My neighbor is not a dago' remains offensive, and can't be used to say the true thing that my neighbor is not a southern European prone to violence. The descriptive content view lacks an explanation of this.
- We next consider a presuppositional view. On this view, 'dago' might just stand for the property of being southern European, but presuppose that all or most southern Europeans are violent (or something like that). An advantage of this view is that it deals well with some embedded use of slurs, but this is only a partial advantage, since the behavior of embedded presuppositions and that of slurs doesn't quite line up.
- We next consider expressivist views, according to which there can be associated with an expression two sorts of content—descriptive meaning and expressive content. An interjection like 'ouch!', for example, has just expressive content, while 'wolf' has just descriptive meaning. Slurs, the thought here goes, have both. This theory can deal with the complex embedding cases, but can't deal with certain other cases.
- The final view is simple to state: it says that slurs are words that one is prohibited from uttering. A good point in evidence in favor of this view is that even *mentioning* slurs is offensive: there are some slurs one can't even talk about by putting quotation marks around them. This is unexpected on every other theory, but can be explained on the prohibitionist view. But we pointed out that this view is perhaps explanatorily lacking. Something is prohibited because it's a slur, not a slur because it's prohibited.

Further Reading and Exercises

FURTHER READING FOR CHAPTER **6**

An overview article that covers much of the same ground as this chapter is Hom (2010). Hom (2008) is a defense of the descriptive content view. Schlenker (2007) makes the case that a presuppositional analysis can capture much of the relevant data, while Potts (2007) defends the expressivist view (it is, however, technically challenging in places). Anderson and Lepore (2013) defends the prohibitionist view. A recent anthology is Sosa (2018).

Comprehension Questions

1. What exactly is the embedding problem for descriptivism?
2. Explain how the presuppositional view does better than the descriptive theory when it comes to some embedding cases.
3. We noted that slurs don't appear to behave entirely in the way they ought to if the presuppositional theory were true. Do you think this holds for other expressive content? Consider somebody remarking to someone whom they don't know well, but know to have a boyfriend:
   * If your boyfriend cheats on you, ditch that asshole asap!
   * You should dump your asshole boyfriend

Is there a difference in acceptability/expressive force between those two sentences? If there is, does it lend support to a presupposition analysis of expressive content? Explain your answer.

4. Which of the views we surveyed do you think is best? Why?
5. In an episode of *Seinfeld*, non-Jewish Elaine attracts the romantic attention of some Jewish men. George explains to her it's because she's a *shiksa*—a non-Jewish woman, whom Jewish men are attracted to because they are different from their mothers. Arguably, in this context, 'shiksa' means 'non-Jewish and deserving of praise because of being so'. It thus seems like a positively valenced slur. Can you think of any other examples of positively valenced slurs? Arguably, 'shiksa' at the same time has a slurring effect toward Jews. Why would that be?

Exploratory Questions

6. The prohibitionist view has an advantage in that it predicts most uses of slurs are bad. But there's a risk that it might still not cover everything we would want it to cover. Thus presumably it will not predict that 'niggardly' is

prohibited, despite the (near) occurrence of a slur inside it, which seems like the right result. But one might think for the same reason it wouldn't predict that the neologism 'unkikey' is prohibited, which seems like the wrong result—that putative word *is* offensive, as when an anti-Semite says of his Jewish friend, 'He may be Jewish, yeah, but he's very...unkikey.' Can you think of a response to this argument?

7. Consider the following dialogue between American Alex and British Beth:
   - Alex: Have you ever had fried eggplant?
   - Beth: No, never had it. Had fried *aubergine*, though.

What Beth seems to be doing, in a slightly obnoxious or jovial manner, is pointing out that something Alex said wasn't quite appropriate: in particular, she was pointing out that she—Beth— doesn't call the shiny purple vegetable 'eggplant'. But she wasn't really responding negatively to the *content* of Alex's question.

What this shows is that you can object to what someone says not by objecting to the content, but by objecting to the way they phrased it, a phenomenon known as metalinguistic negation.

With that in mind, reconsider one of the cases of appropriative slurs that were deemed to cause problems:
   - Alex: You're a dyke
   - Beth: Damn straight, and proud of it!

We were to imagine Alex was using it slurringly, and that made the response of Beth—who is a lesbian—seem odd. But maybe there's a response available: just as in our aubergine dialogue, Beth was responding negatively to the wording rather than the content, could it be that Beth is here responding positively not to the content (which is slurring) but to the wording? We could call this metalinguistic affirmation. What do you think of metalinguistic affirmation as a way to account for such appropriative uses of slurs?

7. *Star Trek* introduces the terms 'Cardie' and 'spoonhead' as pejoratives for the fictional alien race of Cardassians, and *Battlestar Galactica* introduces 'toaster' as a slur for the fictional Cylons. Are these shows successful in creating genuine slurs? (Is it genuinely offensive, for example, to call someone in Cardassian garb at a *Star Trek* convention a 'Cardie'?) Consider the accounts of the meanings of slurs given in this chapter and discuss what these different accounts predict about fictional slurs. What would an author need to do, on these different accounts, to create a new slur, and how successful should we expect authors to be? UrbanDictionary.com claims that 'Cardie' is extremely offensive while 'spoonhead' is only mildly offensive. Could this be right? If so,

what is it about the way the two terms are introduced and used in the shows would create this difference?

8. On Potts's view, all uses of slurs and related terms give voice to a speaker's attitude at the time of utterance. But is this always so? Consider the following sentence:

   • Jack's typically a nice guy, but he can be an arsehole sometimes. When you meet him you never know if you're going to get nice guy Jack (/the nice guy) or asshole Jack (/the asshole).

Does this sentence sound okay to you? Can you think of others like it? If so, does it cause problems for Potts's view?

9. A criminal, like a felon, is a member of a group that has broken the law, and typically criminals are thought to be deserving of bad treatment and negative evaluation (i.e., publicly recorded punishment) as a result of having broken the law. Does that make the words 'criminal' and 'felon' slurs? If not, why not? If so, do they have neutral counterparts?

7

Lexical Effects

7.1 Introducing Lexical Effects: The Non-Cognitive, Associative, Effects of Words

Take a look at these words:

Fart *Sunset* **Pimple** CHOCOLATE <u>Starvation</u> **Coca-Cola**

Imagine yourself looking at one of these words on a big poster. Here is what we know will happen: just the contemplation of these words will trigger in you feelings (happiness, sadness, disgust, amusement, and so on), associations (other soft drinks, Africa), mental images (the image of a sunset or your friend's pimple), and memories (the time you sat in the squeaky chair and it made that embarrassing sound). The mere contemplation of the words can influence your mood and your behavioral dispositions. That is to say: words have all kinds of *non-cognitive effects*. This chapter is about how speakers can exploit the non-cognitive effects of the words they use.

The discussion of slurs in the previous chapter ended with the suggestion that we might need a sharp change from the picture of language that has dominated the earlier chapters and more broadly philosophy of language since its origin at the beginning of the twentieth century. In much of that work, the emphasis has been on the *content* conveyed by language: what is said, what is implicated, and what is communicated. That is to say, the emphasis has been on information—something that can be true or false. There are systematic ways to describe how words can be put together into sentences and how these sentences can say something true (or false) about the world. Efforts to give such systematic theories have been at the core of both semantics and pragmatics (see Cappelen and Dever 2016 for an introductory account of such theories). This emphasis on content, information, and truth has had the result that philosophical studies of language have ignored feelings, emotions, associations, and other non-cognitive effects of language. These have been put aside as somewhat irrelevant side effects. The tacit assumption has been that the real, fundamental, function of language is to convey information, and that non-cognitive effects can be ignored and aren't worth systematic and serious investigation. This is reflected in the idealizations outlined in Chapter 1.

This chapter presents a radically different dimension of language—a dimension completely ignored by all the idealizations. Even though it is true that language at some fundamental level is a device for expressing and exchanging information, the non-cognitive effects are real and play an enormous and poorly understood role in communication. The aim of this chapter is to highlight some of these effects.

In the idealized picture presented in Chapter 1, communication is entirely a matter of speakers using language to build up a body of mutual information. That fact has both a speaker side and a language side.

- On the side of speakers, it means that the communicative intentions of those who make assertions are purely informational. The intention of an idealized speaker is always an intention to express, and to have their audience come to believe, that p, for some p.[1]
- On the side of language, it means that the meanings of words and sentences are well suited to being used to express information. On this view, the meaning of a sentence is always a proposition that p, so that the speaker can make manifest their intention that their audience come to believe that p, by using the sentence that has the proposition that p as its meaning. The meanings of words are meanings that contribute to the propositions expressed by sentences containing those words.

However in the real, non-idealized world, communication isn't always about building up bodies of mutual information. As we saw in the last chapter, one thing real speakers do, for example, is *insult*. When

---

[1] We focus here on the cases where the speaker makes assertions—not when they ask questions, issue orders, make promises, etc. Such phenomena can be accounted for without departing too much from the idealized picture, although to make that case is beyond the focus of this book.

someone says 'that fucking asshole George was at the party last night,' the communicative effect isn't just to add a new piece of information about party attendance to common ground, it's also to insult George. Again, that fact has both a speaker side and a language side.

- On the side of speakers, it shows that the communicative intentions of speakers aren't always intentions that their audience come to believe that some proposition p. We need a better account of the other, non-doxastic, non-informational things that speakers can be up to when they speak.
- On the side of language, we again need meanings of words and sentences that are well suited to being used in pursuit of these non-idealized intentions. We need to consider what the meaning of 'that fucking asshole George was at the party last night' (and hence the meaning of 'fucking asshole') could be that would allow speakers to use that sentence to achieve their non-idealized intentions.

Having made some preliminary examinations on the side of language in the previous chapter, in this chapter we turn to the speaker side.

7.2 Non-Cognitive Lexical Effects: Some Illustrations

To get a sense of what we have in mind when we talk about the non-cognitive effects (lexical effects, for short) of expressions we'll go through four examples of how they are exploited in communication:

- Metaphor
- Brand names (and other names)
- Slurs
- Code words and so-called 'dogwhistles'.

7.2.1 Davidson on the effects of metaphor

Metaphor, in which one talks about something by talking about something else in some way related to it, is ubiquitous in speech. Turn on the TV and you will hear people say that America is a melting pot, or that the GOP is a rudderless ship, for example. Motivational speakers will tell you that time is money. Clearly such metaphors have what we're calling lexical effects. But how do they do so? We like Donald Davidson's view of metaphor. Here is a brief summary of that view.[2] According to Davidson, 'What distinguishes metaphor is not meaning but use... And the special use to which we put language in metaphor is not—cannot be—to "say something" special, no matter how indirectly' (Davidson (1978): 43). At the core of Davidson's view of metaphor is the thesis that *no metaphorical content is conveyed*. Metaphors, according to Davidson, have only their literal meaning, and what they express is typically false ('Juliet is the sun' has only one meaning, namely, that Juliet is the sun—and that is false). The goal of the use of a metaphor is not to convey some special message. Since what the metaphor prompts or inspires in most cases is not entirely, or even at all, recognition of some truth or fact, the attempt to give literal expression to the content of the metaphor is simply misguided. So what is the goal? He compares metaphor to a picture or a bump on the head and says that 'There is no limit to what a metaphor calls to our attention, and much of what we are caused to notice is not propositional in character' (Davidson (1978): 46). Metaphors 'inspire' 'visions, thoughts and feelings'.

Here is what we want to take away from Davidson: words have all kinds of non-cognitive effects and cognitive effects that go far beyond their literal meaning (and their implicatures and presuppositions). Maybe that's not enough for a good theory of metaphor. Don't worry about that for now—our aim here is not to present a full theory of metaphor. What's important is that he's right: Words do have the kinds of effects that he describes. Now, let's ask: is the production of these effects *distinctive* of metaphor? That would be surprising. If Davidson is right about the effects of metaphorical speech—it can inspire visions, thoughts, and feelings—then why not think that language which we would classify as literal speech can't also have *some* of those effects—maybe not to the same extent as good metaphor, but to a more limited extent? It would be extremely surprising if those kinds of effects are restricted to what we naturally classify as metaphor. Suppose we tell you:

---

[2] Just how to interpret Davidson is a matter of some controversy, and what follows is our version of his view.

Nora just made a lemon meringue cookie that she served with a delicious warm cacao.

This is literal speech, but it can inspire thoughts, feelings, associations, and even visions of various kinds. Nothing Davidson says about the effects of metaphor isn't also true about literal speech. That is, words have effects that go far beyond anything they say, implicate, or presuppose.

7.2.2 Brand names and names for people

There is a reason why companies spend an enormous amount of resources protecting their brand names: 80–90 percent of the value of the Coca-Cola company lies in its ownership of the name 'Coca-Cola'.[3] What does that mean? It is of course complicated, but one thing it means is that if Coca-Cola had to change the name of its core product, then the value of the company as a whole would decline dramatically. What's important for our purposes is this: in a scenario where the company was not allowed to put the words 'Coca-Cola' on their product, people's propensity for buying and consuming the product would decline. This is so even among a population that knows about the change in name (and knows that nothing about the drink has changed). The change in lexical item would change their behavior. More generally, one lesson from reflecting on brand names and the theory of brand names (something philosophers of language and linguists should do much more) is that lexical effects are immense. The lexical items themselves have effects on emotions and behavioral motivation that's not captured simply by talking about what is said, what is implicated, or what is presupposed. More generally, the effects are disconnected from meanings. This is so in part because the effects are not entirely, or even for the most part, cognitive effects (they don't add another level of content—it's not about getting more information—the effect is from the lexical item itself).

What, more specifically, are these non-cognitive effects and how are they generated? We don't have a full theory, but it is clear what the beginning of a theory will be: in the positive case, it triggers pro-attitudes, memories, and mental images. Much of advertisement has as its goal to

---

[3] The economist Aswath Damodaran gives an analysis of the value of the Coca-Cola brand name in a blog post at <http://aswathdamodaran.blogspot.com/2013/10/the-brand-name-advantage-valuable.html>.

generate such positive associations and images. Advertisements for Coca-Cola (and many other products) have as central goals to get people to associate Coca-Cola (or the other products) with images of happy people. Part of the aim is also for these images to blend with genuine memories—the images in the advertisement partly shape our memories. Your memories of Christmas, for example, likely involve images of Santa as a kindly man dressed in red with a big beard. This image is also strongly associated with a series of ads, now spanning almost a century, for Coca-Cola. The Coca-Cola company hopes that you'll transfer the positive feelings you have for Christmas to their product, which will make you likely to buy it. The flip side of this is that certain corporate names trigger negative non-cognitive effects. In 2014, two Malaysian Airline flights crashed within four months of each other. As a result, negative emotions were triggered when potential clients saw the words 'Malaysian Airlines' (and the accompanying logo), and the airline's ticket sales declined dramatically. There was of course also cognitive content triggered by seeing 'Malaysian Airlines' (e.g., the thought that there had been two recent crashes), but the decline in sales was at least in part explained by the non-cognitive effects.

This point can be made independently of brand names: just think about ordinary proper names. Suppose that today a child is named 'Hitler'. Imagine the parents didn't know about the evil bearer of that name. It was a typographical coincidence: the ignorant parents happened to like those letters organized in that way. Now imagine people being asked to use that word for the child. Those asked to do so can know what we just said, i.e., there's no connection whatsoever to the evil person. Still, the name will doubtlessly have emotional and associative effects on both speaker and hearer. It will affect how people think about and relate to the child. It is not part of the meaning or sense of the name and it is not related to the referent. It is simply an effect of the name itself. That lexical item triggers certain negative emotional and cognitive effects.

That the sounds of names affect people in interesting ways is shown by a study on how political affiliation affects parents' choice of name for their children. As surprising as it might seem, there is a correlation between what a child is named and the political affiliation of the parents who name it. In particular, a study suggested that parents in liberal neighborhoods are more likely to opt for 'soft' letters in naming their child, such as 'l's and 'm's, while conservative people are more likely to opt for harder sounds like 'k' or 't'. Thus baby Liam is more likely to be the product of liberals while Kurt is more likely to have conservative parents.[4]

The kind of signaling that is involved in name choices is, again, not about the meaning of the name (or the meaning of sentences containing the name). It is about triggering certain kinds of lexical effects, and what the study shows is that parents' choices are guided by lexical effects even when they are not aware of it.

7.2.3 Lakoff on political branding

Some of linguist and political commentator George Lakoff's analysis of political branding is best understood as appealing to what we call lexical effects. Much of his work is about the non-literal effects of combinations of expressions. He has applied this work to what can be described as political branding: calling inheritance tax 'death tax' (in order to make it less attractive), using the expression 'pro-life' (to make laws restricting abortion more attractive) using 'tax relief' rather than 'tax cuts', etc. Here is Lakoff's description in the first pages of his book *Don't Think of an Elephant!*:

When the word *tax* is added to *relief*, the result is a metaphor: Taxation is an affliction. And the person who takes it away is a hero, and anyone who tries to stop him is a bad guy. This is a frame. It is made up of ideas, like *affliction* and *hero*. The language that evokes the frame comes out of the White House, and it goes into press releases, goes to every radio station, every TV station, every newspaper. And soon the *New York Times* is using *tax relief*. And it is not only on Fox; it is on CNN, it is on NBC, it is on every station because it is 'the president's tax relief plan.' And soon the Democrats are using *tax relief*—and shooting themselves in the foot. It is remarkable. I was asked by the Democratic senators to visit their caucus just before the president's tax plan was to come up in the Senate. They had their version of the tax plan, and it was their version of tax relief. They were accepting the conservative frame. The conservatives had set a trap: The words draw you into *their* worldview. That is what framing is about. Framing is about getting language that fits your worldview. It is not just language.
(Lakoff (2014): 4)

Lakoff's account of these kinds of cases is primarily cognitive. He talks about how expressions trigger (or express or are associated with) what he calls 'frames'. He says that '[f]rames are mental structures that shape the

---

[4] <https://www.livescience.com/37196-politics-baby-names.html>.

way we see the world. As a result, they shape the goals we seek, the plans we make, the way we act, and what counts as a good or bad outcome of our actions' (Lakoff (2014): xv). Frames are best understood as also including what we have called lexical effects. The point Lakoff nicely illustrates is that lexical effects are of enormous importance also in politics: the choice of lexical items can make or break a political campaign. This is unsurprising since political branding in these respects is like product branding (and we saw above how important lexical effects are in that domain).

7.2.4 'Code words' and 'dogwhistles'

In a recent paper, Justin Khoo uses the following passage from Donald Trump's book *Time to Get Tough: Making America #1 Again* to illustrate the use of so-called 'code words' in public debates:

> If we keep on this path, if we reelect Barack Obama, the America we leave our kids and grandkids won't look like the America we were blessed to grow up in. The American Dream will be in hock. The shining city on the hill will start to look like an inner-city wreck.   (Trump (2011): 4, quoted in Khoo (2017): 33)

According to Khoo, the passage contains at least three code words: 'hock' (a verb that means to put an item up for pawn), 'the shining city on the hill' (alludes to the Sermon on the Mount, and has been used, going back to the Puritan John Winthrop, as a metaphor for American exceptionalism), and 'inner-city' (which carries racial connotations). According to Khoo, the effect is this:

> Using these code words in close succession, Trump contrasts two outcomes for America: a white, safe, prosperous, Christian, exceptional America, and one dominated by poor, lazy, and criminal black people. Yet, none of this is explicit: on the face of it, all Trump has said is that a second Obama term will result in the American Dream being put up for sale, and that what was once a shining city on the hill will begin to look like a densely populated urban area.   (Khoo (2017): 34)

It's essential to the use of code words that they give the speaker a kind of deniability: he can deny that he has said anything racist. If accused of racism, he can respond that he didn't say anything about poor black people.

So far we have not said what makes an expression into a code word or how in this case the racist attitudes are expressed. Recent work on this topic seeks to answer this question by appealing to informational content. Some theorists think the content is hidden in the text and then decoded by the target audience (Mendelberg (2001)). Others, such as Khoo in the paper just cited, think code words trigger inference. On this view, the words don't have hidden meanings; instead they interact with the beliefs that the target audience has and that triggers inferences. These inferences again lead to the racist content.

Note that this is all an effort to treat code words as tools for getting information across (either by hiding it in a word or by generating it through inferences). We explore those possibilities more in the next chapter. In the context of this chapter, it is important to note that code words have the kinds of non-cognitive lexical effects that we have been drawing attention to in the case of metaphors and brand names. These are effects that are not contents: they trigger pictures, memories, affect your mood, your motivation, and can change 'the way you think about something,' rather than the content of what you think. What this shows is that we can say much the same about code words as Davidson said about metaphor: it may be a mistake to look for a cognitive content to explain the use and effect of code words. An alternative is to analyze code words in terms of the antecedently needed notion of non-cognitive lexical effects introduced in this chapter.

One final illustration of the non-cognitive effects triggered by the use of code words: the series of Willie Horton ads used by G. H. W. Bush's presidential campaign. Horton was a black man who had been convicted of murder and released on furlough While on furlough, he committed a rape. Bush's opponent, Michael Dukakis, had supported the furlough program. Bush wanted to use this against Dukakis and released a series of advertisements featuring Horton, and constantly mentioned Horton in speeches. There was no explicit mention of race in these adverts, but the general consensus is that there was a coded, hidden, racist message. Commenting on this case, Khoo says:

The coded message conveyed by the words and image seemed to be that electing Dukakis would lead to more violent black crime. Perhaps an even stronger conclusion may be warranted, which is that over the course of the campaign, the name 'Willie Horton' itself became a political code word used to stoke fear of increased violent black crime under a Dukakis presidency. (Khoo (2017): 37)

There might be such messages conveyed (we discussed that issue some-what in the previous chapter), but what is indisputable is that the Bush campaign used the term 'Willie Horton' to generate certain non-cognitive effects in the target audience. The words triggered images and emotions associated with Dukakis. These images and feelings could affect people's behavior—for instance make them less inclined to vote for Dukakis.

7.2.5 Pejoratives and slurs

Finally, maybe the easiest way to see lexical effects in action is to return to slurs and pejoratives. The words listed below will inevitably trigger emotions, even though the readers know that we have put them there just as illustrations:

- Kike
- Slut
- Bitch

Some of the world's leading newspapers, such as the *New York Times*, *don't even allow quotations of pejoratives*. Timothy Williamson thinks this is because people don't understand the use–mention distinction (Williamson (2009)). He is right, but even so, it is an indisputable fact that the very presence of the lexical item has an effect on us and it is this effect that these newspapers guard against. These effects are exhibited by the many public debates over uses of the word 'niggardly'. The very appearance of the sequence of letters that (almost) make up a pejorative expression inside another expression that does not itself have any connection to that pejorative has repeatedly been the source of social sanction.[5] Again, any explanation of this will have to talk about lexical effects. There is of course much more to say about slurs and pejoratives and those issues have been addressed in the previous chapter.

7.3 Exploitation of Lexical Effects in Public Debates and Theoretical Work

Above we have emphasized cases that make lexical effects particularly salient. They are, however, ubiquitous. Once you have the category in hand, you find it in all speech (that was in effect the point we made in the

---

[5] See, e.g., <https://en.wikipedia.org/wiki/Controversies_about_the_word_%22niggardly%22>.

section on Davidson on metaphor). Think about public debate and negotiation over certain words, such as 'marriage' and 'rape' (and 'organic', 'hacker', 'refugee', 'immigrant', 'combatant'). Any uses of such words have significant lexical effects. For 'rape' they are far on the negative side of a spectrum and for 'organic' on the positive side. So you can imagine people wanting to exploit these effects (negative or positive).

Those engaged in 'serious' theorizing are not immune to lexical effects. How we label our views and the choice of central theoretical terms have all kinds of non-cognitive effects that scholars exploit (often without being aware of doing it). Our labeling of our views and terms provide a way to indicate allegiances, trigger associations, to make appeals to authority (some famous person used this word), and sometimes just to show off. As David Chalmers says:

> Ideal agents might be unaffected by which terms are used for which concepts, but for nonideal agents such as ourselves, the accepted meaning for a key term will make a difference to which concepts are highlighted, which questions can easily be raised, and which associations and inferences are naturally made.
>
> (Chalmers (2011): 542)

Turning to philosophy (though the point here has nothing specifically to do with philosophy), we suspect that the choice of whether to use terms such as 'reductionist', 'feminist', 'experimental philosophy', 'intuitive', 'anti-realist', 'relativist', 'analytic', etc. is often in large part guided by the non-semantic and non-pragmatic lexical effects those uses will have. Maybe we can imagine a defective intellectual discipline or practice where the primary goal was to choose grammatical combinations of lexical items *with the right lexical effects*—i.e., the primary goal of writing was to exploit lexical effects (as opposed to saying something true or justified). Such people would utter words primarily in order to signal certain kinds of social and intellectual allegiances (and connections). For a possible illustration, see the discussion of Lacan in Chapter 4.

7.4 A General Theory of Lexical Effects?

We've given you some illustrations of lexical effects, but not a general theory. We don't have one. We think they are a hugely varied category. They can inspire, trigger associations of various kinds, make you happy, cheerful, motivated, sad, angry, and so on. They can certainly affect your dispositions to behave. This is a point made particularly vivid by brand names, but if a name like 'Coca-Cola' can make you more likely to spend money on a bottle of liquid, then most likely a name can also make you more disposed to accept, say, a philosophical theory (it is, after all, cheaper to accept a philosophical theory than to buy a bottle of Coke, so we should expect the barriers to behavioral effects to be lower).

In sum: we think the study of lexical effects is potentially enormously significant. It is also deeply empirical. Fields such as sociolinguistics might provide insight. Business schools have entire departments of marketing and one of the things they study is the effects of brand names. They train people to do what we think of as creating and changing lexical effects. We suspect there's a lot philosophers can learn from careful study of that practice.

Some conjectures:

- Lexical effects will be of many kinds, both cognitive and non-cognitive.
- There will not be stable lexical effects across large populations.
- These effects will be temporally unstable, too: they change easily over time.
- Even if you can characterize the lexical effects of two expressions in isolation, you can't predict or calculate the lexical effect of their combination. Suppose you knew everything about the lexical effects of 'fart' and 'rose', that wouldn't give you a theory of the lexical effects of combining them into 'rose fart'. The effects of combinations will be entirely unsystematic and unpredictable.
- Even if you know the lexical effect of an expressions on an individual, that effect will interact with other features of the individual in ways that are largely unpredictable and will vary wildly across individuals.

7.5 Why are Lexical Effects Largely Ignored in Philosophy of Language?

Lexical effects have not been at the center of philosophical reflections about language in the twentieth century. Why not? Since the origins of analytic philosophy, our focus has been on understanding phenomena such as analyticity, the sense–reference distinction, reference fixing, informativeness, substitutivity in opaque contexts, compositionality, and the nature of representation. These clusters of issues more or less ignore the nature of lexical items themselves and their effects. One can, of course, see traces of an interest in this topic here and there. Frege, for example, made a few cryptic remarks about what he called 'coloring', but he didn't do much with it.[6] In short: lexical effects have not been seen as answers to any of the core questions in philosophy of language and mind. That's one important reason why they have been ignored.

Another reason is this: there's a sense in which philosophers of language, at least, have been focused on describing the thoughts expressed by uses of sentences—their content (specified, for example, as truth conditions). This has also, in a sense, been the focus of pragmatics, which has been the study of thoughts expressed in a more indirect way (e.g., through implicatures or presuppositions). All of this is focused on contents and thoughts. Lexical effects bring in another dimension: how the symbols make you feel and affect you. As a result, this topic is very alien to most theorizing about language in the twentieth century.[7]

This is reflected in the idealizations outlined in Chapter 1: They completely ignore lexical effects and focus exclusively on informational content. Anything having to do with the feelings, motivations, and non-informational attitudes of the agents is classified as irrelevant noise to be put aside. If, however, lexical effects are as important to communication as we have argued that they are, this is a significant shortcoming of the idealizations and of most work on language in the twentieth and twenty-first centuries.

CENTRAL POINTS IN CHAPTER 7

- Philosophers of language tend to concentrate on the cognitive content of words: on what they mean, on the thoughts they give rise to. However, words don't merely have cognitive content. They also have the capacity to make you feel things, form mental images, and call to mind memories, among other things. This non-cognitive side of words has been overlooked by philosophers; here we introduce it.

---

[6] According to Frege, coloring has no effect on the logical properties of words, and so he more or less ignored it (see Dummett 1973: 84–5).

[7] This could be a significant mistake even for those of us who have focused on the traditional questions in philosophy of language: if lexical effects affect our judgments about truth and falsity (and it's an empirical question whether they do), then these effects directly influence fundamental data points for semantics.

- We call the non-cognitive effects of words *lexical effects*. We illustrated the notion of a lexical effect by presenting four paradigm and important examples: metaphors, brand names, slurs, and code words and dogwhistles.
- We first talked about metaphor. We looked at Davidson's work on the topic. He argues that just as a bump on a head might make you see stars, so metaphors (metaphorically!) hit you on the head and induce visions, thoughts, and feelings. We endorsed Davidson's view but think it goes further. *All* uses of language can induce visions, thoughts, and feelings. We went on to illustrate this with some non-metaphorical language.
- We considered brand names and names for people. Coca-Cola is in part as successful as it is because it brings with it a raft of positive lexical effects. You shouldn't call your child 'Hitler' because that name has many negative lexical effects.
- We noted that branding and thus the exploitation of lexical effects is ubiquitous in politics, too. For example, conservatives in the US started talking about 'tax relief' instead of 'tax cuts'. 'Relief' has more pleasant associations than 'cut', and thus helped to frame the idea that lowering tax is a good thing. And we considered how code words, dogwhistles, and slurs, have lexical effects too.
- We went on to make some conjectures about the nature of lexical effects: lexical effects are of many kinds, both cognitive and non-cognitive; they will not be stable across people or even for a single person across time; the lexical effect of a sentence won't be determinable on the basis of the lexical effects of its parts; and it will often be unpredictable, even with a lot of information about the lexical effect of a word and a given person, how exactly the word will affect the person at a given time.
- We concluded by explaining why so little attention has been paid to lexical effects given their obvious political, social, and economic importance. We suggested it was because philosophy of language has been misled by the idealizations outlined in Chapter 1.

Further Reading and Exercises

FURTHER READING FOR CHAPTER 7

There isn't much material on lexical effects. Cappelen (2018: chapter 11) introduces the terminology and discusses the role of lexical effects in conceptual engineering. George Lakoff's (2014) is a good place to read about the importance of lexical effects in the wild of political discourse. For Frege's view of coloring one could consult the first chapter of Dummett (1973). There is much interesting material outside of philosophy about the power of branding and words more generally. A classic is Edward Bernays's (1928) book *Propaganda*, which was enormously influential in shaping the practice and importance of advertising as a key feature of economic and social life. More recent books on the same topic include Sedivy and Carlson (2011) and Klein (1999).

Comprehension Questions

1. What is a lexical effect? How does a word's lexical effects differ from its semantic effects?
2. Give an account of Davidson's view of metaphor in your own words.
3. How do you think people in favor of not cutting taxes should respond to the use of 'tax relief'? Can you think of a way to lexically engineer a new word with more appropriate effects? What would it be?
4. Present some examples of pairs of words which have the same meaning but have markedly different lexical effects.

Exploratory Questions

5. We spoke of lexical effects—features of words. Are there also sentential effects, effects that whole sentences have that are in some sense greater than the sum of the lexical effects of their parts?
6. In discussing Frege's view of coloring, Michael Dummett says that a sign that 'and' and 'but' have the same coloring is that replacing one for the other (as a sentential connective, at least) in a sentence always preserves truth value. Do you think this is right?

8

Generics and Defective Reasoning

8.1 Introduction: What are Generics?

A 2016 Gallup poll of United States residents showed that:

- 43 percent of respondents were very or somewhat satisfied with the way immigrants are treated in American society.
- 45 percent of respondents were very or somewhat satisfied with the way Arabs are treated in American society.
- 51 percent of respondents were very or somewhat satisfied with the way blacks are treated in American society.
- 54 percent of respondents were very or somewhat satisfied with the way Hispanics are treated in American society.
- 63 percent of respondents were very or somewhat satisfied with the way women are treated in American society.
- 75 percent of respondents were very or somewhat satisfied with the way Asians are treated in American society.

These sorts of poll results play an important role in setting political agendas, as they determine what problems there is sufficient public support for politicians to address and commit scarce resources to. And the underlying attitudes that individuals are expressing in responding to these polls play an important role in the lives of those individuals, in determining how they will react to, sympathize with, or oppose those around them.

But what do these poll results actually *mean*? What are people agreeing or disagreeing with when they are given poll questions of this sort? Our goal in this chapter is to consider views on which these sorts of *generic* claims have a distinctive kind of meaning. That's then of interest for the study of 'bad language' because it has been suggested that the meanings of generic claims are tied to certain kinds of *cognitive badness*. Something about generics, goes this line, causes us to reason poorly, and in particular makes us susceptible to stereotypical reasoning that can perpetuate unhealthy social structures. Consider the claim 'Immigrants are treated well in American society.' There are tens of millions of immigrants in the United States. Inevitably, some of them are treated well and some of them are not treated well. So:

- If 'Immigrants are treated well in American society' expresses the strong claim that *all* immigrants are treated well, it is trivially false.
- If 'Immigrants are treated well in American society' expresses the weak claim that *some* immigrants are treated well, it is trivially true.

But whatever you think about the treatment of immigrants, it doesn't seem like the *poll* is asking about a *trivial* claim. If the claim were trivial, everyone should be agreeing (or disagreeing, as the case may be) with it.

The claim 'Immigrants are treated well in American Society' is tricky because it deliberately underspecifies *how many* immigrants are treated well. It doesn't say 'all immigrants' or 'some immigrants'; it simply says 'immigrants'. It's thus an instance of a *bare plural* construction, of the same sort as:

1. Prime numbers have exactly two factors.
2. Crows ate the apples from my tree.
3. Dinosaurs are extinct.
4. Earthquakes are common along the Pacific Rim.
5. Philosophers are interested in questions about epistemology and metaphysics.

Bare plural claims are quite complicated in meaning. (Notice that this is itself a bare plural claim.) Some bare plural claims do express universal claims. The claim that prime numbers have exactly two factors is a universal claim, because every single prime number has exactly two factors. (Notice that 'prime numbers are odd' is false, simply because 2 is prime and even.) Other bare plural claims do express existential claims. The claim that crows ate the apples from my tree isn't a claim about all, or even most, crows—it's simply the claim that there are some crows that ate the apples. Some bare plural claims don't express *generalizations* of any sort. The claim that dinosaurs are extinct isn't a claim that any particular number of individual dinosaurs are extinct. It's a category mistake to say that a particular animal is extinct—being extinct is a feature of a *kind* of animal. So the claim that dinosaurs are extinct is a claim about a kind, rather than about the members of the kind.

Our focus here is on *generic* claims made with bare plurals. The claim that philosophers are interested in questions of epistemology and metaphysics is a generalization about individual philosophers, but it's a generalization that (to a first approximation) is intermediate in strength between an existential and a universal claim. We are claiming more than just that *some* philosophers are interested, but less than that *all* philosophers are interested.

8.2   More on the Behavior of Generics

The exact nature of the generalization made by generics is controversial, and we won't attempt to give a full treatment of the controversy here. But a few basic points will be important:

1. Generic claims are typically less strong than universal claims in that they tolerate exceptions. The claim 'Birds fly' is true, even though penguins and ostriches don't fly. The exact nature of this tolerance of exceptions is controversial. We can, for example, distinguish between the question of whether it's *true* that birds fly despite the existence of non-flying birds and the question of whether it's appropriate to *assert* that birds fly once the existence of non-flying birds has been made conversationally salient.

2. However, there is also a sense in which generic claims can be *stronger* than universal claims. Consider the following example. Even if all nine Supreme Court justices have social security numbers that are prime, the generic claim 'Supreme Court justices have prime social security numbers' doesn't look true. The problem is roughly that it looks merely *accidental* that the current justices all have prime numbers, and the generic claim treats the primeness as something more like an *essential feature* of the justices. This suggests that there is a *modal* element to some generic claims; that they discuss how things could be as well as how things are.

3. Many generic claims look like they make something like 'most' claims. To say that basketball players are tall is, roughly, to say that *most* basketball players are tall. But some generic claims definitely don't require majorities. Ducks lay eggs, even though only female

ducks lay eggs, and only half of ducks are female. Generic claims that attribute 'characteristic' features seem to be accepted at lower levels than ones that attribute 'accidental' features. It's true that highways have access roads, even though fewer than half do, because access roads are characteristic of highways, and help distinguish highways from other kinds of roads. It's not true that Canadians are right-handed, even though 90 percent of them are, because being right-handed isn't characteristic of Canadians, and doesn't distinguish them from other nationalities.

4. Some generic claims are made true by only a small number or percentage of instances. Deer ticks carry Lyme disease, even though only about 1 percent of deer ticks actually have the Borrelia bacterium which causes Lyme disease. Generic claims that attribute particularly 'striking' or 'dangerous' properties seem to be accepted at lower levels than most other generic claims. A few shark attacks justify the claim that sharks attack swimmers; a few downloads with malware justify the claim that downloading files from the internet puts malware on your computer.

These example show that there is some kind of important *vagueness* or *underspecification* to generic claims. There is more than one way to understand *why* generic claims have this kind of underspecification.

- Perhaps generic claims are quantified claims with a quantifier that has an underspecified meaning. 'Birds fly' then means something like 'Generically many birds fly' or 'Generally, birds fly' or 'all normal birds fly', where the meaning of 'generically many', 'generally', and 'normal' is underspecified. Maybe these words have a context-sensitive meaning, so that the threshold varies from context to context. Or maybe they have an interactive meaning, where the threshold depends on the objects quantified over and on the property attributed. Or maybe they have a defective meaning, in which case we just haven't done the linguistic work of picking out a precise meaning.

- Perhaps generic claims involve reference to kinds of things and attribute properties to kinds rather than to individuals. 'Birds fly' then means that the *kind* Aves has the property of flying. The underspecification of generics is then a consequence of the flexibility of property possession by kinds. What it takes for the kind Aves to have a property can vary from property to property.

Generic claims appear in political opinion surveys precisely because of their underspecification. Societies are big and complicated things, and we typically aren't in possession of anything like full information about what's going on with them. There are too many immigrants for us to keep track of how *all* of them are treated, or to have reliably statistical information about exactly how many of them are treated well. Often the best we can do is to get a vague general impression of how things are going with immigrants, and form policy preferences on the basis of that vague impression. This is a specific instance of a general fact about our epistemic shortcomings. It's much more efficient for us to know that traffic intersections are generically dangerous and be careful around them than it is to determine for each traffic intersection we encounter exactly how dangerous it is and plan around that precise danger level.

8.3 Some Interesting Experiments

But the underspecification of generic claims has interesting and important consequences for the way that people reason with those claims. Roughly, people tend to *accept* generic claims based on relatively weak evidence, but then *reason from* generic claims to rather strong conclusions. Experiments by Cimpian, Brandone, and Gelman (2010) bring out this asymmetry in reasoning in a striking way. Subjects are told about a fictional species of animal called a *morseth*. Different subjects were told that 10 percent, 30 percent, 50 percent, 70 percent, or 90 percent of morseths had silver fur, and were asked to agree or disagree with the generic claim 'Morseths have silver fur.' From these responses, the average threshold needed for agreement to the generic claim was calculated (by, for each subject, averaging the thresholds at which the generic claim was agreed to be true). The experiment showed that on average, what was required was for 69 percent of the morseths to have silver fur for the generic to be judged true.

(The details of the acceptance data are messy. At the 10 percent level for silver fur, just over 20 percent of subjects judged the generic 'morseths have silver fur' to be true. At the 30 percent level, acceptance rose to about 30 percent. At the 50 percent silver fur level, acceptance jumped to about 60 percent, and then climbed to about 70 percent for 70 percent silver fur, and peaked at about 80 percent acceptance when 90 percent of morseths had silver fur. In contrast, the explicitly quantified claim 'most morseths have silver fur' had essentially no acceptance at the 10 percent and 30 percent silver fur level, jumped to 30 percent acceptance at the 50 percent silver fur level, and then rose to 100 percent acceptance for 70 percent and 90 percent silver fur.)

In the other part of the same experiment, subjects were given the generic claim that morseths have silver fur, and asked to estimate what percentage of morseths have silver fur. Here the experiment showed that on average, subjects expected 96 percent of the morseths to have silver fur. This is a striking result, because that 96 percent level of silver fur *predicted* from the generic is substantially above the 69 percent level of silver fur needed to *establish* the generic. This seems to suggest that generics are the location of a certain kind of cognitive error, that allows us artificially to inflate our information about the world. Someone could start believing that 70 percent of morseths have silver fur, infer on this basis that (generically) morseths have silver fur, and then conclude from the generic that 96 percent of morseths have silver fur. In going through this reasoning, the subject magically ascends from a 70 percent silver fur expectation to a 96 percent silver fur expectation, without in the process acquiring any actual evidence of increased silver fur levels among morseths.

Of course, presumably no one would commit the cognitive error quite so bluntly. If you're aware that you accepted the generic claim about morseths because you thought that 70 percent of morseths had silver fur, you won't immediately conclude from the generic that 96 percent of morseths have silver fur. But we aren't always attending so closely to our reasons. You might just have a general impression, looking at a bunch of morseths, that a lot of them have silver fur. You could then store that general impression for later access in the form of the generic. Accessing the claim later, you could easily (no longer having the morseths before you) use that generic belief to arrive at a higher silver fur estimate than was justified by your original sample. And the problem only gets worse as the reason gets distributed across society. If one person makes some observations, summarizes them, and reports them in generic form, and a second person receives the generic testimony, forms their own generic belief from it, and then arrives at a statistical expectation based on that generic belief, it would be easy for the expected prevalence levels to go up as a result.

The combination of the importance of generics to our ordinary reasoning, and especially our reasoning about general social patterns, and these facts about our tendency to cognitive error in reasoning with generics has led people to suspect that generics may play an important role in the perpetuation of some kinds of social bias. Some prominent instances of Arab terrorism lead people to accept the generic claim 'Arabs are terrorists.' That generic claim gets widely accepted, and perhaps loses track of the exact evidence base on which it was introduced. People then from the generic form an expectation that a large percentage of Arabs are terrorists. The result is bias against Arabs and discriminatory social policy.

Of course, the mere fact that we're inclined to cognitive error with generics doesn't yet show that that error will result specifically in social bias. Maybe cognitive error is always liable to be harmful in some way or other, because it tends to result in false beliefs, which are liable to be harmful. But the false beliefs could be unjustifiably *positive* beliefs as well as unjustifiably *negative* beliefs. Imagine we encounter a critical threshold of kind and generous people, and form the generic belief that people are kind and generous. That generic then leads us to expect a very high proportion of people to be kind and generous. That belief may well lead us into trouble, leaving us open to exploitation by the sadly numerous unkind and ungenerous people, but it's not a trouble specifically of social bias.

However, we noted earlier that generics seem to be acceptable at particularly low statistical levels for striking and dangerous properties ('sharks attack swimmers', 'deer ticks carry Lyme disease'). The Cimpian, Brandone, and Gelman experiments helped confirm this observation, showing that when subjects were told that the silver fur of morseths 'sheds particles that get lodged in your lungs making it impossible to breathe', the acceptance of the generic at lower levels of silver fur increased dramatically. With *dangerous* silver fur, about 55 percent of subjects judged the generic true when only 10 percent of the morseths had silver fur, while with *ordinary* silver fur, only about 25 percent of subjects judged the generic true at the same 10 percent silver fur level. But making the silver fur dangerous did not change how common subjects expected silver fur to be, based on acceptance of the generic claim—that remained at 96 percent.

So striking and dangerous properties are particularly apt to the cognitive error effects. Small initial samples of striking and dangerous properties are more likely to be magnified into unjustifiably high later expectations of prevalence than are small initial samples of neutral or positive properties. We're thus more likely to be misled into having unjustifiably negative views than we are to be misled into having unjustifiably positive views of people's kindness and generosity.

Haslanger (2010a) has suggested that there is a related *modal* cognitive error that we are subject to with generics. As noted above, generic claims at least sometimes have a modal component. The claim that ducks lay eggs looks like it's not just a statistical generalization about ducks, but rather a claim about *how ducks work*. We accept that ducks lay eggs because we think there's a reliable reproductive mechanism in ducks that leads to egg laying. One way of capturing this thought is that the claim that ducks lay eggs has counterfactual consequences. Had there been some more ducks in addition to the ones there actually are, they too would have laid eggs. This counterfactual aspect helps explain why the generic claim that ducks are female isn't acceptable, even though the egg-laying ducks can't be more common than the female ducks: had there been some more ducks, it isn't necessarily true that they would have been female. Similarly, we don't accept that Canadians are right-handed, despite the fact that fully 90 percent of them are, because there's no mechanism connecting being Canadian and being right-handed, and as a consequence it isn't true that had there been some Canadians, they would have been right-handed.

Haslanger thus suggests that we sometimes *accept* generic claims on the basis of merely statistical information, but then *conclude* from the generics that there is a counterfactual-supporting mechanism underwriting the statistical connection. For example, female scores on certain very high-level mathematical tests are significantly lower than male scores. A sequence of qualifying exams leads each year to the selection of 6 high school students to form the United States team for the International Mathematical Olympiad. The initial test is the AMC 12, which is taken by about 50,000 high school students each year. In 2016, the average female score was 53 and the average male score was 59 (both out of a possible 150). High scorers on the AMC 12 advance to the AIME exam, which is taken by about 3,000 qualifying students each year. In 2016, the average female score was 5 and the average male score was 6 (both out of a possible 15). But at the higher end of the score range on the AIME, the gender disparity becomes significant; 4.62 percent of male AIME qualifiers scored 11 or above, while only 1.14 percent of female qualifiers scored 11 or above. As a result, of the 254 qualifiers for the USA

Mathematical Olympiad, 229 were male and 25 were female. Since 1974, 88 percent of the United States 6-person teams to the International Math Olympiad have been entirely male. These statistical facts are arguably enough to accept the generic claim that men outscore women at very high-level math competitions. But there is also good reason to doubt that this statistical correlation is backed by a counterfactual-supporting mechanism. (For example, women who score well on high-level math competitions tend to cluster at a small number of schools, suggesting that good training and environment at those schools is overcoming contingent social obstacles to high female performance on the exams.) So if we conclude from the generic claim that men score higher than women that it's in men's *nature* to score higher, we will make a mistake. And it will be a mistake with important social consequences, because if we conclude that there is a counterfactual-supporting mechanism, we may not bother trying to alter the statistical distribution we find.

Experimental work by Rhodes, Leslie, and Tworek (2012) has provided some apparent confirmation of Haslanger's concern. Rhodes, Leslie, and Tworek read books to toddlers that used a novel category of people ('Zarpies') and then made either generic claims about Zarpies ('Zarpies eat flowers') or particular claims about Zarpies ('This Zarpie eats flowers').They then tested the toddlers for 'essentializing conclusions' about Zarpies, by considering whether the children would appeal to the properties attributed to the Zarpies in explaining the behavior of a new Zarpie, and whether they would predict that a new Zarpie raised in a non-Zarpie environment would also display the feature attributed. The experiment showed that the use of generic language in describing the Zarpies led to substantially higher levels of essentializing conclusions than the use of particular language in describing the Zarpies.

But these experimental results aren't enough to show that there is any *special* connection between generics and essentializing conclusions. Plausibly, there is a defeasible tendency to posit an underlying counterfactual-supporting mechanism any time we discover a regularity in the world. On this view, we notice a pattern of tigers having stripes. This pattern leads us to endorse the generic claim that tigers have stripes. But we will also want an explanation of the observation that tigers frequently have stripes—we don't want it to be just a statistical accident. Of course, that explanation need not be connected to the essence of what it is to be a tiger. We might, for example, suspect that a lover of stripes has been decorating tigers. But explaining the stripes in terms of the nature of tigers will typically provide a simpler explanation, so we'll tend to prefer that kind of explanation unless we have specific reason to doubt that it's available (as, for example, we might have reason to doubt that circuses have natures that require tightrope walkers).

If this is right, we would expect that other regularity claims, in addition to generic claims, often lead to questionable modal conclusions. Further experimental work by Hoicka, Saul, and Sterken (no date) added additional versions of the story saying 'Many Zarpies eat flowers' and 'Most Zarpies eat flowers.' They found that the 'many' and 'most' versions of the story produced essentializing conclusions just as strongly as did the original generic version.

Furthermore, not all generic claims have the kind of essentializing connections that Haslanger focuses on. In some cases, we accept generic claims simply on statistical patterns, and don't read in any underlying mechanism. For example, we might accept:

6. Circuses have tightrope walkers.
7. Presidential campaigns have entertaining scandals.
8. Italian restaurants serve pizza.

just because large numbers of each category have the relevant properties, without thinking that there's anything in the *nature* of circuses, presidential campaigns, or Italian restaurants, that leads to them having those properties. They just accidentally do. Perhaps, then, we only read modal conclusions out of generic claims in the cases in which we had modal evidence supporting the generic in the first place.

8.4 Generics: Interaction of Meaning and Epistemology

Although the exact details remain unclear and controversial, it does seem clear that generics are in some sense implicated in problematic patterns of reasoning that lead to hasty and undersupported generalizations, and that these patterns of reasoning then have some potential for leading to socially undesirable results. The next question is: is there a connection between these *epistemological* features of generics and the *meaning* of generic claims? Are we prone to make mistakes in reasoning about generics because of what generics mean? Can we learn more about the meanings of generics by thinking about the kinds of reasoning errors we make with them, or learn more about our propensity to make mistakes with generics by thinking about what generics mean? There are many possible lessons that could be drawn, depending on how we think generics work. Since there is no dominant and uncontroversial view about the meaning of generics, and since existing competing views are complicated and sophisticated, we'll only sketch some of the options here.

1. The meanings of generics could be given directly in terms of the inferences that they license. Compare how we might give the meaning of the word 'and':

- 'And' licenses an *introduction* rule, saying that if you know that X and you know that Y, then you can conclude that X and Y.
- 'And' licenses an *elimination* rule, saying that if you know that X and Y, you can conclude that X and you can conclude that Y.

On an *inferentialist* view, knowing these two rules just is knowing the meaning of 'and'. Similarly we can give an inferentialist account of 'or':

- 'Or' licenses an introduction rule, saying that if you know that X, then you can conclude that X or Y, and also conclude that Y or X.
- 'Or' licenses an elimination rule, saying that if you know that X or Y, and you know that if X then Z, and you know that if Y then Z, then you can conclude that Z.

But if we can give meanings in this way, we can also give *defective* meaning by giving bad combinations of inference rules. Prior (1960) gives the example of the made-up word 'tonk', which combines the introduction rule of 'or' with the elimination rule of 'and':

- 'Tonk' introduction: if you know that X, you can conclude that X tonk Y.
- 'Tonk' elimination: if you know that X tonk Y, you can conclude that Y.

If we allow ourselves to reason with 'tonk', we can use the introduction rule to reason from X to X tonk Y, and then use the elimination rule to reason from X tonk Y to Y. This is a particularly disastrous form of problematic reasoning: it's reasoning that takes us from anywhere to anywhere. On the inferentialist view, we create a very *bad* language by adding 'tonk' to the language.

Generics aren't as bad as 'tonk', but perhaps they, too, are defective by having mismatched introduction and elimination rules. Perhaps a generic just *is*, by its very meaning, the kind of term that can be introduced by a few instances, and then used to conclude that the great majority of cases follow the same pattern. Generics would then be governed by rules like this:

- Introduction rule: if 70 percent of birds are F, conclude that birds are F.
- Elimination rule: if birds are F, conclude that 90 percent of birds are F.

(More sophisticated versions of these rules might make them sensitive to the kind of property being attributed to the generic.) Reasoning with generics would then inevitably make us vulnerable to bad, overly strong conclusions. On this view, the fault lies not in us but in our language—we have inherited a language with defective rules, and so by following the rules of the language we run the risk of ending up with defective beliefs. The thing to do, then, is to avoid thinking in generic terms (to train ourselves to reason with explicit frequency claims), or to be very cautious in reasoning with generics (to train ourselves to be a bit more reluctant to reach generic conclusions and a bit more cautious about making use of our generic beliefs).

2. The meaning of generics could be given using a special 'generic quantifier', so that saying 'birds fly' is to say 'generically many birds fly', where 'generically many' is a quantifier in the same general category as 'some', 'every', and 'most'. To be faithful to the complexity of the data regarding generics, the generic quantifier needs to be some combination of vague, underspecified, and highly context-sensitive. To say 'generically many birds fly' is perhaps to say something rather imprecise, which merely constrains the frequency of flying birds within some vaguely bounded large region. And it's perhaps to say rather different things in different contexts, as different conversational interests demand different precisifications of that vaguely bounded region.

We aren't very good at reasoning with vague or with highly context-sensitive language. Vagueness, for example, allows us some freedom to sharpen vague boundaries as we go. Manchester is a borderline case of a large city—for some purposes, we can choose to use 'large city' in a way that includes Manchester, and for other purposes, we can use 'large city' in a way that excludes Manchester. But that means that combining beliefs about large cities is epistemically risky, because those beliefs might have been formed under different choices of how to sharpen the boundaries. Context sensitivity means that what content a sentence expresses is shaped by the context in which it's used. If the way that the context shapes content is complicated, or if it's hard to keep track of what context we're in, we'll again be likely to make mistakes. 'Might' claims, for example, such as 'Jones might be a spy,' are plausibly context-sensitive, saying in a given context that it's compatible with the *contextually relevant* evidence that Jones is a spy. But it's not always obvious what evidence is contextually relevant, so we can misunderstand what we are saying and believing when we say or believe that Jones is a spy. It's thus easy for us to make mistakes.

Perhaps we get into similar trouble with generics. Maybe we're right to conclude that morseths have silver fur when we're told that 70 percent of them do, because in that context, 70 percent *is* generically many. And perhaps we're right to conclude that because morseths have silver fur, 90 percent of them do, because in *that* context, 90 percent is generically many. Where we go wrong is in thinking that what we believed when we, in the first context, endorsed 'morseths have silver fur' is the same thing as what we believed when we, in the second context, endorsed the same sentence. On this view, the fault is perhaps shared between us and our language. The language isn't defective, but it is complicated—too complicated for us, so we make semantic errors that then lead us into cognitive error.

3. The previous two approaches to generics put some or all of the fault for our cognitive errors on the language. But perhaps the fault is really all ours. Suppose there is some relatively straightforward meaning theory for generic claims. Because of the complexities in the generics data that we went through above, there would have to be a number of bells and whistles on any such meaning theory. But perhaps at least in some cases, generics simply amount to majority claims. To say that *tigers have stripes*, for example, is just to say that most tigers have stripes. And if that's all *tigers have stripes* means, then there's no (semantic) excuse for bootstrapping our way from a low to a high percentage of striped tigers. So what's going on?

Maybe what the generics themselves mean is unproblematic, but we then make problematic communicative use of generics. Thus consider:

The first hypothesis I'd like us to consider is that with generics of the form Ks are F ('tigers have stripes'), or K1s are more G than K2s ('tigers are more dangerous than cheetahs') there is normally an implication that the connection between the Ks and F or G holds primarily by virtue of some important fact about the Ks *as such* (Haslanger (2010a): 183).

On this view, when we say tigers have stripes, all our words say is that most tigers have stripes. But we *implicate* that (for example) most tigers have stripes because it is in the nature of tigers to have stripes. This is a reasonable and unproblematic suggestion to make when regularly confronted with striped tigers. But it's less reasonable and more problematic in other cases. Haslanger, for example, considers the case 'Women are submissive.' Here an implication that it's in the nature of women to be submissive can be damaging in ways that a mere statistical observation (right or wrong) that most women are submissive is not. If submissiveness is a mere statistical regularity, then we might well take steps to combat it, but if it's something flowing from the *nature* of women, we might be more inclined to accept it as an inevitable and even appropriate feature of the world.

As we've noted above, the fact that implicatures are a form of *devious* communication can make them particularly well suited for serving unhealthy social ends. Since the overt at-issue content of a generic claim, on this account, is just a claim that most items of a type have a certain feature, we might accept generic claims without much challenge, and not realize that we've also tacitly accepted backgrounded content about the natures of the things involved. But it would be helpful to have a full story about how the implicatures are produced. If *tigers have stripes* just means that most tigers have stripes, why should we take speakers using that sentence to be suggesting anything more than that statistical regularity? What Gricean maxim would they be violating if they meant only the regularity?

- Maybe there is a violation of the maxim of quality. Quality requires speakers to say only what they know. How could a speaker come to know that most tigers have stripes? Maybe by surveying all tigers, but that's an implausible hypothesis in most cases. Another possibility is that they know that most tigers have stripes because they know that there is a stripe-producing mechanism in tigers—that tigers have a stripy nature. So by representing himself as knowing that tigers have stripes, the speaker also represents stripes as being part of the nature of tigers.

However, this hypothesis doesn't explain why a speaker's knowledge of a statistical regularity couldn't just come from random sampling. The speaker hasn't seen all tigers, but has seen some large number, and a high percentage of them have been striped. Why wouldn't that be good enough evidence for the claim that most tigers are striped, without appealing to a stripy essence?

- Maybe there is a violation of the maxim of relevance. In many situations, the mere statistical information that most tigers have stripes wouldn't be relevant. If, for example, the speaker is trying to help the audience recognize a previously unseen tiger, the information that *most* tigers have stripes might not be relevant, since the tiger in question might be in the minority. But the information that it's in the *nature* of tigers to have stripes would be relevant, since the tiger in question would share the universal tiger nature.

However, it's not clear that this relevance argument is right. Knowing that the tiger in question has a stripy nature is only going to help the audience recognize it if the stripy nature manifests in a stripy appearance in this case. Since, by hypothesis, generics tolerate exceptions, we must be assuming that stripy natures don't always manifest. So why would the first of the following be more helpful than the second?

- Tigers are by nature striped, and there is a high probability that the tiger in question, sharing that nature, in fact has stripes.
- There is a high probability that the tiger in question has stripes.

A more general worry about the implicature strategy is that if we're looking for an explanation of why generics are particularly prone to produce certain kinds of socially bad reasoning, we need an explanation of why generics are particularly prone to produce the problematic implicatures. And neither of the implicature stories considered above seem to rely on any special features of the meanings of generics.

4. A final possibility is that generics involve no linguistic or communicative failing, but only an epistemological one. Perhaps we are just bad at statistical reasoning. Suppose, for example, that we regularly overestimate the frequency of features that we are looking for. So when the question of whether morseths have silver fur is raised, if we see silver fur on 30 percent of the morseths we observe, we incorrectly conclude that 70 percent of the morseths have silver fur, and walk away from our observations with a greatly inflated estimate of silver fur rate in morseths.

On this view, 'morseths have silver fur' might straightforwardly mean, and communicate, that some high threshold percentage of morseths have silver fur. Our error is then in reaching that conclusion on radically insufficient evidence. Making the view plausible would then require looking for evidence that we are in fact subject to statistical reasoning errors of this sort.

8.5 Summary

The last three chapters have focused on ways that some parts of language can be particularly likely to produce strong, and sometimes deleterious, social effects. One theme running through these chapters has been that it's when language gets *complicated* that we are especially likely to get these effects. In the previous chapter, we saw that slurs and similar terms can have meanings that are complicated because they are multidimensional, combining descriptive, evaluative, expressive, and cultural components. In this chapter, we saw that generics can have meanings that are truth conditionally complicated: saying what it takes for a generic claim to be true or false is a messy and complicated matter. In both cases, when the meanings get complicated, our grip on what our own words mean becomes tenuous, and when our grip is tenuous, we become vulnerable to distinctively linguistic manipulation.

CENTRAL POINTS IN CHAPTER **8**

- In this chapter we look at generics. Generics are interesting both because getting right about their meaning is very tricky, but also because their use has some clear deleterious social consequences. We introduced generics, considered some interesting data about them, and then showed how they can be misused.
- We concentrate on generic statements involving bare plural constructions. 'Prime numbers have exactly two factors', 'ducks lay eggs', 'philosophers are interested in metaphysics and epistemology', and 'deer ticks carry Lyme disease' are some representative examples.
- As these examples indicate, generics differ markedly in their strength: in how many of the things picked out by the bare plural ('prime numbers', 'ducks', and so on) must have the property in question (having exactly two factors, laying eggs, and so on) for the statement to be true. The answers for the generic

sentences in the previous paragraph are something like: 100 percent, ~50 percent, (at a guess) ~30 percent, and 1 percent. This is interesting and unique behavior, and we considered some other interesting linguistic features of generics.

- We next turned to some interesting experiments about how people use generics. In particular, we looked at one which showed that people accept generic claims on weak evidence, but then reason from such claims to strong conclusions. So, for example, people were asked what percentage of objects of a kind K must satisfy a property P for them to accept that Ks P (where, for example, K = *duck*, P = *quack*). They answered, on average, around 70 percent. But then they were asked, assuming that Ks P, how many Ks they thought had the property P, and they answered, on average, 96 percent. So they accept generics when a given level of Ks P, but they assume, hearing that Ks P, that about 40 percent more Ks P.

- Generics thus seem to be a source of systematic cognitive error. This can obviously cause problems, leading us, once we've accepted a generic, to dramatically overestimate how many objects possess the property in question. We pointed out some related experimental data and philosophical argument that supported and/or explained this claim that generics lead to cognitive error. And we noted that this is a cause for concern, given the prevalence of generics in social and political discourse.

Further Reading and Exercises

FURTHER READING FOR CHAPTER 8

Useful overview articles on generics are Leslie and Lerner (2016) and Sterken (2017). Liebesman (2011) defends the view that generics pick out kinds. See Sterken (2015) for the context sensitivity of generics. Nickel (2016) is a recent and sophisticated monograph on the topic. Sarah-Jane Leslie's approach to generics, which is undergirded by some of the work in psychology we sketched, can be found in her (2008) and (2017), the latter of which is explicitly concerned with the bad social consequences generics might produce.

Comprehension Questions

1. Give some features of generics that distinguish them from strong generalizations about all members of a category (such as 'all birds have feathers').
2. Give an example of a generic claim attributing a feature to a kind that is true despite the fact that *no* member of the kind has that feature. Then give an example of a generic claim attributing a feature to a kind that is false despite the fact that *every* member of the kind has that feature.

3. List some malicious uses of generics you've recently encountered in public discourse.

4. Give some more examples like 'dinosaurs are extinct' where we talk about a kind rather than about the members of the kind.

Exploratory Questions

5. Consider negations of generics. Do we get any insight into the semantics of generics from them? What are the truth conditions of 'sharks don't attack swimmers'?

6. We concentrated on bare plurals. But consider the following:
   - A madrigal is polyphonic
   - The average man has 2.4 children
   - Let Pointy be an arbitrary triangle. Pointy has three sides.
   - [in a deportment class] One doesn't say 'what?', one says 'pardon?'

Could one say on this basis that indefinite and definite descriptions ('a madrigal' and 'the average man', respectively), and names and pronouns can be used to express generic generalizations? If so, does this cause problems for any of the views we surveyed?

9

Non-Ideal Speech Acts

9.1 Introduction

In the classroom, conversation is a simple affair. It's one on one, with speaker and audience talking face to face. And it's all just assertions. Alex asserts that Ben Nevis is the tallest mountain in Scotland; Beth uptakes that information. Then Beth asserts that Loch Lomond is the largest lake in Scotland, and Alex acknowledges that information. But outside the classroom, things are not so simple. Speaker and audience can be widely separated in time and space, and that separation can introduce problems of interpretation and understanding. And we do many things with language other than assert. We interrogate, we command, we request, we greet, we speculate. And we do things with language of larger social consequence. We promise, we wed, we volunteer, we apologize, we forgive. On the darker side, we oppress, we silence, we derail, we troll. In this chapter we focus on questions concerning how our speech acts— what we *do*—change as we move from classroom to real world.

One complication that the real world can pose is that of talking to many people at once. In the simplest cases, enlarging the audience doesn't change anything of interest. If Alex says, 'Ben Nevis is the tallest mountain in Scotland' to many people, rather than just to one, then she intends that *all* of them come to believe that Ben Nevis is the tallest mountain in Scotland by recognizing her communicative intention, and if all goes well, all of them *do* recognize her intention, and come to believe that Ben Nevis is the tallest mountain in Scotland.

9.2 Scattered Audiences

When Alex says, 'Ben Nevis is the tallest mountain in Scotland' to many people it is clear what informations he is conveying to each member of his her audience. But when we add context-sensitive language, things get more complicated. When the audience are many, it can be trickier to say what the right context is. If Alex says to Beth, 'You are in Scotland,' then she speaks in a context that has Alex as speaker and Beth as audience, and that context determines Beth as the referent of 'you'. But what happens if she is speaking to *both* Beth and Charles? The simplest thing to say is that she speaks in a context that has Beth and Charles as audience, and that that context determines Beth and Charles as the referents of 'you'. This simple answer, however, doesn't always work. Consider an example due to Andy Egan.

- **Briefing:** In the briefing room before a dangerous mission, the commanding officer says: Look around you. There are 100 people in this briefing room. The mission you're about to undertake is extremely dangerous. It's possible that, two hours from now, you will be the sole survivor of this group. You know your assignment. For security reasons, it's very important that you not tell anyone else about your orders—not even the other people in this room. (Egan (2009): 266)

We get the wrong results if the commanding officer's use of 'you' refers to all 100 people in the room. That, for example, would have the result that the officer says that it's possible that, two hours from then, all 100 will be the sole survivor of the group. Rather, what we need is that the officer speaks directly to each member of the group, saying different things to different people. If Alex and Beth are both in the group, then the officer says to Alex that Alex might be the sole survivor, and says to Beth that she might be the sole survivor. The officer says this with one utterance by speaking in *multiple contexts* simultaneously. The officer is not speaking in one context that has all 100 people as audience, but rather in 100 different contexts each of which has a single soldier as audience.

Once we see that one speaker can speak from multiple contexts, it's easy to produce examples in which the contexts vary even more. Consider another example of Egan's:

Krypton is going to be destroyed by a galactic cataclysm that's about to originate in their system. As they prepare to evacuate, they broadcast a series of warning signals ahead of the wave of destruction, which will reach any civilizations in the endangered area a few years ahead of the cataclysm. . . . The first message says, in part, 'Those who act now can still save themselves.' (Happily, this story takes

place in one of those galaxies in which it's common knowledge that everyone
in the galaxy speaks English.) A subsequent message says, 'By now, it's too late'.
And a final warning says, 'The wave front will arrive ten seconds from now.'

(Egan (2009): 268)

Krypton's warning gets evaluated from contexts differing in their *times*.
Received on Aku, it says that by 2100 it's too late. Received on Timaron,
it says that 2200 is too late. Received on Xudar, it says that 2300 is too
late. Note that the original senders on Krypton might not know who will
receive the message or when it will arrive, so the various contexts in
which the message is evaluated aren't fixed by the communicative intentions of the senders. The full meaning of what the Kryptonians say when
they broadcast is taken out of their hands and placed partly in the hands
of their audience.

When audiences become large and scattered, then, speakers may not
necessarily know what they are saying—not because they are especially
ignorant, but because what they say is shaped by the context, and what
the context is gets fixed partly by the audience. That observation is
straightforward enough when we're considering simple context-sensitive
expressions like 'you' and 'now'. But its consequences expand when we
consider the wider range of context-sensitive language. The sentence 'Alex
has enough cheese' is context-sensitive. In one context, it can mean that
Alex has a sufficient amount of cheese to make a pizza; in another context,
it can mean that Alex has cheese sufficient to feed her pet rat; in a third
context, it can mean that Alex has cheese sufficient to create a life-size
all-cheese sculpture of Winston Churchill. Because of this context sensitivity, a teacher who says, 'If you have enough cheese, you may begin your
project,' will say different things to different people, based on their individual projects and the cheese requirements of those projects.

Similarly, vague terms are context-sensitive, because different contexts
can lead to different local precisifications of the vague terms. There are a
number of reddish-orange shades that are borderline cases of 'red'. In
one context (when, say, sorting apples), we might choose to draw a
relatively precise boundary between the red and the not red in one
way; in another context (when, say, selecting bulbs for traffic lights),
we might choose to draw a different relatively precise boundary in
another way. And once we consider cases with scattered audiences, we
will see that the work of resolving vagueness may rest with the different
audience members (to be done in different ways), and not with the

communicative intentions of the speaker. The manager says to the many employees headed to their several departments, 'It's Christmas—be sure to display the red things prominently.' Those working with apples get one instruction from this; those working with light bulbs get another.

Issues of scattered audiences become especially pressing when the utterances are linguistically complex and when the audiences are highly scattered. Written texts are particularly subject to this combination of worries, since written texts allow the utterance easily to persist over time and space and to be encountered by audiences in many different contexts. Literary and legal interpretation, in particular, are fraught with difficulties deriving from the interaction of scattered audiences and context sensitivity. Consider the Second Amendment to the United States Constitution:

A well regulated militia being necessary to the security of a free state, the right of the people to keep and bear arms shall not be infringed.

This sentence is full of vague and context-sensitive expressions (what counts as 'arms' or as an 'infringement'? 'Necessary' relative to what ends and possibilities?). It is also a sentence deliberately spoken to an ongoing audience, known in advance to consist of people in widely varied and not clearly envisioned circumstances over a future of open and indeterminate scope. This has socially and politically important consequences for how we understand the amendment. The legal position of *originalism*, for example, says that the meaning of the Second Amendment is fully determined by the intentions of the original drafters:

I'm a simple-minded originalist. I believe that given what we accept as legally authoritative, the proper way to interpret the Constitution (and statutes, regulations, and judicial orders as well) is to seek its authors' intended meanings—the same thing we do when we read a letter from Mom, a shopping list from our spouse, or instructions for how to assemble a child's toy made in China.... Suppose someone shows you a piece of paper with marks on it and tells you that the paper contains normative propositions (instructions, do's and don'ts). He asks you to tell him what those normative propositions are (they are to govern him, not you). What would you do? ... If you believed that the marks were in fact made by some person or persons—possibly including God—intending to communicate norms, then you would naturally ask the following: Who were the authors, in what circumstances and with what purposes were they communicating the norms, and what language were they using to do so—English, Esperanto, some idiosyncratic idiolect, a code, and so on? That is what a simple-minded originalist would do.   (Alexander (2011): 87)

The observations about scattered audiences show that even for instructions concerning how to assemble a child's toy, there's more to ask about than the intentions of the speaker. If the instructions say, 'Find a large enough screwdriver,' then how large a screwdriver the instructions call for will depend in part on the situation of the toy assembler (their arm strength, for example), in ways wholly unforeseen by the author of the instructions. From this perspective, the simple-minded originalist about instructions' texts just misses some questions that need to be asked for interpreting the text. Not just who the authors were and what their circumstances were, but also who we are and what our circumstances are.

9.3 Scattered Speakers

Audiences can be many and scattered, but so too can speakers. Moving from one speaker to many puts a different kind of pressure on the notion of a speaker's communicative intention. Collective speech acts can occur when a group of people jointly prepare and release a written statement. In the ideal cases, all of the speakers will share the same communicative intention. In these cases, we can simply appeal to the notion of a *group* or *collective* intention. Suppose the board of Apple releases a statement, on behalf of all eight members, saying that Apple will release a new iPhone in September. If each of the eight board members, in participating in the statement release, intends that people come to believe that Apple will release a new iPhone (by recognizing the intentions of the board members), then the board members converge in their individual communicative intentions. We can then ground an intention of the board in those individual intentions. Here is a popular account of group intention, due to Michael Bratman:

We intend to *J* if and only if

1. (a) I intend that we *J* and (b) you intend that we *J*.

2. I intend that we *J* in accordance with and because of 1a, 1b, and meshing subplans of 1a and 1b; you intend that we *J* in accordance with and because of 1a, 1b, and meshing subplans of 1a and 1b.

3. 1 and 2 are common knowledge between us. (Bratman (1999): 121)

(Note that for the board to collectively intend to communicate the release of the new iPhone, it's not enough that each board member intends to communicate it. They have to know of each other that they have those individual intentions, and they have to mesh those intentions together—it won't be a group intention if, for example, the individual board members are trying to undermine each other's individual intentions.)

Group intentions give a good account of group communication in the lucky cases in which everyone is on the same page, communicatively speaking. But of course in the real world it's not always like that. Again, legal interpretation provides helpful examples. In 1914, Congress passed the Federal Trade Commission Act, which created the Federal Trade Commission (FTC) and declared it (in Section 5 of the Act) to be 'empowered, among other things, to prevent unfair methods of competition, and unfair or deceptive acts or practices in or affecting commerce'. But Congress was far from acting as a unified and cooperative body in passing the Act:

> Senators' views were wide-ranging. Some opposed Section 5 because they preferred the status quo. Some strong antitrust advocates continued to prefer strict statutory standards backed by criminal sanctions; distrusting the proposed commission, they either opposed Section 5 or at best supported it half-heartedly.
>
> (Winerman (2003): 4)

Even among the specific advocates of Section 5 of the Act, there was disagreement about what 'unfair methods of competition' amounted to:

> [Newlands, Hollis, and Cummins] also approached 'unfair competition' from different, if not necessarily incompatible, perspectives. Newlands emphasized a moral basis of the standard, although he drew support for his moral standard from law and economics. Hollis and Cummins focused more directly on economics; for Hollis, unfair competition was competition that succeeded for reasons other than efficiency and, for Cummins, Section 5 would protect the 'competitive force.' (Winerman (2003): 4)

Given all of this, it's clear that Congress didn't have a *group communicative intention* in the strong sense sketched above. The different senators weren't even intending the same thing, much less intending to cooperate in a shared intention. What, then, does the text of the FTC mean? Here are three options:

1. Maybe the text means many different things, corresponding to the differing communicative intentions of the many individual senators. One senator said that the FTC should prevent immoral competition; another said that the FTC should prevent economically inefficient competition. But then what sense are we to make of the *law*? What

legal obligations are created by a law that means dozens of different and inconsistent things?

2. Maybe the text has no *authorial meaning* at all. Since the text is the collective product of the legislators and the legislators failed to have a group intention, the text is just words spoken for no communicative reason—they are like words drawn at random from a hat. In the absence of speaker meaning, we have to rely on audience meaning, so (perhaps) the laws then mean what the courts 'hear' them as meaning.

3. Maybe we need a better theory of group intention. The definition given above is *reductive*, because it defines the intention of the group using a convergence of individual intentions. But we could also give a non-reductive theory of group intention. There is independent reason to want such an intention. Apple can intend to seize Samsung's share of the mobile phone market—that intention can be manifest in Apple's corporate activities. But there needn't be anyone at Apple who intends to seize Samsung's share. Perhaps the way Apple's plan has been implemented within the corporate structure is so distributed over many people that no one knows what the plan is. Perhaps everyone at Apple secretly hates Apple and wants it to lose market share, but their subtle attempts to undermine Apple's activities end up accidentally cancelling each other out.

If the intention of the group is not just the shared intentions of the members of the group, it's then a very hard problem to say what the intention of the group *is*. We won't try to give any non-reductive theory of group intentions here, but we'll note that group intentions are likely to be vague—even vaguer than individual communicative intentions already often are. For example, the text of the FTC was changed during congressional debate from 'unfair competition' to 'unfair methods of competition'. It's tempting to think that there's nothing fully precise that Congress was intending by swapping the one phrase for the other. Rather, some senators, whose votes were crucial for getting the Act passed, thought that regulating 'unfair competition' was somehow a bit too strong, and that switching to 'unfair methods of competition' provided enough softening to make it acceptable to them to vote for the Act. And so the change was made—not out of a communicative plan of individuals, but out of a pragmatic plan to get Congress to do something.

All of this suggests a perspective on which vagueness plays a key communicative role.[1] Once we see that sometimes audiences need to bring additional resources to bear to complete communication (by providing a context in which context-sensitive language is evaluated), and once we also see that speakers, especially but not only in a group setting, might not know exactly what they want to communicate, we see that there is a communicative strategy in which speakers send a *deliberately vague* signal, thus leaving things open for audiences to supply their own context in which to resolve the vagueness. This can be a valuable tactic for providing rules that have the flexibility to provide guidance over changing time and circumstances. The legislators simply pass a law addressing 'unfair competition', and (for example) leave it to the courts to work out what, in any given economic climate, would count as unfair competition.

The above examples show that scattered speakers can create puzzles about communication in cases where it is unclear what the communicative intentions and contexts of scattered speakers are. It can also be unclear who is speaking. Consider a case raised by Ishani Maitra:

An Arab woman is on a subway car crowded with people. An older white man walks up to her, and says, 'Fuckin' terrorist, go home. We don't [want][2] your kind here.' He continues speaking in this manner to the woman, who doesn't respond. He speaks loudly enough that everyone else in the subway car hears his words clearly. All other conversations cease. Many of the passengers turn to look at the speaker, but no one interferes.   (Maitra (2012): 101)

There are a number of interesting issues raised by this case. One begins by focusing on the speaker's use of the word 'we'. Who counts as 'we' in this example? As is so often the case, there is vagueness and the corresponding possibility of negotiation here. The speaker presumably has some probably vaguely delimited group in mind, probably including all or most of the other people in the subway car. But it looks like it is open for other people to protest being included. If Alex is also on the subway, she could respond, 'Don't include me in your "we".' When she says that, which of the following happens?

---

[1] The role of vagueness in *legal* language, for example, has often been observed, as in Waldron (1994) and Tappenden (1995). But see Sorensen (2001) for a contrary view.

[2] We have changed Maitra's use of 'need' to 'want' to make the example suitable for some of our subsequent discussion.

- Alex provides a counterexample to the original speaker's claim, by demonstrating that not everyone referred to by 'we' doesn't want 'your kind here'.
- Alex alters/refines the content of the original speaker's claim, by placing herself outside the group referred to by 'we'.

The second option is more faithful to what Alex says, but requires that control over the content of the original speaker's words is partly in Alex's hands, rather than the speaker's hands.

Suppose now that the speaker doesn't say 'we', but utters only the opening insult. There is then, of course, no question about who counts as 'we'. But there is a related question of *who is speaking*. Of course, in one sense the answer to this question is simple. The 'older white man' mentioned in the example speaks, and everyone else in the subway car remains silent. But further consideration shows that the question *who is speaking?* is not always the same question as *who is uttering words?*

This point is most easily seen with groups and spokespeople. Suppose Charles is an official spokesperson for Apple, and in a press conference says, 'Free iPhones for everyone next Wednesday!' Who has said that there will be free iPhones? Charles, obviously, but plausibly also Apple has said so, through the agency of its spokesperson Charles. Charles, by uttering words, can bring it about that Apple says things. There are certain constraints on Charles's ability to speak on Apple's behalf (that is, to speak, and thereby to bring it about that Apple says what he is saying). When Charles goes out to dinner and orders a salad, it is just Charles, and not Apple, ordering the salad. Charles speaks on Apple's behalf when speaking in his official capacity: at the right times and places and on the right topics. But even when circumstances are appropriate, Apple can prevent Charles from speaking on their behalf. Perhaps Charles has just gone rogue in announcing free iPhones. In this case, Apple can issue an opposing statement, explaining that Charles was not authorized to say this on Apple's behalf. When this happens, it is not the case that Apple first says that there will be free iPhones and then Apple says that there will not be any free iPhones. Rather, Apple's later actions make it the case that Charles wasn't originally speaking on Apple's behalf, and hence that Apple never said that there would be free iPhones.

Suppose, though, that Apple does not issue an opposing statement. Apple's silence then confirms Charles's status in speaking for Apple.

The same sort of thing can happen in a less institutionalized setting. A group of customers coalesces at the airline desk to protest the flight delay. One member of the group, Daniel, starts doing all of the talking for the group. Perhaps at first he is backed up by various sounds of assent from the other group members, but eventually the others fall silent and let Daniel do all the talking. We might then want to say that Daniel speaks on behalf of the group. When he says, 'We demand compensation for the delay,' his use of 'we' picks out everyone in the group, and it's reasonable to report the situation by saying that *they* demanded compensation, rather than just that *Daniel* demanded compensation for them. Again, the other group members can resist Daniel's ability to speak for them. When Daniel says 'We demand compensation,' other people in the group can say, 'Actually, I'm not interested in compensation, I just want the flight to depart as soon as possible.' In so doing, they change *who is speaking* in Daniel's claims, so that it's no longer *all of them* demanding compensation, but just Daniel (or Daniel and some conforming portion of the group).

Because the members of the group *can* opt out from Daniel's statements, their failure to do so may then reinforce Daniel's status as speaking on their behalf. Daniel becomes the spokesperson for the group because the group allows him to become spokesperson. If others had spoken (either agreeing or disagreeing with Daniel), then a single group voice might not have developed. But ongoing silence in the face of someone acting as a spokesperson looks like it can convey spokesperson status. So, returning to Maitra's example, when the other passengers in the subway car remain silent, they may be allowing the 'older white man' to become a spokesperson for the group, and thus may be contributing to it being the case that all of them are verbally attacking the Arab woman.

If all of this is right, there's a double harm in remaining silent in the presence of bad speech. By remaining silent, the other passengers miss the opportunity to combat the harm by resisting the bigotry of the original speaker. But also, by remaining silent, the other passengers risk becoming incorporated into the speech, and thus being active participants in the original bigotry.

9.4 Speech Acts in the Digital Age

Speakers get a bit scattered when groups and mobs are saying things. But they get *really* scattered once we start engaging in extensive online conversations. We are only beginning to see the effects that computers and the internet will have on the nature of language and communication, and theorizing is in its infancy in this area. We'll note a few phenomena of interest.

A range of what look like new speech acts are opening up through online communication. Consider a few examples:

1. What speech act are you performing when you retweet something? The retweet isn't straightforwardly an asserting of the content of the original tweet. One of the most retweeted tweets ever, for example, was 'If the Cleveland Cavaliers win the 2018 NBA finals I'll buy everyone who retweet's this a jersey . . .' Those retweeting this weren't themselves asserting that they would buy jerseys. Perhaps they were asserting that Damarious Randall, the original tweeter, would buy jerseys? (And then incidentally to the speech act they were performing, also making themselves potentially eligible for a jersey?) But this looks less plausible for retweeting of tweets that aren't themselves assertions. When (over two million) people retweet Louis Tomlinson's 'Always in my heart @Harry_Styles. Yours sincerely, Louis,' it doesn't look like there is some information asserted by the original tweet that they could be repeating.

Instead, retweeting looks like it plays a complicated collection of communicative roles. *Sometimes* to retweet is to reassert what the original tweet asserted. Sometimes it is to express the same feelings asserted in the original tweet. Sometimes it is to endorse the contents of the original tweet without asserting that content oneself. (You might endorse the original tweeter's expression of a sentiment without expressing the sentiment yourself, because you think it's appropriate for them, but not for you, to express that sentiment.) Sometimes to retweet is to make a kind of meta-assertion—to say that someone else said something. (You might retweet in this way if you're drawing attention to something odious that someone else tweeted.) Sometimes retweeting is not done to say anything yourself, but to help promote the voice of the original tweeter.

2. What speech act(s) are you performing when you 'like' a post on Facebook? Some of the issues here are similar to those raised by retweeting. When someone posts on Facebook 'The new Avengers movie was an incoherent disaster' and you like their post, are you also asserting that the

movie was a disaster? Are you asserting that you *like* that the movie was a disaster? Or are you just asserting that you like their expression of their view of the movie (even if you disagree with it)? A further complication is that in liking a post, you are restricted (by the nature of the Facebook interface) to only a few types of reaction. Originally the only option on Facebook was the 'thumbs up' liking icon 👍. In 2016, the options were expanded to the six icons 👍, ❤, 😄, 😮, 😢, and 😠. One effect of this expansion was to change the speech act performed by liking with the 👍 icon. Originally, you could 'like' a post in which someone described an encounter with their annoying boss to express your solidarity with their sufferings. But once the 'angry' icon 😠 becomes available, continuing to use the 👍 icon threatens to become a way of saying that you *approve* of their sufferings. Especially since the speech acts performed by the various liking icons are relatively underspecified, the nature of the speech act is prone to be highly context-sensitive and shaped by what the other iconic options are.

Because the speech act you perform by liking a post on Facebook depends on what the iconic liking options are, and because Facebook controls what the iconic options are, it follows that Facebook has a certain level of control over what you can and cannot say on their platform. Not because they engage in censorship by refusing to allow certain combinations of words to be posted (although that happens as well), but because they control the meaning of the language they make available for you to express yourself in. The transition to digital communication thus creates a concern about losing a common public language as a communicative tool not under the control of any one group or individual.

There are significant legal questions related to these questions about speech acts. Courts have ruled, for example, that liking a defamatory post on Facebook can make the liker liable for defamation, partly on the theory that liking a post increases its visibility to other users and thus serves as a form of republishing (retweeting something defamatory can be a form of defamation even more straightforwardly in this way) and partly because liking a post serves as some form of endorsement of the post.[3]

---

[3] A Swiss court in 2017 returned a conviction of defamation for liking Facebook posts, saying 'the defendant clearly endorsed the unseemly content and made it his own' (<https://money.cnn.com/2017/05/31/technology/facebook-like-defamation-switzerland/index.html>). In 2013 a South African court found a man guilty of defamation for being tagged in a post on Facebook, on the grounds that he thereby knew about the post and allowed himself to be associated with it (<https://www.iol.co.za/news/facebook-post-costs-couple-r40-000-1573165>).

3. More generally, social media has seen the rise of extensive non-verbal communication. People often respond to posts not with words, but with GIFs. There is some degree of conventionalization to the meanings of some GIFs (although the conventions aren't very stable and drift around frequently), but many GIFs have the same kinds of indeterminacy of content and speech act type that likings and retweetings do, amplified by the enormous range of GIFs to choose from. GIFs are oriented more toward *expressive* than *informational* roles. The popular 'Drew Scanlon blinks' GIF, for example, isn't used to communicate a bit of information, but to express one's disbelief at something. As with the Facebook 'like' options, there is a concern about the loss of a language as a possession we have in common. Of course anything *can* be a GIF, but images involving celebrities and mass media are more likely to feature in GIFs, which means that control over the language itself is to some extent being ceded to a small collection of individuals. (And that the language itself is to some extent being commodified and made into a vehicle for advertising and self-promotion.)

In addition to giving rise to new kinds of speech acts, digital communication is producing new kinds of speakers. One prominent instance of this is the rise of computerized speakers. Computerized speakers run the gamut from the relatively tame news summarizers (programs that automatically compile and condense information from other human-produced news sources) to more pernicious bots that promote news stories, make disruptive comments, or create and distribute random pseudo-stories. In some cases we don't need to think of the programs themselves as speakers—if a bot is simply widely and repeatedly distributing a bit of text written by a person, then the person is the speaker, and the bot is just an unusual text delivery mechanism. But the degree of distance from human speech, and thus the need to identify a computerized speaker, increases with cases. Automatic news summarizers are relying heavily on speech acts made by the original human producers of the source stories. But different summarizing algorithms can emphasize different aspects of stories, causing quite different outputs. We don't want to hold the original human speaker responsible for the emphasis introduced by the summarizer. Should we think of the programmer of the summarizer as the speaker? But the programmer may never see the summarized text and might have no idea what its content is.

Consider an interesting case moving considerably further along the spectrum. Each November is National Novel Generation Month, during which programmers with literary aspirations, or authors with programming skills, write programs that will then write their own novel. Such programs could leave the programmer very much the speaker, if for example it's a program that simply prints out the full text of a novel the programmer has written and included in the code. Or it could effectively eliminate the programmer's role as a speaker, if for example it just produces pages of randomly selected letters. But many cases are in the murky middle. Darius Kazemi's computer-generated novel *Teens Wander Around a House* was produced by programming in a virtual environment and a collection of virtual characters and then writing algorithms for those characters to wander the environment and comment on what they find. The result includes text like:

After some time Darby found herself in the master bedroom. The next thing she saw was the king-sized bed, which left her feeling disquieted. Part of her, a larger part than she cared to admit, wanted to smash it. She thought about school, and how Gale and Vivianna never talked to her. Why did they leave whenever she entered a room? How could that even be possible? Did they secretly like her after all? It didn't matter anyway. They were queen bees and they knew it. They never invited her to parties; it was a fluke she ended up at this one.

'They were queen bees and they knew it,' for example, appears about 100 times during the novel, always in slightly different party-discussing contexts. Kazemi's program, rather than Kazemi himself, is in some significant sense the author of this text. But understanding speech produced by programs poses considerable difficulties. If, for example, Grice is right that understanding speakers is a matter of understanding their communicative intentions, what would it mean to understand a program which lacks intentions? Or do we need to expand our notion of intention, and of mental states more generally, to allow us to attribute communicative intentions to these sorts of programs?

CENTRAL POINTS IN CHAPTER 9

- In this chapter, we consider departures from the idealized model of communication which arise as a result of the fact that the audience of a given utterance can consist of many people, with different backgrounds and in different circumstances. In addition, we consider the fact that the speaker of a given utterance can be, in a sense, many people, with different intentions. We also consider how speech acts work in the context of social media.
- We first consider scattered audiences. We present examples of speech addressed to multiple people in different contexts, and note that, to make sense of such

utterances, we need (or at least, it's somewhat natural) to assume that the speech act takes place in multiple contexts simultaneously. A problem that arises is that the speaker may not know about all the various contexts in which they speak, and thus may not know all the things they say. Scattered audiences lead to semantic ignorance, and the possibility of saying something other than what one means. This can lead to various extremely momentous political problems. In interpreting the United States Constitution, we need to deal with the fact that its audience—American citizens, past, present, and future—is extremely scattered.

• We then turn to scattered speakers. Consider, for example, the board of Apple putting out a new press release. We can view this as a case in which we have a scattered speaker: all the members of the board. If we assume that in some sense what is said goes by what the speakers intended to say, this sort of case is intelligible. Each of the speakers intended to say what the press release said, and so the press release did so too. However, we noted that there are problem cases here too: for example, sometimes there is no one intention shared by the group. Or one might find oneself corralled into a scattered speaker to which one doesn't want to belong, if someone uses 'we' in your vicinity.

• We end up by considering how speech works on the internet, where these and related problems are acute. What is it to retweet something, or to like a post on facebook, for example? Our idealized model of communication has little to say about this.

Further Reading and Exercises

FURTHER READING FOR CHAPTER 9

Egan (2009) brought the problem of scattered audiences to philosophers' attention. For the semantic theory of context sensitivity underlying it see the textbook presentation in Cappelen and Dever (2016) or go to the source, namely Kaplan (1989). Cappelen (2008) uses Egan cases, among others, to argue that we need to overturn some fundamental assumptions in the philosophy of language. Zakkou (2017) argues that the standard Kaplanian theory can account for such uses. A helpful overview of collective intentionality is Schweikard and Schmid (2013), and a defense of the claim that organizations like Apple can have intentional states is Tollefsen (2002), and a book-length investigation of group agency, which, among other things, helps frame the debate, is List and Pettit (2011).

Comprehension Questions

1. What is the problem of scattered audiences?
2. What is constitutional originalism? Do you think we should be originalists?
3. In your view, are retweets endorsements? Under what circumstances do you 'like' posts?
4. Do you speak as part of any scattered speakers? Have you ever had any problem(s) of speaking in this sense without intending to?
5. Are our emoji semantics correct? Is it indeed the case that 👍-ing someone's complaint about their boss indicates one's happiness with the person's suffering?

Exploratory Questions

6. Consider the sentence 'cane nero magna bella persica.' This means, in Latin, 'sing, o nero, the great Persian wars.' However, it also means 'the black dog eats a nice peach' in dialectical Italian. Imagine someone uttering it in an Egan-style scenario, with a scattered audience consisting of both Latin and Italian speakers. Should we want to say that the speaker said both the translations? If not, how do we draw the line between this bad case and Egan's good cases?
7. The twitter bot @papertitlebot generates analytic philosophy title papers by replacing words at random in a few templates. While it is programmed typically to produce somewhat implausible titles ('Stalnaker's account of Lacanian psychoanalysis', for example), it has, at least once, come up with a paper title that makes an original contribution to the literature (the paper title is 'Does Davidsonian quotation have a Frege–Geach problem?', although to explain why it contributes would take us too far afield). If one were to cite this in a paper on quotation, whom would one credit? The bot? Its creator?

10

Linguistic Oppressing and Linguistic Silencing

One of the great advantages of language is that it gives us a reliable mechanism for doing things at a great distance. *Visiting* Rome is difficult—you have to make plane, train, and taxi arrangements, and you are highly dependent on causal cooperation from the rest of the world. But *talking about* Rome is easy—you just use the word 'Rome' and you've done it, and you don't need anyone's permission or assistance. But that advantage becomes a disadvantage when language is put to malignant purposes. Some of the disadvantage follows immediately on the advantages we've just noted. Language lets you easily talk about Rome, pass on information about Rome, and praise Romans. But it equally (as we've discussed in earlier chapters) lets you lie about Rome, slur Romans, and threaten Romans.

In this chapter we turn to ways that language makes easy some less obviously linguistic malignant acts. We'll focus primarily on *oppressing* and *silencing*, and then close with some more general observations. There is a great deal of oppressing going on in the world. Much of it, of course, is wholly non-linguistic. When Africans were taken prisoner, shipped in horrible conditions over the ocean, and sold into slavery, they were thereby oppressed, and that oppression was achieved by chain and whip, not by word. Similarly, there is a great deal of silencing going on in the world. Much of it, too, is non-linguistic. When the leaders of a dissident political movement are jailed, their protesters chased from the streets by police, and their printing presses seized and destroyed, the movement is silenced, and the silencing is achieved by gun and boot, not by word.

But oppressing and silencing can be done linguistically as well. Linguistic oppression and silencing, as we'll see, may be less violent than the non-linguistic varieties, but they may also, because of the nature of language, be more directly under the control of the oppressor or silencer, and hence harder to resist. Before plunging into the details of oppression and silencing, we begin with some more general observations about doing things with language.

10.1 A Brief Introduction to Speech Acts

In the classroom, the focus is less on what we are doing with language and more on the information carried by the language. The informational focus means that in the classroom there are only two kinds of *speech acts* we need to consider: *asserting*, in which a speaker says something in order to put information into the conversational common ground, and *questioning*, in which a speaker asks something in order to help direct the informational investigation. But outside the classroom, we quickly find that asserting and questioning aren't the only speech acts we perform. To help focus attention on the idea of the speech act performed, consider the various things that can be done with the single sentence 'You'll never leave this room':

- It can be a simple *assertion*, providing a piece of information to someone uncertain about their future locations.
- It can be a *threat*, made not to provide a piece of locational information, but to reveal the speaker's intentions to thwart the audience's movements.
- It can be a *promise*, made to an acrophobe, creating commitments by the speaker to keep the audience indoors.
- It can be a *plan*, made as part of a cooperative attempt to work out where to place guards.

If we are interested in the social and political effects of language, speech acts other than assertion are of central importance.

Speech act theory separates out three things that a speaker does in uttering a sentence: Suppose Beth is considering whether to fly to Toronto to visit her mother, and Alex says, 'I'll give you a ride to the airport.' We can distinguish three actions Alex thereby performs:

1. The Locutionary Act: Alex utters some words with a particular meaning, and thereby *says that* she will give Beth a ride to the airport. What she says is a bit of potential information; the sort of thing that

can be true or false. In general, the locutionary act performed by a speaker is the act of saying some words with some meaning.

2. **The Illocutionary Act**: Alex isn't just making a prediction about her future actions. She is *promising* to give Beth a ride to the airport. Her locutionary act—her saying that she will give Beth a ride—constitutes the promising. It is *in saying* what she does that she promises.

3. **The Perlocutionary Act**: Alex's promising as she does then has psychological consequences for Beth. With the difficulty of getting to the airport removed, Beth decides she will visit her mother in Toronto. Alex has thus *persuaded* Beth to visit her mother. Alex's saying that she will give Beth a ride doesn't constitute a persuading in the same way that it constitutes a promising. Rather, it achieves a persuading through its subsequent effects on Beth.

As a rough guideline, we can say that a speaker's locutionary act is *saying something*, their illocutionary act is *doing something in saying that thing*, and their perlocutionary act is *doing something by saying that thing*. There is an element of decreasing control by the speaker over the act as we proceed along the sequence:

1. A speaker has considerable but not complete control over what locutionary act they perform. They can select what words to say. They don't control what those words mean—we don't have a Humpty Dumpty theory of meaning on which words mean what the speaker wants them to mean. No matter how much the speaker wants 'glory' to mean 'a nice knock-down argument', it doesn't, because the meanings of words are fixed by factors outside the speaker's control. But if they know the meanings of words in advance, they can pick words that mean what they want. If, as we've considered repeatedly, there is an element of social negotiation over the meanings of words, this negotiation will further limit the speaker's control over their locutionary act.

2. Illocutionary acts are somewhat less under the control of the speaker. Merely wanting, trying, or intending to perform a given illocutionary isn't enough to perform it. Illocutionary acts typically require an appropriate social setting. Alex can try to perform the illocutionary act of marrying Beth and Charles in performing the locutionary act of saying *I now pronounce you man and wife*. But if

Alex doesn't occupy the right social role to perform the ceremony of wedding people, or if Beth and Charles haven't agreed to be wed, or if Beth and Charles aren't present, the desired illocutionary act won't be achieved. And merely *not* wanting to perform an illocutionary act isn't always enough to avoid performing it. If Alex says to Beth (in the right setting) 'I promise to bring you to the airport,' then even if she doesn't really want to promise (never intends to bring Beth to the airport, for example), she nevertheless has promised, because the social setting is one of promising.

3. Perlocutionary acts are even further outside the domain of control of the speaker. Once the social setting is correct, a speaker can bring about illocutionary acts that she promises something, or names a baby something, largely under her own control, by using the right form of words. There's no danger that the speaker (appropriately situated) will say, 'I hereby name the baby Elizabeth,' but the baby will remain strangely unnamed. But perlocutionary acts are different. The speaker can say, 'I hereby persuade you that I am right' in the context of an argument, but still completely fail to persuade the speaker. With illocutionary acts, saying more or less makes it so (given the appropriate context), but not so with perlocutionary acts. Whether Alex performs the perlocutionary act of persuading Beth depends very much on Beth—if she comes to agree with Alex, then Alex has persuaded her, but if she does not, Alex has not persuaded her. The success or failure of perlocutionary acts, then, is at the mercy of the world, and depends on whether certain desired causal consequences of the saying are achieved.

Let's return briefly to the classroom, and consider the case of asserting. Alex says, 'Ben Nevis is the tallest mountain in Scotland.' What are the locutionary, illocutionary, and perlocutionary acts? There is no universally agreed-upon way of splitting things up, but perhaps:

- Locutionary Act: Alex expresses the content that Ben Nevis is the tallest mountain in Scotland.
- Illocutionary Act: Alex updates the common ground with the proposition expressed in the locutionary act.
- Perlocutionary Act: Beth updates her beliefs with the new content of the common ground.

Or alternatively:

- Locutionary Act: Alex expresses the content that Ben Nevis is the tallest mountain in Scotland.
- Illocutionary Act: Alex proposes updating the common ground with the proposition expressed in the locutionary act.
- Perlocutionary Act: The common ground is successfully updated following the proposal made in the illocutionary act.

The choice between these two characterizations is the choice between (i) a picture of conversational common ground as a theoretical posit of the theory of meaning, so that the common ground is automatically updated by an assertion, meaning that there is an open (perlocutionary) question of how audience members cognitively react to the changed common ground, and (ii) a picture that reduces the conversational common ground to facts about the mental states of conversational participants, so that an assertion can only change the common ground by being accepted by the audience, changing their mental states, and thereby changing the common ground.

When we think about *types* of speech acts, we are usually characterizing them in terms of illocutionary acts. Promises can vary greatly in locutionary act. We can promise by saying, 'I'll take you to the airport,' or by saying, 'I promise to bake you a cake.' And promises can vary greatly in perlocutionary act. Some promises have the perlocutionary effect of convincing Beth to visit her mother, other promises have the perlocutionary effect of cheering up Charles. But all promises have the same illocutionary effect: the effect of promising. Or, if we want a less trivial answer, of creating a binding obligation to another person (or whatever our preferred theory of promising is). Similarly, *threats* are unified by having the illocutionary effect of threatening (attempting to control someone's behavior by making clear that bad consequences will follow on non-compliance).

Many speech acts are great things. Using language to assert, promise, wed, praise, apologize, and name adds much that is good to life. In this chapter, however, we want to explore some of the dark underbelly of speech acts. We have already looked extensively at lying and bullshitting, and mentioned threatening in passing. We'll now consider *oppressing* and *silencing*.

10.2 Linguistic Oppressing

Let's start with oppressing. Pretty much every human artefact has been pressed into the service of oppression at one time or another, and language is no exception. Many of the oppressive uses of language happen through the perlocutionary effects of language. The king says, 'Increase the taxes!', in so doing issuing an order that taxes be increased, and the perlocutionary effect is that the peasantry is (further) oppressed. The oppression happened by way of language, but indirectly. The king's utterance was an imperative and its illocutionary act was an ordering. The downstream causal consequences of that ordering—the perlocutionary act performed—was then an oppressing.

However, it has been suggested that sometimes oppression is an *illocutionary* act. Consider the following example due to Mary Kate McGowan:

Suppose, for example, that the proprietor of a certain restaurant makes the following declaration, 'From now on, any employee of mine who serves a non-white customer will be fired!' This utterance makes it impermissible for his employees to serve a non-white person (and hence for a non-white person to be served in his establishment). This example illustrates several important points. First, mere speech can be an act of oppression. One of the things this utterance does is enact a policy whereby non-whites are not permitted to patronize a certain establishment. Since this policy systematically disadvantages non-whites and since it does so in virtue of membership in a socially marked group (i.e. non-white), this policy is (racially) oppressive.   (McGowan (2009): 392)

It's important to be clear on why this kind of oppression is illocutionary, rather than perlocutionary. We can distinguish in this example two stages of oppression. First it is made impermissible for non-whites to be served. Then, as a consequence of this impermissibility, non-whites in fact are not served. These are two separate things, as we can bring out by imagining variants of the case in which we have each without the other:

- The proprietor could declare the new policy, thereby making it impermissible for non-whites to be served, but his employees could decide to break the policy and continue serving non-whites. We would then have the oppression of impermissibility without the oppression of non-service.
- The proprietor could leave the restaurant's policy as it is, leaving it permissible for non-whites to be served, but the employees could take it on themselves to refuse to serve non-whites. We would then have the oppression of non-service without the oppression of impermissibility.

The impermissibility is an illocutionary effect of the proprietor's utterance, while the actual non-service is a perlocutionary effect. The proprietor only indirectly brings it about that non-whites aren't served. In the end, stopping service to non-whites requires cooperation from the employees, and nothing the proprietor says can in itself directly achieve that cooperation. But the proprietor *directly* brings it about that serving non-whites is impermissible. As the owner, the proprietor has the appropriate authority to issue and withdraw permissions regarding service in his restaurant, so nothing more is needed to make service impermissible than for the proprietor to declare it impermissible.

Let's consider three questions about this example:

1. Is the purported *illocutionary oppression* really a form of oppression? Being unable to get service at a restaurant because of one's race is, of course, a form of oppression. But that's the perlocutionary effect of the proprietor's act. If we focus specifically on the illocutionary change in permissibility, is *that* an oppression? Are there two oppressions here: an initial oppression when the permissions are changed, and a second oppression when the changed permissions are put into effect? Or, to put the same point another way, if the perlocutionary effect fails (if the employees refuse to stop serving non-whites), has there been any oppression *just* from the change of permission?

Better to be served impermissibly than to be denied service while having the permission to be served, presumably. So there's some reason to think that the perlocutionary oppression here is *worse* than the illocutionary oppression. But that doesn't mean that the change in permission isn't also a form of oppression. First, we often care about *what is allowed* as well as *what happens*. Just as it can be upsetting to be denied service, it can be upsetting to be denied permission to be served (even if you are then actually served). Second, facts about permissions can have practical consequences. In this case, the primary effect of the illocutionary change in permission is the typical perlocutionary change in service, but even if that perlocutionary effect fails, there are other bad consequences that a change in permission can have. Making service impermissible is a step toward normalizing different treatment for non-whites. Even if no actual change in treatment follows in this case, the normalization may make it easier for other people to change their behavior in oppressive ways.

2. Is the change in permission really an illocutionary act? Does the proprietor really change what is permissible simply in saying that serving

non-whites is now impermissible? If everyone ignores what he says, has he really effected a change in permission? This is similar to the question of whether a law that is never followed or enforced is really a law. We might helpfully distinguish between thin and thick senses of permitting and forbidding here. To forbid something in the thin sense is just to put it on the conversational record (with the proper authority, setting, and so on) that it is not allowed. As we've seen, conversational contexts do track what possibilities are relevant, and linguistic acts can change those conversational features. Merely by saying, 'You might put the public interest first for once,' a speaker puts possibilities in which the public interest is put first into the conversational context, and those possibilities will then influence what must and must not be the case. But of course changing the conversational context doesn't force other people to conform to the new context. They can try to change the context back, or proceed *as if* the context has remained unchanged, or drop out of the conversation and start a new one. To forbid something in a thick sense is not just to update the conversational context, but to take steps to get the other conversational participants to *acknowledge* the changed context, and to *treat* the forbidden thing as forbidden. It's only in the thin sense that the proprietor's change in permission is an illocutionary act. So in thinking about whether there is illocutionary oppression in this case, we should be attentive to whether the *thin* change in permission is oppressive.

3. Does it matter whether we classify linguistic acts of oppression as perlocutionary or illocutionary? As we've seen, deciding how to sort the various features of speech acts into the illocutionary and perlocutionary bins is a messy matter, and we might wonder why we're supposed to care in which of these rather theoretical categories we put whatever oppressing the proprietor has done in saying, 'From now on, any employee of mine who serves a non-white will be fired!' It's uncontroversial that the use of language can be involved in oppressing people—is there a reason to care just how intimately connected to the language the oppressing is?

One reason the distinction might matter is that it connects to how we think about freedom of speech. Defenders of free speech recognize that bad things can happen as a result of people speaking, but think that in creating legal prohibitions, we need to distinguish between the bad result and the speech that gives rise to the bad result. So when Alex says to the hitman, 'I'll pay you $1,000 to kill Beth,' she brings about the death of Beth through her speech. But what should be prohibited here is *hiring hitmen*, not *saying certain things*. Alex hires the hitman *by* saying what she said (i.e., the hiring was a perlocutionary act), but the hiring was a separate thing from the saying, and thus can be regulated separately. But illocutionary effects are more intimately connected to sayings. The illocutionary effect is what the speaker does *in speaking*; it is constituted by and is an automatic consequence of the speaking (in a suitable context), and the two thus can't be separated. If, then, certain speech acts are themselves oppressing—they illocutionarily oppress—then it might be reasonable in these cases to restrict freedom of speech to prohibit saying those sentences which are associated with the problematic illocutionary acts, since here we can't separate the saying and the doing.

10.3 Pornographic Linguistic Oppressing

Some (illocutionarily) oppressive speech is overt and easy to spot. The 'No Irish!' sign in the window of the bed and breakfast illocutionarily changes permissions for staying in the bed and breakfast, and thereby oppresses the Irish. But recent literature has been interested in cases in which there is less obvious linguistic oppression. A case of particular interest has been pornography, which some writers have claimed can be a form of oppressive speech which illocutionarily oppresses women.

Everyone agrees that pornography might oppress women. To say this is just to say that pornography might have causal consequences that lead to women's rights and freedoms being infringed. Pornography might cause men to engage in acts of violence toward women at an increased rate, for example. Whether pornography in fact has these oppressive consequences is an empirical question requiring careful investigation. It's thus a sociological matter that falls outside the scope of our philosophical investigation of the role of language. The illocutionary view says something more: it says that pornography says something the very saying of which is oppressive.

We thus need two questions answered: (i) what is it that pornography is saying, and (ii) how does the saying of that constitute oppression? Consider an example from Langton and West:

We illustrate with an example, not particularly extreme, but typical, perhaps, of the kind of pornography MacKinnon has in mind. The story, from *Hustler*, is called 'Dirty Pool'.

Example. A waitress is pinched by a male pool player, while his companions look on with approval. The captions to the series of sexually graphic pictures read:

Though she pretends to ignore them, these men know when they see an easy lay. She is thrown on the felt table, and one manly hand after another probes her private areas. Completely vulnerable, she feels one after another enter her fiercely. As the three violators explode in a shower of climaxes, she comes to a shuddering orgasm.

The story is an example of what is sometimes described in the social science literature as a 'favorable' rape depiction. It is not explicitly said in the story that the female waitress says 'no' when she really means 'yes'; that, despite her protestations to the contrary, she wanted to be raped and dominated all along; that she was there as an object for the men's sexual gratification; that raping a woman is sexy and erotic for man and woman alike. Nevertheless the conversation—if we can call it that—follows certain patterns of accommodation which render acceptable these things that are not explicitly said. These presuppositions are required in order to make sense of what is explicitly said and illustrated.   (Langton and West (1999): 311 reprinted in Langton (2009): 184)

The thought, then, is that pornography sometimes says oppressive things by presupposing them. Let's focus on the specific content *it is permissible to treat women as sexual objects*. Of course, pornography could say this explicitly (it would be a rather theoretically inclined pornography that did), but it can also, on Langton and West's view, presuppose that content.

It's worth being careful about the notion of presupposition here. Earlier in this book we considered a clearly linguistic notion of presupposition. 'Alex doesn't regret stealing Beth's car' presupposes that Alex stole Beth's car, and it presupposes that because of specific features of the meaning of the word 'regret', which is a presupposition *trigger*. Using presuppositional language in this sense can, through accommodation, place information in the common ground. This will then have predictable linguistic consequences. For example, because the information that Alex stole Beth's car has been put in common ground, using a pronoun to pick out Beth's car is made possible:

- Alex doesn't regret stealing Beth's car. It's a Mercedes, so it was worth it.

But there is a broader use of presupposition available, in which something is presupposed if it's just something we assume everyone is thinking. In this sense, for example, *The Lord of the Rings* presupposes that there are no plane flights from the Shire to Mordor, and thus that for

Frodo to get the Ring to Mordor he has to walk. We can assume that everyone reading the stories thinks this, and certain aspects of the stories won't make sense to someone who doesn't. But this is a less specifically linguistic sense of presupposition. There's no presupposition trigger in *The Lord of the Rings* that serves to introduce the information that there are no plane flights to Mordor, and the stories don't seem to *say* in any sense that there are no plane flights to Mordor. The narrowly linguistic sense of presupposition persists, as we've seen, under negation. If we negate the content of *The Lord of the Rings* ('Here's what didn't happen:...'), then it's not at all clear that the stories continue to presuppose that there are no plane flights to Mordor.

If a work of pornography presupposes that it is permissible to treat women as sexual objects, it looks like it does so in the broader rather than in the narrower sense. It doesn't look like there is a linguistically encoded presupposition trigger in the pornography that introduces the presupposition. (Would a negated work of pornography still presuppose that it's permissible to treat women as sexual objects?) Rather, it's just that the pornographic story wouldn't make sense if the viewers aren't thinking that it's permissible to treat women as sexual objects. This matters for two reasons. First, presuppositions in this broader sense, as we've seen, don't seem to be *said*. So it will be harder to extract from this account the conclusion that the work of pornography says something that could constitute a linguistic oppressing. Second, presuppositions in this broader sense don't have to be *believed*. In reading *The Lord of the Rings* we in some sense presuppose that there are no plane flights to Mordor—we read the story on the assumption that that's a feature of the world of the story. But we don't thereby actually *believe* that Frodo has to walk from the Shire to Mordor. We don't think there really are such places, and thus we don't think there really are any facts about how one gets from one such place to another. But if that's the sense of presupposition that's active in pornography, then if it is presupposed that it's permissible to treat women as sexual objects, it will be presupposed *within the story*, not as a feature of reality. Of course, it's always possible that viewers of pornography will get confused and carry over that presupposition to reality, just as a reader of *The Lord of the Rings* might. (There might well be features of pornography, or of the claim that it's permissible to treat women as sexual objects, that make it particularly easy to get confused in this way.) But oppression that resulted from that confusion wouldn't be a direct illocutionary effect of the pornography.

Let's turn to the second question now. Suppose (setting aside the above concerns) that a work of pornography does say, in this presuppositional sense, that it is permissible to treat women as sexual objects. How does this saying constitute oppression? Following the earlier example of the racist proprietor, the suggestion is that pornography, when it presuppositionally says that it is permissible to treat women as sexual objects, thereby illocutionarily changes the permissions so that it *really is* permissible to treat women as sexual objects. Since it's oppressive to be treated as a sexual object, it's also oppressive for it to be permissible to treat one as a sexual object.

But the idea of changing permissions needs to be examined carefully here. Things can be permissible and impermissible in many senses. It's *legally* permissible to address someone with a racist slur (because of free speech protections), but it's not *morally* permissible to do so. It's legally and morally permissible to move a rook diagonally on a chess board, but it's not permitted *by the rules of chess*. In the racist proprietor case, it's reasonably clear what the relevant sense of permissibility is. The proprietor's declaration makes it impermissible to serve non-white customers *according to the rules of the workplace at that restaurant.* The proprietor can illocutionarily change permissibility in this sense because he's properly situated to control those permissions, since it's his restaurant. He can declare what the workplace rules are, but he can't, for example, declare what's legally or morally permissible. And other people can't declare what the workplace rules are—an employee couldn't undo the proprietor's bad work by declaring, 'Now it is once again permissible to serve non-whites.'

When a work of pornography declares that it is permissible to treat women as sexual objects, what notion of permissibility is involved? The difficulty is in finding a sense of permissibility that brings together two requirements: it's a notion of permissibility that the pornographic work is situated to control (can speak authoritatively about), and that it would be oppressive to have enacted. Consider some options:

1. *It is morally permissible to treat women as sexual objects.* It would clearly be oppressive to have this permission enacted, but there's no reason to think that a pornographic work can, in speaking, enact a change in moral permissions.

2. *It is legally permissible to treat women as sexual objects.* Again, it would clearly be oppressive to have this permission enacted, but there's again no reason to think that a pornographic work can, in speaking, enact a change in legal permissions (unlike, for example, a legislative body).

3. *It is permissible in the pornographic fiction to treat women as sexual objects.* It's plausible that the pornographic work can speak authoritatively on this permission—authors of fictional works have broad authority to say what's true in the fiction. But it's less clear that it would be oppressive *just* to have it be permissible *in the fictional world of the pornographic work* to treat women as sexual objects.

4. *It is culturally permissible to treat women as sexual objects.* This looks like the most promising option for an illocutionary account of pornographic oppression. It would be reasonable to view it as oppressive to make it culturally permissible to treat women as sexual objects. Can a pornographic work speak authoritatively on cultural permissions? Things are murky here, largely because the status of cultural rules is murky. It's certainly true that people *declaring* something to be culturally permissible can help bring it about that that thing is in fact culturally permissible, since cultural rules are sustained largely through our ongoing collective endorsement of them. And media voices plausibly have a particularly powerful role in doing that sustaining, so a pornographic work probably has more power than the average citizen to shift and shape cultural norms. But it's less clear that this amounts to the ability to change the rules *illocutionarily*. Can the pornographic work simply declare what the cultural rules are and thereby change them, in the same way that the proprietor can simply declare what the workplace rules are and thereby change them?

Again, none of this is to deny that people's behavior can change, and change for the worse, by interacting with pornography. People and societies are enormously complex things, and their behaviors are always subject to often-unpredictable change as they get poked and prodded in various ways. And one possible reaction to encountering fiction is always emulation—the Star Trek fan might start speaking Klingon and guiding their behavior by the Prime Directive. (But another possible reaction to encountering fiction is rejection; taking the fiction as a model of what to avoid.) Our boundaries between fiction and reality can be complex and permeable. But these changes, although triggered by language, aren't constituted by linguistic acts. How much that matters to the social question of dealing with the causal consequences of such speech is a hard question, but it does matter in thinking about what the boundaries of theorizing specifically about language are.

10.4 Silencing

Our second example of the dark underbelly of speech acts is silencing. As we emphasized earlier, there are of course many ways of silencing people without the use of speech (jailing them, blocking their access to public fora and media). There are also ways of silencing people that do involve language. Threats, of course, can be used to silence someone by stopping them from speaking. A speaker can also be silenced simply by being shouted over. This shows that there is an important difference between being *silent* and being *silenced*. A speaker who is shouted over isn't silent—they are still speaking; it's just that their speech can't be heard. And being heard is a requirement for communicating, so they can't communicate successfully. In that sense they are being *silenced*.

To be silenced by being shouted over is to be silenced by speech, but only in a rather trivial way. It's not the *linguistic* nature of the shouting that does the silencing, but just the *auditory* nature. The same effect could be achieved using a siren or a jackhammer. But it has been suggested that there are cases of silencing that are achieved through the linguistic nature of speech—cases in which there is something like a speech act of silencing, in which the silencing is an illocutionary act.

To see how illocutionary silencing might happen, consider the following case. Alex has decided to kill Beth. Being linguistically inclined, she's chosen a rather convoluted way of doing so. Alex becomes the director of a play, with Beth one of the actors. Alex institutes a very strict policy, during rehearsals, of saying 'Begin action' to start a bit of rehearsal and 'End action' to end that bit of rehearsal. This is important because the play contains substantial improvisation, and the clear markers make it possible to tell when the actors are speaking in their roles (and thus not really asserting anything) and when they are speaking for themselves (and thus really asserting). Alex then arranges for Beth to drink a glass of poisoned water. Beth, feeling the poison starting to take effect, is about to say 'Help, I've been poisoned. Someone call a doctor.' But before she can say this, Alex says 'Begin action.' In saying this, Alex prevents Beth from *asserting* that she has been poisoned. She can, of course, still say the words, but now she says them as lines in the play, not as an assertion. Alex has silenced Beth—prevented her from asserting what she wants to assert. Alex's silencing is genuinely linguistic. She silences Alex directly by means of what she says—it's crucially a consequence of the *content* of her utterance, and not just (for example) the loudness of it, and it's an immediate effect of the utterance.

The idea here is that there are necessary social conditions for making an assertion, and that Alex (in her role as the director) has the ability to manipulate the social conditions so that the required conditions for asserting come and go. For example, assertion might require a background social readiness to take on board the asserted information (into the conversational common ground, or into the beliefs of the audience). Where the audience lacks this readiness (because, for example, they think they are listening to a play), assertion becomes impossible.

It's important to note that this picture of what's going on with assertion isn't inevitable. We could instead say that to assert is just to speak with certain kinds of intentions. This will make asserting a private matter, wholly under the control of the speaker, and not at the mercy of social conditions. On this alternative picture, Beth *does* assert when she says 'I've been poisoned.' Because of Alex's deceptive plans, Beth's audience doesn't *realize* that she is asserting, and hence they don't properly receive her statement—there is no uptake of her assertion. That's of course just as bad for Beth—she'll be just as dead whether she (i) can't even assert that she's been poisoned or (ii) can assert it, but can't get anyone to realize that she is really asserting. The question is how tightly linguistic is the explanation of Beth's death.

We want, then, to distinguish between being *silenced* (prevented from performing the linguistic act one wants to perform) and being *ignored* (performing one's linguistic act, but not having it taken up in the way that one wanted). Alex, for example, could instead have spread scurrilous rumors that Beth is a paranoid hypochondriac. Then when Beth says 'I've been poisoned,' her audience receives it as an assertion, but doesn't believe what she has asserted, and thus rejects the assertion and doesn't act on it. In this case Alex hasn't silenced Beth, she's caused Beth to be ignored. Again, that's still bad for Beth, but the badness isn't directly linguistic. The ignoring of Beth is a perlocutionary downstream causal consequence of Alex's speech, not a constitutive feature of what Alex is saying.

It's not hard to see that there are real examples of illocutionary silencing. Consider first a trivial example. Alex says, 'Charles is coming over for dinner.' She is about to utter the sentence 'He is bringing a bottle of wine,' but before she says that, Beth says, 'We should invite Daniel, too.' Once Beth says this, Alex can no longer say that Charles is bringing a bottle of wine using the sentence 'He is bringing a bottle of wine.' That's because in the new conversational context created by Beth's utterance about Daniel, the pronoun 'he' will no longer pick out Charles, and will pick out Daniel instead. So there's been a kind of very small-scale silencing of Alex—she can't, as a direct linguistic consequence of what Beth says, use the words she wanted to use to say what she wanted to say.

Of course, this silencing isn't particularly serious, because Alex can just pick an alternative method of saying what she wants to say (for example, by saying 'Charles is bringing a bottle of wine'). But once we see the pattern, we can find more serious examples. We've emphasized in earlier chapters that the meanings of words are often subject to ongoing conversational negotiation and dispute. Suppose that Alex wants to declare exploitation of phobias to be torture, but the conversational negotiation proceeds in a way that shifts the meaning of the word 'torture' so that exploitation of phobias is no longer included under the new meaning. Alex could try to say what she wants to say in a different way. But first, there might be no other way in the language to make her claim. She had been relying on a word 'torture' that had a subtle and complicated meaning whose boundaries had been shaped through a long history of use. She had no way to characterize those boundaries herself, so when the old meaning was taken away through conversational negotiation, she was left with no way to say what she wanted to say. And second, she was also counting on the *lexical effects* of the specific word 'torture'. Part of what she wanted to do in her assertion was to say that exploitation of phobias was torture and invoke the associations of that word in her audience. With the shift in meaning, she's blocked from doing this.

In general, the more we come to think that our language is not a stable tool that we pick up and use, but instead a dynamic and flexible thing that we shape and are shaped by, the more we will come to think that there are many ways that people can be locally silenced—prevented from saying what they want to say by having the linguistic means for saying it yanked out from under them. If it's words of central social import that are particularly likely to be the foci of linguistic negotiation, and if social power differences show up as differences in ability to affect the outcome of that negotiation, then there's a real possibility of malignant silencing as a linguistic act.

It has been suggested that pornography, in addition to performing a speech act of oppression, also performs a speech act of silencing.[1] Suppose that Charles encounters repeated pornographic narratives in which a woman says that she does not want to have sex, but is clearly characterized in the work as actually wanting sex. Charles then comes to believe that there's a social practice of women saying they don't want to have sex when they in fact do. He then ends up in an intimate situation with a woman, who when she's asked if she wants to have sex says 'No, I don't want to have sex.' Charles, as a result of his belief acquired from pornography, doesn't treat this utterance as a real assertion—he takes it to be a bit of play acting involved in the sexual encounter (much like the audience in the play-acting example above). The suggestion is then that the woman has been silenced—she has been prevented from asserting anything in this situation, so that she cannot in fact refuse the sexual encounter.

As with earlier cases, there's no doubt that speech can have *causal consequences* along these lines. Charles could definitely, as a causal consequence of encountering pornographic narratives, be led to *disregard* what the woman says. (How common or likely this sequence of causation is is then a question for sociology rather than for the theory of language.) The question is whether this will count as an illocutionary silencing. Has the woman been silenced, or is she not silenced but ignored in what she says?

Consider Langton and West's discussion of ways in which women can be silenced in sexual contexts:

She may utter words of protest, but her intended move may fail to count as correct play. An example of the latter is provided by the case of Linda Marchiano (Lovelace), who wrote a book, *Ordeal*, intended as an indictment of the pornography industry. In it she tells the story of how she was abducted, beaten, tortured,

---

[1] Most famously by MacKinnon (1992), but the idea has been explored by a number of philosophers in recent years, including Langton (199), McGowan (2003), and Maitra (2009).

and hypnotized in order to perform her starring role in the successful porno-graphic film 'Deep Throat'. Now although *Ordeal* was meant to be a protest against the pornography industry, it has in fact been marketed *as pornography*. This case appears to be one example in a familiar pattern to be found in the language games of many, including the sex offenders who twist women's words—who 'always reinterpret the behavior of their victims [and] will say the victim encouraged them, or seduced them, or asked for it, or wanted it, or enjoyed it'.

Women often find themselves unable to alter the score of language games in the ways that they intend—and find themselves altering the score in ways they did not intend—in both public and private sexual conversations, conversations whose score includes the presupposition, introduced and reinforced by pornog-raphy, that a woman's no often means yes. A woman's testimony in court about sexual violence and sexual harassment often goes awry. Judges and juries some-times acquit men of sexually-related charges on the grounds that the victim was wearing a short skirt and so 'asking for it', or—in cases where the alleged offence was photographed or filmed—that she looked like she was enjoying it, or that, despite her words, she couldn't really have been refusing. In the private contexts of date rape, a woman's 'no' sometimes fails to count as correct play—fails to count as the refusal it was intended to be.

(Langton and West (1999): 313–14, reprinted in Langton (2009): 188)

All of these distressing things can and do happen. But many of these examples look like examples of what we have called *ignoring*, rather than *silencing*. The problem in many of these cases is not that the women are *unable* to speak, but rather that when they do speak, they are not listened to. (It has been observed that a worrying consequence of the view that women in these situations are silenced is that it requires denying women's claims that they *did* refuse. A view that says instead that their refusal was ignored doesn't have that consequence.) If that's right, then these aren't uniformly cases in which malignant social effects are a direct consequence of language.

As with the cases of oppressing, it does look like it's *possible* to have real cases of silencing along these lines. Words, for example, are often highly context-sensitive in their meanings. If pornographic works enter into the ongoing process of linguistic negotiation to shift the meaning of 'no' so that in specifically sexual situations, it means 'yes', then there would be real silencing occurring—people would have the linguistic tools of refusal taken away from them. Whether it's plausible that porno-graphic works could have this effect is then a question that would need to be answered by a full theory of linguistic negotiation.

CENTRAL POINTS IN CHAPTER 10

- We have considered, in previous chapters, ways of linguistically wronging people: by insulting them or using slurs to describe them. These are essentially linguistic acts: you can't slur someone without language. In this chapter, we consider using language as a means to effect not-necessarily-linguistic wrongs. We concentrate on two such wrongs: oppression, and silencing. You can oppress someone by locking them up; you can silence someone by cutting out their tongue. But we consider oppressing and silencing by saying things.

- We began by briefly running through some material from the theory of speech acts. We introduced the distinction between the locutionary, the illocutionary, and the perlocutionary dimensions of speech. In saying something, one often performs three different sorts of acts. The most obvious is that one says something with a particular content: this is the locutionary act. But one can also do something in saying the thing one says: by saying 'I'll drive you to the airport' you *promise* to drive someone to the airport. In saying 'I thee wed' you wed the person. These sorts of acts—promisings and weddings—are illocutionary acts. Finally, one performs a perlocutionary act: these are the things that one does by saying something. By saying 'I thee wed,' for example, you (hopefully!) make the addressee happy. But you don't simply make them happy in so saying.

- It should be obvious that one can perlocutionarily oppress someone by saying something. If the king says 'Increase the taxes!' he thereby oppresses his citizens (provided the order is obeyed and the taxes are collected). An interesting question is whether one can *illocutionarily* oppress someone. McGowan thinks so: if a restaurant owner says, 'Anyone who serves black people will be fired,' she argues, they illocutionarily make it impermissible for black people to eat at the restaurant, and being unable to eat at a restaurant is a form of oppression. We queried whether that's the right way to explain this case, and noted that it is important to get right about such things. If it is an illocutionary effect, then it might have ramifications for our theory of free speech.

- We went on to consider one purported instance of linguistic oppression that has been the subject of quite a lot of debate, namely pornography. The idea here is that pornography presupposes that it's permissible to treat women as sex objects—that as a viewer one *can't understand* what is going on in pornography without making that assumption, and so one does make it. We considered various ways of understanding the notion of permissibility at issue in the above sentence such that what pornography presupposes manages to oppress women.

- We then turned to a second form of not-necessarily-linguistic wronging, namely silencing, and again considered whether one can achieve it illocutionarily (one can certainly silence perlocutionarily). Can you silence someone in saying something? Again, we considered the case of pornography, where it's been argued, essentially, that pornography presupposes that a woman's 'no's in fact mean 'yes', the thought being that this silences women by preventing them from saying no to a sexual advance. We asked whether, in a case in which a women says no to sex but her partner acts as if she hadn't, we should say that's because she has in fact been prevented from saying no (and so silenced), or because she is able to say it but has been ignored.

Further Reading and Exercises

FURTHER READING FOR CHAPTER 10

The classic and at least superficially readable work on speech acts is Austin (1962). A useful overview is Green (2017). A highly relevant recent anthology of papers is Fogal, Harris, and Moss (2018). Langton (1993), Hornsby (1995), and Langton and West (1999) are seminal on pornography as speech. Wieland (2007), and references therein, is helpful on the sort of authority pornographers would require. Langton (2009) contains several helpful papers responding to objections to the pornography as oppressive/silencing speech view. Saul and Diaz-Leon (2018) is a good overview and bibliography of topics in this area.

Comprehension Questions

1. What is it to oppress someone?
2. What is the difference between locutionary, illocutionary, and perlocutionary acts?
3. I look at my new lizard and say:
   * I name you Betsy

Betsy is the name of my mother, who is in the room. What are the locutionary, illocutionary, and perlocutionary acts I have performed?

4. Explain why some think that pornography linguistically oppresses. Do you agree?
5. What is silencing? Are you often silenced?

Exploratory Questions

6. We suggested that any presupposing imposed by pornography might be more similar to the presupposing works of fiction do than the presupposition language does. What do you think? Are there significant differences between presupposing

in fiction and presupposing in language? What are they? Is pornography better thought of as fiction or as language, or as yet something else?

7. Do you think that pornography silences women or causes them to be ignored (or neither)? What about pornography aimed at gay men or women?

8. Why is it important to get clear one way or the other about this?

11

The Speech Act of Consent

The cluster of questions we'll be concerned with in this last chapter include: What *is* it to give consent? What *should* it be to give consent? What are the conditions under which one can or should give consent?

Recall again the idealizations in Chapter 1. They focus on speakers who utter sentences in order to convey information to each other. That's one thing speakers can do with language. Throughout this book, we have looked at a variety of other things that speakers can do with language (implicate, presuppose, lie, bullshit, obfuscate, insult, slur, etc.) This chapter is about another thing we can do with words: consent. A very simplistic view of consent takes it to be a speech act whereby we agree that something is true. If that were true, it would involve minimal divergence from the idealized picture. However, the simplistic picture is a mistake. As we will see, a deeper understanding of the phenomenon will reveal consent as a massively complex, hard to understand, and essentially controversial issue. In understanding the nature of consent we can draw on many of the lessons from earlier in the book. Our conclusion will be that much of the controversy surrounding consent will remain unresolved by an investigation into language and speech acts. The lesson will be that the nature of consent is dynamic and continuously up for negotiation: linguistic investigation will reveal no stable essence. If we want to understand this part of language, the idealizations again fall short.

11.1 Paradigms of Consent: Home-Visits, Medical Procedures, Consent Forms, and Sex

We start with some illustrations to help identify the phenomenon. There are indefinitely many instances of consenting to various things, and a central claim below is they might not have very much in common, or at least that the aim of finding a common core they all share is misguided.

Paradigm 1: Letting people enter your home. Consider something as commonplace as letting a person into your home. Imagine walking with someone, remembering that you have to pick something up at home, then stopping by, letting your friend come into your home. In so doing, you are consenting to your friend being in your home. Here are some notable features of such cases:

(i)   The consent is often tacit. Walking together and opening the door for the friend can constitute consent. Giving consent doesn't have to take the form of saying: 'I agree to you entering my home right now.'

(ii) There are massive restrictions on the consent: minimally, the friend can assume that she has been given permission to stand inside your home. It would also be natural to think that she is allowed to sit down on relevant and salient furniture and also to move around a bit. But there are limits: the friend hasn't been tacitly invited to fall asleep in your bed, raid your refrigerator, look through your drawers, or take a shower. The range of admissible actions associated with inviting someone into your house will vary between contexts and cultures.

Paradigm 2: Medical exams and treatments. When we enter a doctor's office, we tacitly agree to let the doctor do things to us that other people are not allowed to do. The doctor can touch us, ask us to undress, put needles in us, etc. In the case of medical treatments, we encounter a range of tacit and explicit consents. In some litigious countries, medical procedures require a great deal of explicit consent. In other cultures and at other times, visiting the doctor involves tacit agreement to a wide range of actions. What's within the range of admissible actions is often unclear and a matter of dispute.

Paradigm 3: Signing agreements online. In order to use various internet services we have to sign consent forms. This type of consent differs radically from the cases discussed above. The consent forms are often very long texts written in a technical language that few of us would fully understand. We are asked/required to express our consent to what it says by clicking a little button next to 'I agree'. None of us read and understand all those texts: it is in fact humanly impossible to read everything that we consent to. Researchers at Carnegie Mellon found that it would take each of us around seventy-six full workdays to read the whole text of the various privacy policies we consent to each year.[1] None of us can spend that time. Moreover, if we did, we could not understand most of it.

Paradigm 4: Sex. This is an area where the debate about consent is intense. There's little agreement, the stakes and emotions are high, and the intellectual challenges immense. The issue is closely related to how we are to understand the nature of rape because a natural definition of 'rape' is non-consensual sex. A crucial component of understanding when someone has been raped is to know the answer to the question: 'What constitutes sexual consent?' Settling this issue is not just an intellectual exercise. It has massive practical implications. As a result, all legal systems have put effort into defining sexual consent. The definition of consent varies between countries, and even within countries: for example, in the US, there are great variations between states. Institutions such as universities have also had to decide on definitions. The results are varied and constantly evolving. We'll give just a few illustrations here. The first is from Harvard University. Their Office of Sexual Assault Prevention & Response gives the following definition (as of August 2017):

Consent is:

- an ongoing physical and emotional process between people who are willing, equally free of coercion, communicating unambiguously, and sincere in their desires.
- a mutual agreement to be fully present with one another throughout all interactions, to prioritize both yourself and your partner's needs, and to understand that someone may choose to disengage from the experience at any time.
- knowing and feeling—without a doubt—that the other person is excited to engage with you in whatever activities you agree upon, regardless of whether the experience is amazing or mediocre.

We can be confident that a great deal of effort went into reflecting on this definition, both because Harvard cares about its students' extracurricular lives and because important legal issues are at stake. The definition has a number of striking features: it implies that one cannot consent to a sexual activity one isn't excited by (so it is, according to this definition, *impossible* to consent to non-excited sex). The definition also requires that consensual sexual partners communicate unambiguously, though it

---

[1] <https://www.theatlantic.com/technology/archive/2012/03/reading-the-privacy-policies-you-encounter-in-a-year-would-take-76-work-days/253851/.>

is left unclear how much unambiguous communication is required and the notion of 'communication' is not defined.

It's interesting to compare this to a similar institution's effort to define consent. Yale University's rule as of August 2017 focuses primarily on continuous explicit consent:

> Under Yale's policies, sexual activity requires affirmative consent, which is defined as positive, unambiguous, and voluntary agreement to engage in specific sexual activity throughout a sexual encounter. Consent cannot be inferred from the absence of a 'no'; a clear 'yes', verbal or otherwise, is necessary. Consent to some sexual acts does not constitute consent to others, nor does past consent to a given act constitute present or future consent. Consent must be ongoing throughout a sexual encounter and can be revoked at any time.

So Yale explicitly rules out tacit consent. Importantly, it requires explicit consent to *every* sexual act. A lot will depend on how one individuates sexual acts: is each kiss a new sexual act? If so, it looks like the administrators at Yale advocate a view where most sexual encounters will consist mostly of a massive amount of affirmative consenting. If not, sexual partners are put in the very difficult situation of tacitly agreeing on what counts as a new sexual act.

11.2 Some Questions about Consent

The examples above illustrate the varieties of consent, and the disagreements that can arise in connection with each of them. The disagreement between Yale, Harvard, and others about what constitutes sexual consent can be replicated in the other cases. What can philosophy, and philosophy of language in particular, contribute to this debate? We think that's a largely open question and in what follows we address three sets of issues:

1. The nature of tacit consent: how one can communicate something by not doing something (and how not doing something is different from doing nothing).
2. How to characterize the content of consent (whether it be tacit or explicit).
3. Whether deception can undermine consent.

Before moving on, we should mention that there's a small minority of philosophers and legal theorists who deny that consent is a speech act. On this alternative view, consent doesn't require any form of communication: to have a consenting-intention is sufficient for consenting (even if this consenting intention isn't communicated). To see why this view is wrong, consider the following exchange:

Stage 1: A asks: 'Can I use your car today?'

Stage 2: B thinks about it, goes back and forth a bit, and then decides, without speaking, that it would be ok if A used his car.

Stage 3: B says: 'That's fine, you can use it.'

Whatever intention or thought went through B's head at Stage 2, the following is true about that stage:

(i) B has not yet agreed to let A use his car

(ii) B has not given his consent

(iii) if for some reason Stage 3 never occurred, even B can't say later: I gave her permission to use my car

(iv) all that's true at Stage 2 is that B intends or plans to, or has decided to, consent to A using the car.

This case shows that it's clearly insufficient for consent to occur that one merely have a consenting-intention.

11.2.1 Tacit consent: perils and advantages

We have to distinguish between (i) non-communicated consent and (ii) consent that is communicated tacitly. For example opening the door for someone and letting them in is a tacit, non-verbal, way to consent to someone entering a home. Taking off your shirt at the doctor's office can be a sign of tacit consent to the doctor putting a stethoscope on your body. Often, not performing an act, or not objecting to the performance of an act, can be a tacit sign of consent. If A is invited into B's home, and sits down on a chair, then B's not objecting is a sign of consent that it is okay for A to sit on that chair. When consent is given tacitly, much of what is permitted and what is not permitted is left non-explicit. The consent for you to walk on the floor has been given tacitly, and it's understood that letting you in isn't a license to raid the refrigerator and take a shower. Some of the same is true in a doctor's office: in most countries, patients are not presented with lists of permissible and impermissible acts to give explicit consent to. On the other hand, we have seen that in the case of two people having sex, the administrators at Yale University think that explicit consent is required for every new act and for every moment of the sexual act. The Yale proposal, taken literally, is absurd because you can't literally ask for consent every new moment—there has to be some time limit. And you can't literally ask for consent for every new movement you make during sex—there has to be a restriction on what counts as a new act. Nonetheless, there are reasons why it's important to be explicit in many cases. In what follows we briefly look at what might seem to be advantages of explicit consent over implicit consent.

11.2.2   The difficulty of distinguishing between tacit consent and silencing

It is difficult to tell the difference between tacit consent and an inability to object. Here is how the philosopher Eric Swanson puts the point:

> Consider the slogan 'Silence is consent.' This has a natural reading on which it says that we should voice our objections—if we do not, we are passively consenting to practices we may abhor. This sounds plausible enough when it would be genuinely feasible for those who are silent to express their dissent. But it's clearly wrong when one is coerced into not saying S. For example, silence clearly does not constitute or implicate consent to sexual activity if the silent party has been coerced into silence.   (Swanson forthcoming)

It helps here to distinguish between (i) *being silenced* (unable to perform the action of speaking) and (ii) *being silent* (choosing not to speak). The latter is in effect to perform an action—to choose to not say something. The former is to not perform an action (because one is prevented from speaking up). In general, we need to distinguish between *performing the action of not doing A*, and *not performing the action of doing A*. An analogy might help. Suppose Nora has the following job: she checks if there's danger around the camp and if there is danger she has to lower our flag (that is currently flying high). On the first day she looks around, finds no danger, leaves the flag up, and so communicates that there is no danger. The second day, she forgets about her job, she doesn't look around and she forgets about the whole flag business. In this latter case she hasn't lowered the flag, as in the first case, but on the other hand, she has not performed the action of not lowering the flag.

In many cases we want to figure out whether a person is silenced or being silent, and it can be very hard to tell the difference. Swanson draws on work by Miranda Fricker for some strategies for improving our communicative and interpretive abilities in these respects. Swanson says:

What should we do when omissions *might* be the result of coercion? Miranda Fricker suggests that 'virtuous hearers' can sometimes 'help generate a more inclusive hermeneutical micro-climate' through a dialogue that 'involves a more pro-active and more socially aware kind of listening than is usually required in more straightforward communicative exchanges. This sort of listening involves listening as much to what is *not* said as to what is said' (2007, pp. 171–2). When this is not possible, Fricker goes on to suggest, a virtuous hearer can try '*reserving* judgement, so that the hearer keeps an open mind as to credibility'.

(Swanson forthcoming)

Does the problem of distinguishing silencing from being silent show that explicit consent is in some sense better than implicit consent? One might think that tacit consent is too easily confused with silencing (or that it's too hard to distinguish between being silenced and being silent)—and maybe insistence on explicit consent (as at Yale University) can help to alleviate that problem. This, however, might be too quick a conclusion. Just as silence can be forced, speech can be forced. Consider someone who utters the words 'yes' or 'I agree', but does so because of being coerced (in much the same way someone can stay silent because of being silenced). Rachel McKinney talks about what she calls 'extracted speech' and coerced consent to illustrate the phenomenon:

One version of extracted speech already familiar to moral philosophers is that of coerced 'consent' to sexual activity. Sarah Conly, for instance, describes the case of Tess in *Tess of the d'Urbervilles*. On Conly's interpretation of the story, Tess is worn down by Alec d'Urberville's persistence, flattery, subterfuge, and psychological pressure, finally relenting (on Conly's view, consenting) to have sex with him. Lois Pineau, arguing for a conclusion opposite to Conly's, describes a similar interaction between two young people on a date: the young man needles, cajoles, guilts, and shames the young woman into having (unpleasant) sex that she otherwise has no interest in.   (McKinney (2016): 261)

So if the move to explicitness is done to alleviate the worry about forced consent, it's unclear that we have made much progress.

11.3 The Imprecision/Vagueness of Implicit Consent

Another worry about tacit consent is that it is vague and imprecise. It's unclear exactly what is being agreed to and for how long. When you let someone into your home, are you tacitly allowing her to touch or look into a book on your table? To sit down on the floor? To stretch out on the floor? There's obviously a range of unclear and unsettled cases. Sex is of course a very salient domain where this imprecision becomes significant and often litigated. The imprecision might, in part, be what underlies the Yale definition of consent: it insists on the participants giving explicit consent for each new moment in time and for each sexual act (each new kiss and touch, presumably). More generally, one might think that the content of an implicit consent is typically so imprecise that if there are high stake actions involved (where significant damage can be done if something goes wrong), we're better off making the content of the consent explicit.

This line of thought is tempting, but we think ultimately it's unconvincing. Even if we were to agree that imprecision in what is consented to is a drawback, it is a mistake to think that making consent explicit will reduce imprecision. On the contrary, making it explicit can often *increase* imprecision. Here is a way to see that: we have *practices* that enable us to recognize consent and what is consented to. As participants in those practices we have developed abilities to recognize what constitutes tacit consent within those practices. Illustration:

> *Illustration of our ability to tacitly recognize what is permitted*: when letting someone into your house, you're able to recognize acts that are permitted (covered by the consent), and very many things that are impermissible (not covered by the consent). As lifelong participants in this practice, we have developed such recognitional capacities which enable us to make such judgments without much reflection.

Note that if we were asked to make these rules explicit, we might simply be incapable of doing so. The practice may be too complex, too subtle, for us to articulate it into words. Making it explicit would make us worse off, not better: the language would likely be less precise and more vague than our tacit abilities are.

Trying to make our practices of consenting explicit is similar to trying to make our ability to ride a bike explicit: we can ride a bike effortlessly, but were we to write down the rules for bike-riding and act in accordance with those rules, we couldn't do it. Our ability to recognize consent is often like that: it's better left implicit and any effort to make it explicit will reduce precision and clarity. Tacit consent that is embedded in an established practice can be infinitely superior to anything we can do with words.

None of this is to say that explicit consent is never an advantage: in certain legal contexts, it's unavoidable, and in many other contexts it might be helpful to make the content of the consent explicit. This is especially so in contexts where there is no agreed and shared practice. Where sexual intercourse lies on this spectrum, we will leave for the reader to reflect on.

What the points above suggest is that making the content of tacit consent explicit is difficult, often impossible, and often pointless. One way to see this is to note that, in general, it's very hard to make explicit the content of desire. A case (based on Delia Graff Fara (2013)) that illustrates this:

Suppose Emilia tells you she wants an apple. You give her an apple, but it's poisoned. Did you give her what she wanted? Not really. She didn't want a poisoned apple. Well, what exactly did she want? A normal apple. Many normal apples have worms in them. Did she want that? Did she want one covered in ketchup? Saying exactly what Emilia wanted is hard.

John Searle illustrates this with the example of someone who orders a hamburger at a restaurant ((1994): 641). He's served a hamburger, but it's enclosed in cement. Did he get what he ordered? In both cases, there's an inclination to say that the real content is richer than just 'an apple' or 'a hamburger'. However, it's impossible to fill out either of those desires' descriptions so that no such deviant cases can be constructed. There are just too many 'weird' ways to give someone an apple. To explicitly rule them all out is something we don't know how to do. Nonetheless, we're able to easily recognize when someone got an apple or a hamburger. It's an ability we have, but one that we can't put into words. The relevance of this to consent is the following: If we were to try to make what we consent to when we consent, say to sex, fully explicit, we just couldn't do it. In many cases it is better to rely on our abilities to recognize what we consented to. That, however, is not to say that this strategy won't result in very complex and controversial cases (where there's fundamental and high-stakes disagreement about what has been consented to). This might be inevitable.

11.4 Can Deception Invalidate Consent?

A allows B to come into her home. Suppose the consent was based on certain assumptions about B, for example, that B is an exterminator.

Question: What if B has misrepresented herself and she isn't really an exterminator? B has been deceptive and the deception triggered the consent. One thing is clear about this case: other things being equal, B can be blamed in some way for deceiving A. But that's not the interesting point for our purposes. The question we're now focusing on is this: Can that kind of deception *invalidate* A's consent? Can the result of deception be that A didn't really consent? Note that if we say 'yes' to that, then in this case B is not only deceptive, she is also trespassing (since A never genuinely consented to letting B enter the house—there was the illusion of consent, but the deception stands in the way of real consent).

Here is the sexual analog of that question: Can misrepresentation by one sexual partner have as a consequence that the other partner didn't consent? If so, it means that the sex was non-consensual and that has potentially important legal implications. This kind of issue has been litigated. Tom Dougherty gives the following example:

Even though April Fool's day is an inauspicious day for a wedding, you still would not expect the marriage to end with the bride suing the Cuban government for non-consensual sex. Yet that was the conclusion of Ana Margarita Martinez's marriage to Juan Pablo Roque, after he left their Florida residence, never to return (Bragg 1999). The mystery of his disappearance was resolved a few days later when he appeared on television broadcast from Havana, unveiling himself as an undercover spy sent to infiltrate the dissident community in the United States. This was surprising, and unwelcome, news to Martinez, who thought she had married a fellow dissident. Consequently, she filed a lawsuit about the deception against his employer. Since Cuba was not accustomed to defending itself in Florida's courts, it did not contest the suit, and Martinez was awarded millions of dollars in damages. Part of her case was based on her claim that the fraud meant that she did not give valid consent to sex with Roque. As her lawyer put it, 'She would not have given her consent, had she known.' (Dougherty (2018))

Cases where consent to medical procedures is based on fraudulent information are frequently litigated. We can ask the same kind of question there: is the crime in such cases the fraudulent presentation of the procedure, or *also* that the procedure was performed without the patient's consent (since the fraudulent information invalidated (or canceled) the consent)?

The issues raised here are complex and the complexities are illustrated by the sexual consent case: many sexual encounters are engaged in by partners who have false (or very little) information about each other. Many people who have sex meet somewhere, talk briefly, and then have sex.

In those kinds of encounters, the participants often lie about who they are or what they do. Nonetheless, we typically don't think that undermines consent and no jurisdiction treats all such misinformation as the basis for an accusation of sexual assault (because consent is invalidated by the false information). That, however, doesn't mean that *no* misinformation can invalidate consent. When (if ever) is consent invalidated by misinformation? It's an open question and we know of no clear and precise answer.[2] The reason why there's no such answer might be explained by the view we outline in the next section: the Dynamic Conception of Consent.

11.5 The Dynamic Conception of Consent

This chapter has already given illustrations of consent from different domains. If one thought that 'consent' denoted an immutable and fixed kind of act, one would start looking for what all these cases have in common and aim to come up with a set of context-insensitive necessary and sufficient conditions for an act's being one of consent. A philosopher engaged in such a project would think that there is an essence to consent, and the philosopher's aim is to articulate this eternal essence. As should be clear from our discussion of conceptual engineering, we think that this is a mistaken view of both concepts and language. Many of our concepts are constantly in flux and are being negotiated in particular contexts for particular purposes. Consent is clearly one such notion. The various instances of consent that we have outlined above differ and there might not be a common core to all of them. What consent is will vary between cultures and between contexts within cultures. So our goal is not to find the essence of consent. Instead our goal should be to articulate issues and features that are useful to engage with in many contexts where consent is being negotiated.

On this view, philosophy of language—e.g., the study of the meaning of 'consent'—will do nothing to settle for example the issue of whether consent can be invalidated by deception. What philosophy of language

---

[2] For a helpful discussion of both the legal and philosophical issues (as far as sex is concerned) see Rubenfeld (2013) and the response paper Dougherty (2013). The law is clearer when it comes to, e.g., entering a house by deception. See the first few pages of Rubenfeld and its references.

will tell you is that the notion is dynamic: in some contexts a certain act (e.g., Juan having sex with Ana) will be considered an action of coercion, and in other contexts it can be considered consensual. That depends on how 'consent' is fixed in those varied contexts. No one way of fixing the meaning is more linguistically correct than the others. One way of fixing the meaning of 'consent' might be morally superior to the others, but that's an issue settled by moral reflections, not by an investigation into the speech act of consenting.

What we are advocating here is not a form of relativism about truth. It is not that the truth of 'Ana didn't consent' can vary between contexts. What follows from the dynamic view is that the meaning of, for example, the sentence 'Ana didn't consent' can vary in meaning between contexts (depending on contextual negotiations). So what is said in different contexts will be different. Given the different meanings, it is possible that a speaker can say something true by uttering 'Ana didn't consent' in context C, and another can say something false by uttering 'Ana didn't consent' in context C*. This is no more surprising than that 'The ball is to the left' can be true for one person and false for another. That's not a form of relativism about truth, but instead a corollary of the fact that meanings can vary between contexts.[3]

11.6 Consent as an Illustration of How the Idealizations Fail

According to the idealizations in Chapter 1, communication is essentially a tool for the cooperative exchange of information. What we have seen in this chapter is yet another illustration of the shortcoming of that picture. Saying 'I agree' or 'Yes' is often to allow people to do things to you. What you have let them do to you will depend on complex and largely tacit practices and abilities we have. These are often impossible to make explicit. The idealized picture doesn't answer important practical questions such as:

- What has been consented to?
- What constitutes tacit assent?
- Is explicit consent better than tacit consent?
- Can false information invalidate consent?

[3] For more on relativism see Cappelen & Huvenes (forthcoming).

One thing to say in favor of the idealized picture is this: maybe the answer to these and related questions should not be answered by a theory of language or communication. Maybe they are best treated as political or moral questions, to be settled not by the study of language, but by some other fields. One worry we have about that answer is that it delineates 'language' and 'communication' too narrowly and that what it leaves behind is insufficiently connected to the real world of people speaking. We have more to say about this in the last chapter, where we reflect further on the relationship between ideal and non-ideal theories of language and communication.

CENTRAL POINTS IN CHAPTER 11

- In this chapter, we consider the speech act of consent. This is a topic of intrinsic social importance but it is also a useful case study in the way that words have extra-linguistic consequences (to consent is often to let someone do things to you), and in how the idealized model of communication we sketched in the first chapter falls short.
- We began by considering four paradigms of consent: letting people into your home, undergoing medical treatments, agreeing to websites' terms and conditions, and sex. We pointed out that each of these familiar phenomena, when looked at closely, poses difficult questions. We then went on to consider some important questions about consent.
- It's important that one can tacitly consent, just because obtaining explicit consent for everything would be incredibly time-consuming and pointless (if you invite someone into your home, should you say 'I consent for you to stand in the living room and sit in the living room and use the bathroom and . . . but not eat from the fridge and not take a shower and not . . . '?).
- Nevertheless, explicit consent is also clearly important. One concern is that tacit consent might be confused with silencing: in particular, someone's silence could be interpreted as tacit consent whereas in fact it is a result of their being silenced. If that's a risk in a particular case, we should opt for explicit consent in that case.
- Another worry with tacit consent is that it is vague and imprecise. It will often be unclear to what precisely one has tacitly consented. We noted that one might think this again supplies an argument for explicit consent, but again noted that things aren't so simple. Sometimes explicit consent can increase imprecision and vagueness. This might be because making what is consented to implicitly explicit is too difficult, or it might interfere with our familiar and for the most part successful practice of implicitly consenting to things.

- We went on to consider whether deception can invalidate consent. We noted that in some salient cases, people have tried to make the argument that this is so. But we also noted that holding that deception invalidates consent will give counterintuitive verdicts for many cases. If two people meet in a bar or on Tinder, they may misrepresent or even outright lie about themselves in greater or smaller ways. If they consent to and have sex, should the fact that they've lied to each other invalidate their consent? Arguably, no, although there is certainly room for debate.
- We ended by putting forward our own view about consent: that it's a dynamic phenomenon, which is different in different circumstances. There is no fixed essence of consent. We tied things up by considering how the idealized model of language gives us little guidance as to the nature of consent and the speech act of consenting.

Further Reading and Exercises

FURTHER READING FOR CHAPTER 11

A recent anthology on consent is Müller and Schaber (2018). Alexander (2014) defends the claim, which we didn't spend much time on, that consent is not a speech act but a mental state. See also Manson (2016) for discussion of what kind of thing consent is. For consent in bioethics, which we didn't concentrate on, see the overview article Eyal 2012 and references therein. Dougherty (2013) argues that deception vitiates consent; for a response and discussion see Liberto (2017).

Comprehension Questions

1. Did you consent to anything while going about your daily business before reading this text/sitting in this class?
2. We gave some paradigms of consent. Give some more.
3. You give someone your phone to look at a photo of your cat. You thereby give them permission to touch and look at your phone. You do not thereby give them permission to swipe to the next photo in your camera roll. This seems like an example of quite precise tacit consent-granting. Can you think of any other such precise tacit consent-granting?
4. Are there other speech acts we can tacitly perform? Can we tacitly assert, promise, or name, for example?

5. We argued that making consent explicit will often interfere with our well-understood tacit consent granting practice. Give an example of this.

6. Sex is clearly a very important domain in which tacit consent is important. Can you think of other domains in which tacit communication is so fraught?

Exploratory Questions

7. Do you think there's a clear answer to whether, if you let someone into your home who has misrepresented themselves, your consent is rendered invalid by their misrepresentation?

8. What are the conditions under which you can give consent on behalf of others?

12

Thoughts on Ideal vs Non-Ideal Theories of Language

We began this book with a simple picture of how theorizing about language is often driven by a number of idealizing assumptions about language, language users, and language use. From that starting point, we have gone on to examine a wide variety of decidedly non-ideal ways in which language gets used. Where then does this leave theorizing about language? Are theories of how languages work under idealized conditions a waste of time, since real language use never occurs under ideal conditions? Or are these theories good first steps toward an eventual improved theory of language that deals with both ideal and non-ideal conditions? Or, again, are theories of ideal languages perfectly fine in their own right, a theoretical enterprise to be kept separate from the very different project of constructing something like a total theory of psychology that will handle all the messy details of what people actually *do* with the languages?

Before trying to answer these questions about language, we'll spend some time thinking about the role that idealization plays in other areas—both natural sciences and social sciences. This will lead us to distinguish two importantly different kinds of idealization and to reach some conclusions about when these kinds of idealization do and don't make sense. With these tools in hand, we'll wrap up by returning to language and then we'll say something about the above questions in light of those tools.

12.1 Are Idealized Theories Absurd?

Suppose you've been feeling a bit under the weather and so pay a visit to your doctor. He runs a few blood tests and comes back to the examination room. The following dialog ensues:

DOCTOR: Looks like a case of the marthambles. I'm prescribing a course of azoth for you.

YOU: Will that fix me up?

DOCTOR (AFTER A PAUSE): Well, azoth completely cures the marthambles under ideal conditions. Of course, your body doesn't present ideal conditions. Nothing personal—none of our bodies present ideal conditions. All these other chemicals are floating about in them.

YOU: So what happens when azoth is used under non-ideal conditions?

DOCTOR: Oh, I have no idea. I'm a doctor of ideal medicine. My medical theory deals entirely in questions of what happens under ideal conditions; it's silent about curing diseases under non-ideal conditions.

YOU: Um, thanks. I think I'll go get a second opinion.

When you go for a second opinion, the new doctor agrees that it's marthambles, but thankfully isn't interested in treatment with azoth. Instead, she decides that your marthambles are advanced enough that you need heart surgery. You pick a local surgeon, but when you go in for a preliminary appointment, you end up in another peculiar conversation:

YOU: I need heart surgery as a result of marthambles.

SURGEON: Oh, I'm afraid I don't operate on hearts.

YOU: What kind of surgery do you do? Brain? Eye? Liver?

SURGEON: Oh, none of those. I specialize in surgery on the corona pollentia.

YOU: The corona pollentia? I don't think I've heard of that.

SURGEON: Well, I'm not too surprised. It's an organ that could only be found in a person who had developed under ideal conditions. Wouldn't actually be a human being, strictly speaking, I suppose. It's just as well that no one actually has a corona pollentia, I guess. The surgical procedures require instruments made of a metal that's only created under ideal astronomical conditions that don't occur in our non-ideal universe.

Considering examples like this can make it seem that the idea of 'ideal conditions medicine' is a pretty silly one. It's silly, we might think, because we want doctors to *do* something. A doctor who can only recommend treatments that won't actually work for us, or who can only operate on organs we don't actually have, is *useless*. Similarly, the engineer who tells you that she can build a bridge that supports traffic under ideal conditions, but may or may not collapse immediately under real non-ideal conditions, doesn't seem like much of an engineer, and the bridge certainly isn't of much use. The central concern here is:

> **The Prediction Worry**: One of the things we want from theories is the ability to make reliable predictions about what is going to happen. But if our theory is limited to telling us what happens under ideal conditions, then we won't be able to use it to make predictions about what happens under non-ideal conditions. Since real conditions are typically non-ideal, we'll be left with a theory that's useless for predictive purposes.

This is what's disturbing about the doctor prescribing azoth for the marthambles. His theory makes him unable to predict what the medicine will do under the non-ideal conditions that the actual patient presents, and we don't want to be treated by a doctor who is unable to predict what the treatment will do.

12.2 Prediction and Galilean Idealization

The Prediction Worry isn't always a serious worry. Science is full of idealizations that don't interfere with our doing useful things with the results of the science—in fact, often the idealizations are *essential* for doing the useful things. To take an example that wears its idealization on its sleeve, consider the ideal gas law. The ideal gas law tells us that the pressure and temperature of a gas are directly proportional (when one doubles, the other doubles as well), that the volume and temperature of a gas are directly proportional, and that the pressure and volume of a gas are inversely proportional (when one halves, the other doubles). The ideal gas law is an idealization. It is derived by assuming that gases are made up of point-size particles that don't exert any force on each other except when colliding. Real gases aren't like that, and thus the behavior of real gases doesn't conform to the ideal gas law. However, in many cases the difference between what the ideal gas law predicts and the way the actual gas behaves is very small. And getting a more accurate prediction is very difficult. We need to take into account an enormous number of facts about the sizes of the various gas molecules and the way those sizes affect the collisions among the molecules. Those facts are close to impossible to get in the first place, and the mathematics needed to figure out how they affect the gas behavior vastly exceeds the capacities of our best computers. In practice, then, the predictions from the ideal gas law may be the best we can do.

Of course, 'the best we can do' isn't very interesting if that best isn't very good. Your doctor may be doing the best he can do in prescribing azoth, but that's no reassurance and no reason to pay attention to the doctor's prescription. But we don't always need *perfect* predictions. If we're trying to build a refrigerator and the ideal gas law lets us get a close estimate of what temperature the coolant will reach if we expand its volume, we will have what we need to make something that keeps food acceptably cold. If the refrigerator's final temperature is a tiny fraction of a degree off of what the ideal gas law predicts, it won't matter for our practical purposes.

Michael Weisberg (2007), in discussing types of idealization in scientific theory, identifies a category of *Galilean idealizations*. Galilean idealizations are idealizing assumptions that make calculating predictions from the theory easier to do. Galilean idealizations are *risky* when we are using our sciences. The divergence of the idealized prediction from what actually happens may not matter when we're just building a refrigerator, because it's not important exactly how cold we keep the food, but it could be tremendously important when we're trying to calculate thrust for a rocket, because in this case the divergence could make the difference between the rocket reaching orbit or not, or between the fuel container exploding or not.

12.3 Understanding and Minimalist Idealization

Galilean idealization can make sense when our goals are practical—if we want to build a bridge, we can use a Galilean idealized theory of bridges so long as the predictive inaccuracies of the idealized theory aren't so large that they threaten to make the bridge collapse. But good predictions aren't the only thing we want from our theories. Evolutionary theory, for example, is notoriously predictively unhelpful. If you want to know what pigeons will look like 10,000 years from now, evolutionary theory isn't going to tell you anything helpful. That doesn't mean that evolutionary theory is useless, though. It's still a good theory, because it lets us retrospectively make sense of what did happen by showing us what the mechanisms were that made things happen as they did. It helps us *understand*, rather than predict.

If our goal in theorizing is to understand rather than to predict, then Galilean idealization doesn't seem well motivated. We can't just overlook some aspect of reality because it's very computationally complicated—it could turn out that that aspect of reality is crucial for really understanding what's going on. But there is another kind of idealization that is common, and perhaps even essential, in building theories meant to help us understand.

Consider the common use of frictionless planes in physics. On a frictionless plane, we can derive results about how objects will move and interact with each other in collisions, without worrying about the further fact that these objects are always slowing down due to friction. Of course, there are no real frictionless planes—a theory of motion on a frictionless plane is an idealized theory. Why would we bother having a theory of how objects move under frictionless conditions that never actually show up? This *could* be another instance of a Galilean idealization— the mathematical computations involved in determining how things will move under frictionless conditions are much easier than the computations involved in determining how things move with friction included. But it's not a very good Galilean idealization. Frictional forces are generally too significant to be simply disregarded. If we try to build cars and roads using a theory in which friction has been idealized away, we (like the idealized cars) will get precisely nowhere.

But there is another *conceptual* reason to disregard friction. Without friction, movement is determined by a small body of information about masses and a few forces, such as gravity, normal forces, and externally applied accelerating forces. We can get a simple and explanatory theory of those forces that help us *understand* why objects move in the ways they do. It won't be a very predictively useful theory. But if we try to improve prediction by including friction, we discover that frictional forces are the result of an enormously complicated collection of facts about tiny details of the shape and composition of the surfaces of objects and the small electrostatic forces that result when those surfaces travel past each other. In that vast hoard of detail we lose sight of the simple general patterns that are made visible through the frictionless generalization. By considering the frictionless plane, we can get a cleaner picture of how motion is influenced by specific factors.

A theory of motion under frictionless conditions is thus theoretically helpful. It's not a theory of the motion of any real objects, but it's a theory of how certain real forces behave—it's idealized in *ignoring* some factors that exist under all real conditions, while examining the behavior of other real forces. Weisberg calls this kind of idealization a *minimalist* idealization (2007). Minimalist idealizations are motivated by a desire for understanding and explanation, not by a desire for predictive utility. If predictions are what we want, we may need to combine the idealized theory with something more like an *art* of producing predictions. We find coefficients of friction not by figuring them out on theoretical grounds, but by actually going into the lab and trying sliding different kinds of objects on each other, and then we use those experimentally determined coefficients of friction to apply a computational fix to the frictionless theory. We aren't getting a real *understanding* of friction out of this—part of the picture here is that frictional forces are too messy and idiosyncratic for there to be much understanding of them—but we're just doing some ad hoc patching of the frictionless theory to let us get some decent predictions out.

12.4 What to Idealize Away?

Minimalist idealization is a risky business. The goal of a minimalist idealization is to look at a messy collection of data and choose certain parts or aspects of that data to disregard as not helpful in understanding what's really going on. We might disregard some specific data points. ('It looks like exposure to someone with the plague causes the plague. That person was exposed and didn't get sick, but we'll write him off as an anomaly.') Or we might disregard certain parts of all of the data points. ('It looks like parent eye color explains offspring eye color, but only if we group eye colors into a few big categories and ignore small variations in hue.') But either way, we will end up with a good theory, one which aids understanding and explanation, only if we make the right choices about what to disregard.

Friction is a good thing for a theoretical scientist to ignore. That's because friction isn't part of the deep joints of reality, but instead is noise obscuring our view of the deep joints of reality. The important categories of forces are (for example) gravitational and electromagnetic forces. Paying attention to frictional forces makes it harder for us to see what's going on with those important forces. But consider another instance of a minimalist idealization. In introductory physics classes, students also spend time learning how objects move under idealized Newtonian conditions, on the assumption that there are no Einsteinian relativistic effects. Later, they're told that this is incorrect, and that the real scientific truth involves Minkowskian spacetimes on which length, mass, and duration are dependent on velocity and frame of reference. Newtonian mechanics is a theory of a universe that doesn't really exist, one obtained by idealizing away bits of the data about how objects at high speed act in slightly unexpected ways.

Interest in Newtonian mechanics can easily be justified as a Galilean idealization. Relativistic theory requires learning conceptually difficult mathematics of non-Euclidean geometries, and it's just easier to start with a theory that uses a familiar Euclidean geometry. And in many situations—when all the objects are moving slowly compared to the speed of light—the Newtonian theory produces pretty good predictions, off by only small amounts. We could also view Newtonian mechanics as a minimalist idealization—the choice, for purposes of understanding and explanation, to disregard relativistic effects. As a minimalist idealization, though, it's not a very good idealization. That's because the relativistic theory is, from a theoretical point of view, much more interesting than the Newtonian theory. The Newtonian theory is a decent starting point, because *some* of the ideas that will be important in a relativistic setting are more or less present in a Newtonian theory. But it is only a stopping point along the way to a relativistic theory of motion. As theoretical scientists, we aren't going to be happy sticking with the Newtonian theory and writing off the relativistic effects as small predictive errors, because that would cause us to misunderstand what reality is really like and what the deep structure of space and time is.

A frictionless theory, on the other hand, isn't just a theoretical stopping point. (You can keep taking more advanced classes in physics without getting to a 'now we always include friction' point.) That's because, roughly, there is no interesting theory of friction. We don't learn more about what the fundamental structure of reality is like by thinking about friction; we just get bogged down in a mass of boring particular facts.

Importantly, there was no way to know in advance that friction could be helpfully minimalist-idealized away and that high-velocity effects could not be helpfully minimalist-idealized away. Sometimes little bits of things turn out to be theoretically central and sometimes they don't. If we're out to understand genetics, idealizing away the details about what's going on in the molecular structure of the cytosol of cells is probably helpful, but idealizing away the details about what's going on in the molecular structure of DNA is a disaster. Again, we can't tell that in advance—we just have to try building theories under different kinds of minimalist idealizations and see which theories end up being powerfully explanatory and get onto important aspects of the structure of reality.

12.5 Ideal and Non-Ideal Theory in the Social Sciences

In the case of natural sciences, we can usually get at least a decent idea about how much our Galilean idealizations distort predictions. But when it comes to the social sciences, it can be much harder to see how much effect Galilean idealizations have. For this reason, political philosophers have worried that idealized theorizing can have a dangerous distorting effect. John Rawls, in discussing the structure of a just society in *A Theory of Justice*, makes two kinds of idealizing assumptions. First, he assumes that there will be complete compliance with the rules of the society. Second, he assumes that the society exists 'under favorable circumstances', with (for example) an adequately educated population in possession of adequate natural resources. In light of these assumptions, he sets out a view of how social structures ought to be organized. But, of course, no real human society is going to meet those Galilean idealizations. That's not a big problem if the right way to organize the real-world non-ideal societies is sufficiently similar to the right way to organize idealized societies—in that case, the theory may offer practical guidance that is good enough. But if the right way to organize a real-world non-ideal society is radically different from the right way to organize an idealized society, then the idealized theory might offer advice that is useless or even damaging.

Consider a toy example. Suppose that one of our idealizations in political theory is that our society is made up of individuals who make rational judgments based on the evidence. That idealization can then lead us to conclude that a good judicial system in that society allows citizens as jurors to have a great deal of freedom in reaching verdicts. But if in our actual non-ideal societies, people's judgments are systematically distorted by various biases about race, gender, wealth, education, and so on, that kind of judicial system might have disastrously unjust effects, and a system that required jurors to consider only certain kinds of evidence and questions might instead be the just way to structure things. As a result, many political theorists have concluded that we should be constructing *non-ideal* rather than *ideal* political theories.

When we move outside the natural sciences to the social sciences, the language of 'ideal' and 'non-ideal' becomes ambiguous and can give rise to confusions. The ideal gas law tells us about the behavior of ideal gases. Ideal gases are *ideal because* they are *idealizations*—they ignore some of the messy and complicated realities of actual gases. But they aren't ideal because they are *especially good gases*. There's nothing about an ideal gas that makes it more of a gas, or a better gas, than actual gases. It's just a simplified case, not in any sense a *perfect* case. But Rawls's idealizations look for ideals in both senses. Rawls's ideal society is, *like* ideal gases, a simplifying idealization. The ideal society is easier to theorize about because it doesn't have messy and complicated features that real societies have. But Rawls's ideal society, *unlike* ideal gases, is also an especially good society. The things that Rawls abstracts away from are various of our imperfections, so he is addressing not only the question 'how should society be structured were we less complicated in various ways?', but also the question 'how should society be structured were we the way we ought to be?'

Call these two notions of idealization *simplifying ideals* and *guiding ideals*. When we use guiding ideals as our simplifying ideals in making Galilean idealizations in our theorizing, there's a special danger of getting sucked into the appeal of ideal theorizing. After all, our political theory aims to tell us how we ought to structure our societies. If there is a guiding ideal for how we ought to be, shouldn't the way we ought to structure our societies be the way societies ought to be structured for people who are the way we ought to be? Shouldn't we strive to make things the way they ought to be for the people we ought to be? Not necessarily. Stemplowska and Swift give the analogy of mountain climbing:

In mountaineering, the climber who myopically takes immediate gains in height wherever she can is less likely to reach the summit than the one who plans her route carefully. The immediate gains do indeed take her higher—with respect to altitude she is closer to the top—but they may also be taking her away from her goal. The same is true of normative ideals. To eliminate an injustice in the world is surely to make the world more just, but it could also be to take us further away from, not closer towards, the achievement of a just society. ((2012): 379)

Trying to pattern what you ought to do on what guiding ideals say you ought to do isn't always a good idea. The ideal athlete might escape danger by leaping over the chasm. It doesn't follow that you, with your non-ideal athletic abilities, ought to try to leap the chasm—that could lead to disaster.

Whether the ideals of language use with which we started this book are simplifying ideals or guiding ideals isn't a straightforward question. Some of the ideals look like they are saying something about how we ought to be. Isn't a cooperative communicator a *better* communicator than an uncooperative one, not just a simpler communicator to theorize about? But others look less guiding. It's not clear that it's a normatively *better* language that has stable meanings—it's just a more convenient one. If, then, we want to justify ideal language theorizing as a Galilean idealization, we need to make sure that's because we think the ideal theory is useful (enough) in predicting how things go with our actual non-ideal linguistic practice, not because we think we ought to be striving to become idealized communicators.

12.6 Ideal and Non-Ideal Theories of Language

Let's return now to the question of idealization in theories of language. This idealization might be a Galilean idealization or minimalist idealization. If it is Galilean idealization, we need to be careful that it does not introduce too much theoretical distortion in exchange for its predictive simplifications. The various examples of bad language we have been considering in this book can then serve as test cases for the predictive limitations of the idealized linguistic theory. However, we would suggest that Galilean idealization is not the best way to think about idealization in linguistic theories. Galilean idealization makes sense for the engineer, not for the theorist—we idealize to improve computational ease because we want to use our theory to build things. But linguistic engineering looks like something too hard for us even under idealized conditions. Languages are too big and complicated for us to exercise any great control over them.

Instead, idealization in linguistic theories should rather be seen as minimalist idealization. We've seen in this book that the idealizations we started the book with are indeed wild idealizations. Real people having real communications aren't particularly similar to our idealized class-room participants. This leads us to the crucial question is: is the idealizer idealizing away things that ought to be ignored, or things that are theoretically important? Are the many kinds of non-ideal phenomena we've been considering in this book a kind of 'linguistic friction' or a kind of 'linguistic relativity'?

Here's what those two options amount to:

1. To say that the non-ideal phenomenon of the rough and tumble of the real world is a kind of linguistic friction is to say that there's no interesting theory of the non-ideal stuff to be had. We've seen hints of this perspective from time to time, when we've suggested that various communicative effects just merge into a general theory of psychology, sociology, and history. If, for example, all there is to say about lexical effects is that different words have different impacts on people because of some compli-cated mess of facts about those people's psychologies, the cultures those people live in, and the history of the uses of those words, then there may be no theoretically interesting account of lexical effects. We might not be able to produce anything like helpful predictions about which words will have which lexical effects, and we might not learn anything theoretically inter-esting about how languages work by trying to grapple with a huge morass of idiosyncratic psychological and sociological details.

We might end up with a view on which the idealized theory of communication we sketched in the first chapter is our 'frictionless' theory of communication, and on which that's the only real *theory* of communication. Or we might end up with a view on which it's 'all friction', and we have to give up the idea that there's anything that's helpfully isolated as the 'linguistic' part of the theoretical project. Maybe all there is is the enormously messy project of figuring out which people will do what under which conditions.

2. To say that the non-ideal phenomena is a kind of linguistic relativity is to say that we've been misled about the deep structure of communication by considering only 'low-velocity' cases, as it were. What we're seeing in the non-ideal cases is not some unstructured collection of messy details that we should ignore as theoreticians and confront only ad hoc when we want to get some decent predictions out—rather, what we're seeing is a collection of phenomena that point us to a deeper and richer theory of what communication, information, and language are really about. On this way of thinking about things, the important lesson to take from this book is that we need to continue to develop formal tools of expressive content, non-cooperative speech situations, and so on that diverge from the simple picture of contexts and contents we started with, so that our theoretical picture of language more closely matches the real structure of language and communication.

So which is it? Are we looking at the first steps of an Einsteinian revolution in the theory of language, or have we just been charting some of the messy details of linguistic friction? We don't have an answer to that question, but we do think it is one of the deep and important questions that confronts philosophy of language at this point. Answering the question is in large part a matter of *trying* to construct theories of the many non-ideal phenomena we've been discussing here, and seeing whether those theories reveal new tools and concepts that shed new light on how we think about language. Sometimes we find surprising and robust patterns in how things behave under non-ideal conditions. In these cases we should suspect that there's some deep explanation for what's going on, and that uncovering that deep explanation may require deeply rethinking our basic toolkit of linguistic ideas. In other cases we find patterns breaking down. We find that there's not much to say to the question 'what's going to happen when people say these sorts of things under these sorts of situations' than 'who knows? People might do just about anything under those conditions.' In these cases we should suspect that we're dealing with mere linguistic friction, and that we're at the limits of what a *theory of language* can helpfully say. We have seen, we think, suggestions of both of these things in this book, and weighing the balance between them is a task for ongoing investigation.

- *Bad Language* began by setting out some idealizations about how communication occurs and then subsequently presented a range of linguistic phenomena which don't obey those idealizations. A natural question is what use idealizations are, if they don't apply to the non-ideal real world. We considered this question here.

- *We idealize*, at least in the physical sciences, at least sometimes, in order to predict. We idealize away from the particularities of gas molecules when specifying laws about how gases behave, because measuring the particularities would be impossible, and computing with them intractable. Such an idealization, however, is of no cause for concern because it yields accurate and usable predictions. Such idealizations, made in order to simplify predicting, are called *Galilean idealizations*.

- We then went on to briefly consider the role of idealization in social science. We noted that Rawls's famous *A Theory of Justice* makes the idealizing assumptions that the society he discusses has an adequately educated population and commands adequate natural resources. And he assumes that the population will obey the rules of the society. These are ideal both in the sense of making theorizing easier by stripping away complications, but also because these are features of an ideal society. A society which has these features is *better* than one which doesn't; by contrast, there's no sense in which a gas which obeys the ideal gas law is better than actual gases which in fact don't.

- A natural question is then to ask what our idealizing assumptions about language are like. Are they merely *simplifications* to yield better predictions, or are they like Rawls's assumptions, features that it would be ideal for communication to have? Arguably some are of the former kind and others of the latter.

- We then turned to a different sort of idealization. While Galilean idealizations are made in the service of making prediction more tractable, *minimalist idealizations* are made to yield better understanding of how some *bits* of a given phenomenon work, while ignoring others (even if those other bits are predictively important). For example, in physics we frequently assume that planes are frictionless. In so doing, we can explain the movements of objects along them neatly using a few key features. But if we tried to make predictions about how actual objects move along actual planes using the frictionless plane theory, our predictions would be way off.

- What one can ignore when doing minimalist idealization is a tricky question. We can ignore friction, because, in a sense, it's boring: *friction plays no deep theoretical* role in formulating the laws that govern how objects move and interact. But there are some things that, if we ignore them, we should only do so temporarily. Just as we ignore friction in introductory physics courses, so we ignore relativistic effects (the effect on an object's length and mass of its velocity, for example). And unlike friction, doing so still leaves us with decent predictive theories, for the most part. But we're missing out something very important if we don't introduce relativistic effects at some point, because they, unlike friction, *do* play a deep theoretical role in our understanding of physics.

- We finally turned to the question how exactly we should understand our idealizations. We suggested we should understand them as minimalist idealizations. Then the crucial question becomes: are they a kind of 'linguistic friction' or a kind of 'linguistic relativity'? Is there any interesting theory of non-ideal language use, or is it too messy? We don't have an answer to this question right now, but we think that it's an important question for philosophers of language to be asking, and we hope this book has shown why.

Further Reading and Exercises

FURTHER READING FOR CHAPTER 12

Ladyman (2010) is an overview on idealization which covers the material in this chapter (and more). Cartwright (1980) and McMullin (1985) are early classics on idealization in science while Strevens (2017) is a more recent contribution. A helpful overview of non-ideal political theory is Valentini (2012). Appiah (2017) is an enjoyable and erudite discussion of idealization as it occurs in many domains.

Comprehension Question

1. What are 'Galilean idealizations'?
2. What are 'minimalist idealizations'?
3. Can you think of any more examples of such idealizations from disciplines you know (which could be psychology, economics, sociology, etc.)?
4. Can you think of idealizations in other areas of philosophy?

Exploratory Questions

5. Does the philosophy of language aim for near-enough predictions, the sort that would be delivered by Galilean idealization? If so, of what sort are they?
6. Which, if any, of the topics we have covered do you think are 'linguistic friction', i.e. can safely be discarded when providing theories of language?

7. Which, if any, of the topics do you think are 'linguistic relativity', i.e. are important to focus on when providing theories of language?

8. If you think we should aim for a theory of non-ideal language, which topic in this book is most pressing?

9. If you think we shouldn't, how should we understand things like slurs and lexical effects and pornography?

References

Aikin, Scott and Talisse, Robert (2018) On 'Fake News'. *3 Quarks Daily* May 21 2018, <https://www.3quarksdaily.com/3quarksdaily/2018/05/on-fake-news.html>.

Alexander, Larry (2011). Simple-Minded Originalism. In Grant Huscroft and Bradley W. Miller (eds), *The Challenge of Originalism*, 87–98. Cambridge University Press, 2011.

Alexander, Larry (2014). The Ontology of Consent. *Analytic Philosophy* 55 (1): 102–13.

Allcott, H. and Gentzkow, M. (2017). Social Media and Fake News in the 2016 Election. *Journal of Economic Perspectives* 31 (2): 211–36.

Anderson, Luvell and Lepore, Ernie (2013). Slurring Words. *Noûs* 47 (1): 25–48.

Appiah, Anthony (2002). Race, Culture, Identity: Misunderstood Connections. In P. H. Coetzee and A. P. J. Roux (eds), *Philosophy from Africa: A Text with Readings*. Oxford University Press.

Appiah, Anthony (2017). *As if: Idealizations and Ideals*. Harvard University Press.

Ashwell, Lauren (2016). Gendered Slurs. *Social Theory and Practice* 42 (2): 228–39.

Austin, J. L. (1962). *How to Do Things with Words*. Clarendon Press.

Ayer, A. J. (1936). *Language, Truth and Logic*. Gollancz.

Beaver, David I. (2001). *Presupposition and Assertion in Dynamic Semantics*. CSLI Publications.

Beaver, David I. and Geurts, Bart (2014). Presupposition. In Edward N. Zalta (ed.), *The Stanford Encyclopedia of Philosophy*. <https://plato.stanford.edu/archives/win2014/entries/presupposition/>.

Bernays, Edward (1928). *Propaganda*. Routledge.

Blome-Tillmann, Michael (2013). Conversational Implicatures (and How to Spot Them). *Philosophy Compass* 8 (2): 170–85.

Bragg, Rick (1999). Ex-Wife Is Suing Cuba Over a Spy's Deception. <https://www.nytimes.com/1999/08/15/us/ex-wife-is-suing-cuba-over-a-spy-s-deception.html>.

Bratman, M. (1999). *Faces of Intention: Selected Essays on Intention and Agency*. Cambridge University Press.

Bricmont, J. and Sokal, A. (1999). *Fashionable Nonsense: Postmodern Intellectuals' Abuse of Science*. Picador.

Bronston v. United States, 409 US 352 (1973).

Brownmiller, Susan (2000). *In our Time: Memoir of a Revolution*. Dial Press.

Burgess, Alexis and Plunkett, David (2013a). Conceptual Ethics I. *Philosophy Compass* 8 (12): 1091–101.

Burgess, Alexis and Plunkett, David (2013b). Conceptual Ethics II. *Philosophy Compass* 8 (12): 1102–10.

Burgess, Alexis, Cappelen, Herman, and Plunkett, David (eds) (forthcoming). *Conceptual Engineering and Conceptual Ethics*. Oxford University Press.

Camp, Elisabeth (2013). Slurring Perspectives. *Analytic Philosophy* 54 (3): 330–49.

Camp, Elizabeth (2018). Insinuation, Common Ground, and the Conversational Record. In Fogal, Harris, and Moss (2018).

Cappelen, Herman (2008). The Creative Interpreter: Content Relativism and Assertion. *Philosophical Perspectives* 22 (1): 23–46.

Cappelen, Herman (2011). Against Assertion. In Jessica Brown and Herman Cappelen (eds), *Assertion: New Philosophical Essays*. Oxford University Press.

Cappelen, Herman (2013). Nonsense and Illusions of Thought. *Philosophical Perspectives* 27 (1): 22–50.

Cappelen, Herman and Dever, Josh (2016). *Context and Communication*. Oxford University Press.

Cappelen, Herman and Dever, Josh (2018). *Puzzles of Reference*. Oxford University Press.

Cappelen, Herman and Dever, Josh (forthcoming). Untitled fourth book in this series. Oxford University Press.

Cappelen, Herman and Huvenes, Torfinn (forthcoming) Relative Truth. In M. Glanzberg (ed.), *Oxford Handbook of Truth*. Oxford University Press.

Cappelen, Herman (2018). *Fixing Language*. Oxford University Press.

Cappelen, Herman and Plunkett, David (forthcoming). A Guided Tour of Conceptual Engineering and Conceptual Ethics. In Burgess, Cappelen, and Plunkett (forthcoming).

Carnap, Rudolf (1959). The Elimination of Metaphysics through Logical Analysis of Language. In A. J. Ayer (ed.), *Logical Positivism*. Simon and Schuster.

Carson, Thomas L. (2006). The Definition of Lying. *Noûs* 40 (2): 284–306.

Cartwright, Nancy (1980). Do the Laws of Physics State the Facts? *Pacific Philosophical Quarterly* 61 (1/2): 75.

Chalmers, David J. (2011). Verbal Disputes. *Philosophical Review* 120 (4): 515–66.

Charlow, Nate (2014). Logic and Semantics for Imperatives. *Journal of Philosophical Logic* 43 (4): 617–64.

Cimpian, A., Brandone, A. C., and Gelman, S. A. (2010). Generic Statements Require Little Evidence for Acceptance but Have Powerful Implications. *Cognitive Science* 34: 1452–82. doi:10.1111/j.1551-6709.2010.01126.x

Cohen, G. A. (2002). Deeper into Bullshit. In S. Buss and L. Overton (eds), *Contours of Agency: Themes from the Philosophy of Harry Frankfurt*. MIT Press.

Collins English Dictionary (2017). Definition of 'Fake News'. <https://www.collinsdictionary.com/dictionary/english/fake-news>.

Cross, Charles and Roelofsen, Floris (2018). Questions. In Edward N. Zalta (ed.), *The Stanford Encyclopedia of Philosophy*. <https://plato.stanford.edu/archives/spr2018/entrics/questions/>.

Davidson, Donald (1978). What Metaphors Mean. *Critical Inquiry* 5 (1): 31–47.

Davis, Wayne (2014). Implicature. In Edward N. Zalta (ed.), *The Stanford Encyclopedia of Philosophy*. <https://plato.stanford.edu/archives/fall2014/entries/implicature/>.

Dougherty, Tom (2013). Sex, Lies, and Consent. *Ethics* 123 (4): 717–44.

Dougherty, Tom (2018). Consent and Deception. In Andreas Müller and Peter Schaber (eds), *The Routledge Handbook of the Ethics of Consent*. Routledge.

Dummett, Michael (1973). *Frege: Philosophy of Language*. Duckworth.

Egan, A. (2009). Billboards, Bombs and Shotgun Weddings. *Synthese* 166 (2): 251–79.

Eyal, Nir (2011). Informed Consent. In Edward N. Zalta (ed.), *The Stanford Encyclopedia of Philosophy*. <https://plato.stanford.edu/archives/fall2012/entries/informed-consent/>.

Fara, Delia Graff (2013). Specifying Desires. *Noûs* 47 (2): 250–72.

Faulkner, Paul (2007). What is Wrong with Lying? *Philosophy and Phenomenological Research* 75 (3): 535–57.

Fogal, Daniel, Harris, Daniel, and Moss, Matt (eds) (2018). *New Work On Speech Acts*. Oxford University Press.

Frankfurt, Harry G. (2005). *On Bullshit*. Princeton University Press.

Frege, Gottlob (1879). *Begriffsschrift: Eine der arithmetischen nachgebildete Formelsprache des reinen Denkens*. Verlag L. Nebert. English translation by S. Bauer-Mengelberg in J. van Heijenoort, *From Frege to Gödel: A Source Book in Mathematical Logic*, 1–82. Harvard University Press, 1967.

Gelfert, Axel (2018). Fake News: A Definition. *Informal Logic* 38 (2): 84–117.

Green, Mitchell (2017). Speech Acts. In Edward N. Zalta (ed.), *The Stanford Encyclopedia of Philosophy*.

Grice, H. P. (1989). *Studies in the Way of Words*. Harvard University Press.

Gupta, Anil, Definitions. In Edward N. Zalta (ed.), *The Stanford Encyclopedia of Philosophy* (Summer 2015 Edition). <https://plato.stanford.edu/archives/sum2015/entries/definitions/>.

Habgood-Coote, Joshua (2019). Stop Talking about Fake News! *Inquiry: An Interdisciplinary Journal of Philosophy*: 1–33.

Haslanger, Sally (1999). What Knowledge is and What it Ought to Be: Feminist Values and Normative Epistemology. *Philosophical Perspectives* 13 (s13): 459–80.

Haslanger, Sally (2000). Gender and Race: (What) are They? (What) do we Want them to Be? *Noûs* 34 (1): 31–55.

Haslanger, Sally (2006). What Good are our Intuitions? Philosophical Analysis and Social Kinds. *Aristotelian Society Supplementary Volume* 80 (1): 89–118.

Haslanger, Sally (2010a). Ideology, Generics, and Common Ground. In Charlotte Witt (ed.), *Feminist Metaphysics: Essays on the Ontology of Sex, Gender and the Self*, 179–207. Springer.

Haslanger, Sally (2010b). Language, Politics, and 'The Folk': Looking for 'The Meaning' of 'Race'. *The Monist* 93 (2): 169–87.

Haslanger, Sally (2012). *Resisting Reality*. Oxford University Press.

Hoicka, Elena, Saul, Jennifer, and Sterken, Rachel (n.d.) Quantified Generalisations and Social Essentialism (MS).

Hom, C. (2008). The Semantics of Racial Epithets. *The Journal of Philosophy* 105 (8): 416–40.

Hom, Christopher (2010). Pejoratives. *Philosophy Compass* 5 (2): 164–85.

Hom, Christopher (2012). A Puzzle about Pejoratives. *Philosophical Studies* 159 (3): 383–405.

Hornsby, Jennifer (1995). Disempowered Speech. *Philosophical Topics* 23 (2): 127–47.

Kaplan, David (1989). Demonstratives. In Joseph Almog, John Perry, and Howard Wettstein (eds), *Themes From Kaplan*, 481–563. Oxford University Press.

Khoo, Justin (2017). Code Words in Political Discourse. *Philosophical Topics*.

Klein, David and Wueller, Joshua, (2017). Fake News: A Legal Perspective. *Journal of Internet Law* (Apr. 2017), <https://ssrn.com/abstract=2958790>.

Klein, Naomi (1999). *No Logo: Taking Aim at the Brand Bullies*. Knopf Canada.

Kripke, Saul A. (1980). *Naming and Necessity*. Harvard University Press.

Ladyman, James (2010). Idealization. In Stathis Psillos and Martin Curd (eds), *The Routledge Companion to Philosophy of Science*. Routledge.

Lakoff, George (2014). *Don't Think of an Elephant!* Chelsea Green Publishing.

Langton, Rae (1993). Speech Acts and Unspeakable Acts. *Philosophy and Public Affairs* 22 (4): 293–330.

Langton, Rae (2009). *Sexual Solipsism: Philosophical Essays on Pornography and Objectification*. Oxford University Press.

Langton, Rae and West, Caroline (1999). Scorekeeping in a Pornographic Language Game. *Australasian Journal of Philosophy* 77 (3): 303–19.

Lazer, D. M., Baum, M. A., Benkler, Y., Berinsky, A. J., Greenhill, K. M., Menczer, F., and Schudson, M. (2018). The Science of Fake News. *Science* 359 (6380): 1094–6.

Levy, Neil (2017). The Bad News about Fake News. *Social Epistemology Review and Reply Collective* 6 (8): 20–36.

Leslie, Sarah-Jane (2008). Generics: Cognition and Acquisition. *Philosophical Review* 117 (1): 1–47.

Leslie, Sarah-Jane (2017). The Original Sin of Cognition: Fear, Prejudice, and Generalization. *Journal of Philosophy* 114 (8): 393–421.

Leslie, Sarah-Jane and Lerner, Adam (2016). Generic Generalizations. In Edward N. Zalta (ed.), *The Stanford Encyclopedia of Philosophy*.

Lewis, David (1978). Truth in Fiction. *American Philosophical Quarterly* 15 (1): 37–46.

Lewis, David (1979). Scorekeeping in a Language Game. *Journal of Philosophical Logic* 8 (1): 339–59.

Lewis, David (1996). Elusive Knowledge. *Australasian Journal of Philosophy* 74 (4): 549–67.

Liberto, Hallie (2017). Intention and Sexual Consent. *Philosophical Explorations* 20 (sup2): 127–41.

Liebesman, David (2011). Simple Generics. *Noûs* 45 (3): 409–42.

Lilleker, Darren (2017). Understanding Fake News: The Nature of the Problem and Potential Solutions, Submission to the UK Parliament Culture, Media and Sport Committee 'Fake news' inquiry, <http://eprints.bournemouth.ac.uk/28610/3/Evidence%20Submission%20-%20Fake%20News%20FINAL.pdf>

List, Christian and Pettit, Philip (2011). *Group Agency: The Possibility, Design, and Status of Corporate Agents.* Oxford University Press.

Ludlow, Peter (2014). *Living Words.* Oxford University Press.

Lycan, William G. (1999). *Philosophy of Language: A Contemporary Introduction.* Routledge.

McGowan, Mary Kate (2003). Conversational Exercitives and the Force of Pornography. *Philosophy and Public Affairs* 31 (2): 155–89.

McGowan, Mary Kate (2009). Oppressive Speech. *Australasian Journal of Philosophy* 87 (3): 389–407.

McIntyre, L. (2018). *Post-truth.* MIT Press.

McKinney, Rachel Ann (2016). Extracted Speech. *Social Theory and Practice* 42 (2): 258–84.

MacKinnon, Catharine A. (1993). *Only Words.* Harvard University Press.

McMullin, Ernan (1985). Galilean Idealization. *Studies in the History and Philosophy of Science* 16: 247–73.

Mahon, James Edwin (2015). The Definition of Lying and Deception. In Edward N. Zalta (ed.), *The Stanford Encyclopedia of Philosophy*.

Maitra, Ishani (2009). Silencing speech. *Canadian Journal of Philosophy* 39 (2): 309–38.

Maitra, Ishani (2012). Subordinating Speech. In Mary Kate McGowan and Ishani Maitra (eds), *Speech and Harm: Controversies over Free Speech*, 94. Oxford University Press.

Mallon, Ron (2004). Passing, Traveling and Reality: Social Constructionism and the Metaphysics of Race. *Noûs* 38 (4): 644–73.

Manson, Neil C. (2016). Permissive Consent: A Robust Reason-Changing Account. *Philosophical Studies* 173 (12): 3317–34.

Mendelberg, Tali (2001). *The Race Card: Campaign Strategy, Implicit Messages, and the Norm of Equality*. Princeton University Press.

Michaelson, Eliot and Stokke, Andreas (2018). *Lying: Language, Knowledge, Ethics, and Politics*. Oxford University Press.

Montgomery-McGovern, J. B. (1898). An Important Phase of Gutter Journalism: Faking. *Arena* 19 (99): 240–53.

Morgan, Appleton (1890). What Shall We Do with the Dago? *Popular Science Monthly* 38 (December) <https://en.wikisource.org/wiki/Popular_Science_Monthly/Volume_38/December_1890/What_Shall_We_Do_with_the_Dago%3F>.

Mueller, Andreas and Schaber, Peter (eds) (2018). *The Routledge Handbook of the Ethics of Consent*. Routledge.

Nickel, Bernhard (2016). *Between Logic and the World: An Integrated Theory of Generics*. Oxford University Press.

Nietzsche, Friedrich (1968). *The Will to Power*. Vintage Books.

Plunkett, David and Sundell, Timothy (2013). Disagreement and the Semantics of Normative and Evaluative Terms. *Philosophers' Imprint* 13 (23): 1–37.

Potts, Christopher (2007). The Expressive Dimension. *Theoretical Linguistics* 33 (2): 165–98.

Prior, A. N. (1960). The Runabout Inference-Ticket. *Analysis* 21 (2): 38.

Pullum, Geoffrey (2018). Slurs and Obscenities. In David Sosa (ed.), *Bad Words*. Oxford University Press.

Rhodes, Marjorie, Leslie, Sarah-Jane, and Tworek, Christina (2012). Cultural Transmission of Social Essentialism. *Proceedings of the National Academy of Sciences* 109 (34): 13526–31.

Rini, Regina (2017). Fake News and Partisan Epistemology. *Kennedy Institute of Ethics Journal* 27 (S2): 43–64.

Rubenfeld, Jed (2013). The Riddle of Rape-by-Deception and the Myth of Sexual Autonomy. *Yale Law Journal* 122: 1372.

Saul, Jennifer (2006). Gender and Race. *Aristotelian Society Supplementary* 80 (1): 119–43.

Saul, Jennifer (2012). *Lying, Misleading, and What is Said*. Oxford University Press.

Saul, Jennifer and Diaz-Leon, Esa (2018). Feminist Philosophy of Language. In Edward N. Zalta (ed.), *The Stanford Encyclopedia of Philosophy* <https://plato.stanford.edu/archives/fall2018/entries/feminism-language/>.

Scharp, Kevin (2013). *Replacing Truth*. Oxford University Press.

Schlenker, Philippe (2007). Expressive Presuppositions. *Theoretical Linguistics* 33 (2): 237–45.

Schweikard, David P. and Schmid, Hans Bernhard (2013). Collective Intentionality. In Edward N. Zalta (ed.), *The Stanford Encyclopedia of Philosophy*.

Searle, John (1994). Literary Theory and its Discontents. *New Literary History* 25: 637–67.

Sedivy, Julie and Carlson, Greg (2011). *Sold on Language: How Advertisers Talk to You and What This Says about You*. Wiley-Blackwell.

Silverman, C. (2017). I Helped Popularize The Term "Fake News" And Now I Cringe Every Time I Hear It. Buzzfeednews, December 31 2017. <https://www.buzzfeednews.com/article/craigsilverman/i-helped-popularize-the-term-fake-news-and-now-i-cringe>

Silverman, C. and Alexander, L. (2016). How Teens in the Balkans Are Duping Trump Supporters with Fake News. Buzzfeed News, November 3, 2016. <https://www.buzzfeed.com/craigsilverman/how-macedonia-became-a-global-hub-for-pro-trump-misinfo?utm_term=.ybgwZKQVa#.fcjbDYNOZ>.

Simons, Mandy (2006). Foundational Issues in Presupposition. *Philosophy Compass* 1 (4): 357–72.

Sokal, Alan and Bricmont, Jean (2003). *Intellectual Impostures* (2nd edn), trans. Alan Sokal and Jean Bricmont. Bookmarque.

Sorensen, Roy (2001). Vagueness Has No Function in Law. *Legal Theory* 7: 387–417.

Sosa, David (ed.) (2018). *Bad Words*. Oxford University Press.

Sperber, Dan and Wilson, Deidre (1986). *Relevance*. Blackwell's.

Stemplowska, Z. and Swift, A. (2012). Ideal and Nonideal Theory. In David Estlund (ed.), *The Oxford Handbook of Political Philosophy*. Oxford University Press.

Stalnaker, Robert (1978). Assertion. *Syntax and Semantics* (New York Academic Press) 9: 315–32.

Stalnaker, Robert (1984). *Inquiry*. Cambridge University Press.

Stalnaker, Robert (2014). *Context*. Oxford University Press.

Stanley, Jason (2008). Philosophy of Language in the Twentieth Century. In *Routledge Companion to Twentieth Century Philosophy*. Routledge.

Sterken, Rachel Katharine (2015). Generics in Context. Philosophers' Imprint 15: 1–30.

Sterken, Rachel Katharine (2017). The Meaning of Generics. *Philosophy Compass* 12 (8): 1–13.

Sterken, Rachel Katharine (forthcoming). Linguistic Intervention and Transformative Communicative Disruptions. In Burgess, Cappelen, and Plunkett (forthcoming).

Stokke, Andreas (2013). Lying, Deceiving, and Misleading. *Philosophy Compass* 8 (4): 348–59.

Stokke, Andreas (2018). *Lying and Insincerity*. Oxford University Press.

Strevens, Michael (2017). How Idealizations Provide Understanding. In S. R. Grimm, C. Baumberger, and S. Ammon (eds), *Explaining Understanding: New Essays in Epistemology and the Philosophy of Science*. Routledge.

Swanson, Eric (forthcoming). Omissive Implicature. *Philosophical Topics.*

Tappenden, Jamie (1995). Some Remarks on Vagueness and a Dynamic Conception of Language. *Southern Journal of Philosophy* 33: 193–202.

Tollefsen, Deborah (2002). Organizations as True Believers. *Journal of Social Philosophy* 33 (3): 395–410.

Trump, Donald (2011). *Time to Get Tough: Making America # 1 again.* Regnery Publishing.

Valentini, Laura (2012). Ideal vs. Non-ideal Theory: A Conceptual Map. *Philosophy Compass* 7 (9): 654–64.

Van Inwagen, Peter (2008). *Metaphysics.* Routledge.

Weisberg, Michael (2007). Three Kinds of Idealization. *Journal of Philosophy* 104 (12): 639–59.

Wieland, Nellie (2007). Linguistic Authority and Convention in a Speech Act Analysis of Pornography. *Australasian Journal of Philosophy* 85 (3): 435–56.

Williams, Bernard (2002). *Truth and Truthfulness: An Essay in Genealogy.* Princeton University Press.

Williamson, Timothy (2000). *Knowledge and its Limits.* Oxford University Press.

Williamson, Timothy (2009). Reference, Inference and the Semantics of Pejoratives. In Joseph Almog and Paolo Leonardi (eds), *The Philosophy of David Kaplan*, 137–58. Oxford University Press.

Wilson, Deirdre and Sperber, Dan (2002). Truthfulness and Relevance. *Mind and Language* 111 (443): 583–632.

Winerman, M. (2003). The Origins of the FTC: Concentration, Cooperation, Control, and Competition. *Antitrust Law Journal* 71 (1): 1–97.

Zakkou, Julia (2017). Jesus Loves you! *Philosophical Studies* 174 (1): 237–55.

Index

and nonsense 63–4
and slurs 78
and pornography 171–3
of lying 43, 46
Morgan, Appleton 92
Moss, Matt 179
Müller, Andreas 194

Nickel, Bernard 142
Nietzsche, Friedrich 76–7, 88
Nonsense *see* deep bullshit

Obama, Barack 18–19, 31–2, 52, 55, 118
Oppressing (linguistic) 165–8
via pornography 168–73
Originalism (philosophy of law) 147, 159

Pejoratives *see* slurs
Perlocutionary act *see* speech act
Pettit, Philip 158
Plunkett, David 74, 80, 88
Politics *see also* fake news, branding, codewords, dogwhistles
Bullshit in 52–3, 55
Philosophy of as ideal 203–5
Relation to conceptual engineering 79–80, 86–7
Pornography 168–73, 176–7
Potts, Christopher 100–2, 108, 110
Pragmatics
relation to lexical effects 111–12, 123
Presupposition
And Lying 45
Nature of 20–6
View of slurs 97–9
Prior, Arthur 136–7
Pullum, Geoffrey 90

Race
And conceptual engineering 80
And meaninglessness 66–9
Rawls, John 203–4, 208
Rhodes, Marjorie 134
Rini, Regina 58
Roelofsen, Floris 27
Rubenfeld Jed 191

Saul, Jennifer 46, 50, 81, 82, 135, 179, 183, 191
Scattered audiences 144–8
Scattered speakers 148–54
Schaber, Peter 194

Scharp, Kevin 78–9, 88
Schlenker, Philippe 108
Schmid, Hans Bernhard 158
Schweikard, David P. 158
Scoreboard, conversational 4–5, 26–32
Searle, John 189
Sedivy, Julie 45, 125
Silencing 173–7
and consent 186–7
Silverman, Craig 58–9
Simons, Mandy 34
Slurs
appropriative uses 96–7
descriptivism 91–7
expressivist views 99–102
presuppositional views 97–9
prohibitionist views 102–6
Social Media 55, 154–6
Sokal, Alan 64–6
Sorensen, Ray 151
Sosa, David 108
Speech Acts 161–4 *see also* Scattered audiences, Scattered speakers, Social Media, Consent
Sperber, Dan 48–9, 51
Stalnaker, Robert 11, 159
Stanley, Jason 11
Stemplowska, Z. 204–5
Sterken, Rachel 82, 135, 142
Stokke, Andreas 41, 45–6, 50
Strevens, Michael 209
Sundell, Tim 74
Swanson, Eric 186–7
Swift, A. 204–5

Talisse, Robert 58
Tappenden, Jamie 151
Tollefsen, Deborah 158
Trump, Donald 38, 56, 57, 59, 118
Truth *see also* fiction, lying, presupposition, implicature
and bullshit 52–4
and the idealizations 35
and lying 41–2
(supposed) importance for communication 46–9
Tworek, Christina 134–5

Vagueness 78, 129, 137, 146, 151
of implicit consent 187–9
Valentini, Laura 209
van Inwagen, Peter 78